D1220707

Societal Impact on Aging Series

K. Warner Schaie, PhD, Evan Pugh Professor of Human Development and Psychology College of Health and Human Development, Series Editor
The Pennsylvania State University, University Park, PA

2006 **Social Structures, Aging, and Self-Regulation in the Elderly**
K. Warner Schaie and Laura L. Carstensen, Editors

2005 **Historical Influences on Lives and Aging**
K. Warner Schaie and Glen H. Elder, Jr., Editors

2004 **Religious Influences on Health and Well Being in the Elderly**
K. Warner Schaie, Neal Krause, and Alan Booth, Editors

2003 **Impact of Technology on Successful Aging**
Neil Charness and K. Warner Schaie, Editors

2002 **Personal Control in Social and Life Course Contexts**
Steven H. Zarit, Leonard I. Pearlin, and K. Warner Schaie, Editors

2002 **Effective Health Behavior in Older Adults**
K. Warner Schaie, Howard Leventhal, and Sherry L. Willis, Editors

2000 **The Evolution of the Aging Self: The Societal Impact on the Aging Process**
K. Warner Schaie and Jon Hendricks, Editors

2000 **Mobility and Transportation in the Elderly**
K. Warner Schaie and Martin Pietrucha, Editors

1997 **Impact of Work on Older Adults**
K. Warner Schaie and Carmi Schooley, Editors

1997 **Societal Mechanisms for Maintaining Competence in Old Age**
Sherry L. Willis, K. Warner Schaie, and Mark Hayward, Editors

1996 **Older Adults' Decision-Making and the Law**
Michael Smye, K. Warner Schaie, and Marshall B. Kapp, Editors

1995 **Adult Intergenerational Relations: Effects of Societal Change**
Vern L. Bengtson, K. Warner Schaie, and Linda K. Burton, Editors

1993 **Societal Impact on Aging: Historical Perspectives**
K. Warner Schaie and W. Andrew Achenbaum, Editors

About the Authors

K. Warner Schaie, Ph.D., is the Evan Pugh Professor of Human Development and Psychology at the Pennsylvania State University. He also holds an appointment as Affiliate Professor of Psychiatry and Behavioral Science at the University of Washington. He received his PhD in psychology from the University of Washington, an honorary Dr. phil. from the Friedrich-Schiller University of Jena, Germany, and an honorary ScD degree from West Virginia University. He received the Kleemeier Award for Distinguished Research Contributions from the Gerontological Society of America, the MENSA lifetime career award, and the Distinguished Scientific Contributions award from the American Psychological Association. He is author or editor of 48 books including the textbook *Adult Development and Aging* (5th edition, with S. L. Willis) and the *Handbook of the Psychology of Aging* (6th edition, with J. E. Birren). He has directed the Seattle Longitudinal Study of Cognitive Aging since 1956, and is the author of more than 275 journal articles and chapters on the psychology of aging. His current research interest is the life course of adult intelligence, its antecedents and modifiability, the early detection of risk for dementia, as well as methodological issues in the developmental sciences.

Laura L. Carstensen, Ph.D., is Professor of Psychology at Stanford University, where she is also Chair of the Psychology Department. She has published extensively about emotional, cognitive, and motivational changes with age and formulated socioemotional selectivity theory. She is a fellow in the American Psychological Society, American Psychological Association, and the Gerontological Society of America. Dr. Carstensen received the Kalish Award for Innovative Research from the Gerontological Society in 1993, and was selected as a Guggenheim Fellow in 2003.

Social Structures, Aging, and Self-Regulation in the Elderly

Edited by
K. Warner Schaie, PhD
Laura L. Carstensen, PhD

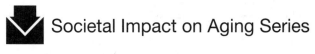 Societal Impact on Aging Series

SPRINGER PUBLISHING COMPANY
New York

Springer Publishing Company, Inc.
11 West 42nd Street
New York, NY 10036

Acquisitions Editor: Sheri W. Sussman
Managing Editor: Mary Ann McLaughlin
Production Editor: Emily Johnston
Cover design by Joanne E. Honigman
Composition: Apex Covantage

06   07   08   09   10/   5   4   3   2   1

Library of Congress Cataloging-in-Publication Data

Laura L Carstensen
    Social structures, aging and self-regulation in the elderly/edited by K. Warner Schaie,
Laura L Carstensen
        p. cm.—   (Societal impact on aging)
    Edited conference papers.
    Includes bibliographical references and index.
    1. Aging—Social aspects—Congresses.   2. Cognition in old age—Congresses.
I. Schaie, K. Warner (Klaus Warner), 1928–   II. Carstensen, Laura L.
III. Pennsylvania State University. Gerontology Center.   IV. Series.

    HQ1061.S6486 2006
    305.26—dc22   2006012820

Printed in the United States of America by Edwards Brothers.

Contents

Contributors   *vii*

Preface   *ix*

1. Societal Influences That Affect Cognitive Functioning in Old Age   1

Selam Negash and Ronald C. Petersen

Commentary: Societal Factors in Cognitive Aging: One Eye Wide Shut?   9

Naftali Raz

Commentary: Societal Influences on Cognition in Historical Context   13

K. Warner Schaie

2. Wisdom in Social Context   33

Ursula M. Staudinger, Eva-Marie Kessler, and Jessica Dörner

Commentary: The Dynamic Relationship Between Age Stereotypes and Wisdom in Old Age   55

Becca R. Levy and Corey Pilver

3. Social Influences on Adult Personality, Self-Regulation, and Health   69

Daniel K. Mroczek, Avron Spiro III, Paul W. Griffin, and Shevaun D. Neupert

Commentary: From Kindling to Conflagration: Self-Regulation and Personality Change   85

Brent W. Roberts

Commentary: Can Self-Regulation Explain Age
Differences in Daily, Weekly, and Monthly Reports of
Psychological Distress?   95

David M. Almeida, Daniel K. Mroczek, and Michelle Neiss

**4. Social Norms, Rules of Thumb, and Retirement:
Evidence for Rationality in Retirement Planning**   123

Gary Burtless

Commentary: Modeling the Retirement Decision   161

Joseph F. Quinn

Commentary: Numbers Are Just Numbers   175

Ellen Peters

**5. Race and Self-Regulatory Health Behaviors: The Role of
the Stress Response and the HPA Axis in Physical and
Mental Health Disparities**   189

James S. Jackson and Katherine M. Knight

Commentary: Mechanisms of Health Disparities:
Variations in Health Care Provider Attitudes and
Their Impact on Older Minority Adults   209

Stephanie L. Garrett and Toni P. Miles

Commentary: Adding Paths to Resilience and Daily Accounts
to an Already Rich Field of Inquiry: A Brief Commentary
on James Jackson's "Social Structure and Health Disparities"   215

Alex J. Zautra, Kate E. Murray, and Brendt P. Parish

Index   *240*

Contributors

David M. Almeida, PhD
The Pennsylvania State University
State College, PA

Gary Burtless, PhD
The Brookings Institution
Washington, DC

Jessica Dörner, PhD
Jacobs Center for Lifelong
Learning and Institutional
Development
International University Bremen
Bremen, Germany

Stephanie L. Garrett, MD
University of Louisville
Louisville, KY

Paul W. Griffin, PhD
Pace University
Pleasantville, NY

James S. Jackson, PhD
Institute for Social Research
University of Michigan
Ann Arbor, MI

Eva-Marie Kessler, PhD
Jacobs Center for Lifelong
Learning and Institutional

Development
International University Bremen
Bremen, Germany

Katherine M. Knight
Institute for Social Research
University of Michigan
Ann Arbor, MI

Becca R. Levy, PhD
Yale University
New Haven, CT

Toni P. Miles, MD, PhD
Wise-Nelson Chair, Clinical
Geriatrics Research
Professor, Family & Geriatric
Medicine
University of Louisville
Louisville, KY

Daniel K. Mroczek, PhD
Purdue University
West Lafayette, IN

Kate E. Murray, M.S.
Arizona State University
Tempe, AZ

Salem Negash, PhD
Alzheimer's Disease Research

Center
Mayo Clinic College of Medicine
Rochester, MN

Michelle Neiss, PhD
Oregon Health and Science
University
Portland, OR

Shevaun D. Neupert, PhD
North Carolina State University
Raleigh, NC

Brendt P. Parish
Arizona State University
Tempe, AZ

Ellen Peters, PhD
Decision Research
University of Oregon
Eugene, OR

Ronald C. Petersen, PhD, MD
Alzheimer's Disease Research
Center
Mayo Clinic College of Medicine
Rochester, MN

Corey Pilver, PhD
Yale University
New Haven, CT

Joseph F. Quinn, PhD
Boston College
Chestnut Hill, MA

Naftali Raz, PhD
Institute of Gerontology
Department of Psychology
Wayne State University
Detroit, MI

Brent W. Roberts, PhD
University of Illinois
Urbana-Champaign
Champaign, IL

Avron Spiro III, PhD
Boston VA Health System &
Boston University School of Public
Health
Boston, MA

Ursula M. Staudinger, PhD
Jacobs Center for Lifelong
Learning and Institutional
Development
International University Bremen
Bremen, Germany

Alex J. Zautra, PhD
Arizona State University
Tempe, AZ

Preface

This is the 18th volume in a series on the broad topic of "Societal Impact on Aging." The first five volumes of this series were published by Erlbaum Associates under the series title of "Social Structure and Aging." The present volume is the 13th published under the Springer Publishing Company imprint. It is the edited proceedings of a conference held at the Pennsylvania State University, October 4–5, 2004.

The series of Penn State Gerontology Center conferences originated from the deliberations of a subcommittee of the Committee on Life Course Perspectives of the Social Science Research Council, chaired by Matilda White Riley in the early 1980s. That subcommittee was charged with developing an agenda and mechanisms that would serve to encourage communication between scientists who study societal structures that might affect the aging of individuals and those scientists who are concerned with the possible effects of contextual influences on individual aging. The committee proposed a series of conferences that would systematically explore the interfaces between social structures and behavior, and in particular to identify mechanisms through which society influences adult development. When the first editor was named director of the Penn State Gerontology Center in 1985, he was able to implement this conference program as one of the center's major activities.

The previous seventeen volumes in this series have dealt with the societal impact on aging in psychological processes (Schaie & Schooler, 1989); age structuring in comparative perspective (Kertzer & Schaie, 1989); self-directedness and efficacy over the life span (Rodin, Schooler, & Schaie, 1991); aging, health behaviors, and health outcomes (Schaie, House, & Blazer, 1992); caregiving in families (Zarit, Pearlin, & Schaie, 1993); aging in historical perspective (Schaie & Achenbaum, 1993); adult intergenerational relations (Bengtson, Schaie, & Burton, 1995); older adults' decision making and the law (Smyer, Schaie, & Kapp, 1996); the impact of social structures on decision making in the elderly (Willis, Schaie, &

Hayward,1997); the impact of the workplace on aging (Schaie & Schooler, 1998); the evolution of the aging self (Schaie & Hendricks, 2000); mobility and transportation in the elderly (Schaie & Pietrucha, 2000); societal impact on health behavior in the elderly (Schaie, Leventhal, & Willis, 2002); mastery and control in the elderly (Zarit, Pearlin, & Schaie, 2002); impact of technology on the elderly (Charness & Schaie, 2003); religious influences on health and well being in the elderly (Schaie, Krause, & Booth, 2004); and historical influences on lives and aging (Schaie & Elder, 2005).

The strategy for each of these volumes has been to commission reviews on three major topics by established subject-matter specialists who have credibility in aging research. We then invited two formal discussants for each chapter—usually one drawn from the writer's discipline and one from a neighboring discipline. This format seems to provide a suitable antidote against the perpetuation of parochial orthodoxies as well as to make certain that questions are raised in regard to the validity of iconoclastic departures in new directions.

To focus each conference, the organizers chose three aspects of the conference topic that are of broad interest to gerontologists. Social and behavioral scientists with a demonstrated track record were then selected and asked to interact with those interested in theory building within a multidisciplinary context.

The present volume focuses on the interplay of social structures and self-regulation in the elderly. No one doubts that the social contexts in which individuals develop exert strong influence on life trajectories. Those born into environments that provide high quality education, supportive social relations, and economic assets do better in old age than those born into environments bereft of the same resources. However, the extent of this influence is only beginning to be revealed. Recent research shows that life experiences influence basic brain structures (e.g., the influence of musical training on neural organization) and functions (e.g., inflammatory processes), and that social embeddedness may even protect against Alzheimer's disease. Similarly, education increasingly appears to have a real effect on neural integrity. Thus, societal contexts may not simply open or close doors for individuals; they may influence self-regulatory processes at the most basic levels of functioning.

Although social structures are generally thought of as the independent variables that affect individual aging, it is also possible to think of a lifetime development of self-regulatory processes leading to behaviors in old age that can have impact on and modify societal structures. Hence, we first consider self-regulation as the dependent variable, asking how social contexts influence cognitive, emotional, and self-regulatory processes. We then reverse the question, by treating self-regulation as the independent variable and consequences for retirement and physical health as dependent variables. This approach allows us to consider the question as to how the effectiveness of self-regulation influences physical and economic outcomes in old age.

The first topic in this volume is concerned with the complex bidirectional influences between brain and environment. In particular, consideration is given to the effects of lifelong experiences as they affect cognitive functioning in old age. The major review lists a variety of societal contexts and in particular focuses on the protective role of education. Two commentaries caution, first, that many individuals who profit from favorable environments seek out or are selected into such environments because of genetic predisposition, and second, that the environmental impact may differ across historical contexts and in subsets of the population studied.

The second topic is concerned with individual resilience in societal context. A major impact of societal context on individual aging is through providing the experiences necessary for learning how to navigate one's life, adapting to the complex societal and cultural rules and mores within which the individual life course progresses. It is well known that the attainment of wisdom requires not only high levels of cognitive competence, but also the successful experience of many complex life situations: a lifelong process. However, experiential learning not only affects problem-solving behavior, it also affects the development of life-stage-appropriate identity and self-schemas that affect adult personality organization. It is also likely to affect personality processes such as assimilation and accommodation in old age. While the first review chapter on this topic considers the acquisition of wisdom in societal context, the second directly addresses the role of self-regulation as an important personality construct.

The third topic addresses the physical and economic outcomes of effective self-regulation across the adult lifespan. The issues and literature on certain behaviors that may have major impact on major societal structures are explored. The position is taken that successful aging results from effective self-regulation over the lifespan; that is, functional status in old age reflects, in large part, the lifelong culmination of economic decisions, health behaviors, and health care utilization. It also reflects social standing and the favorable or adverse consequences that social status affords. Specifically, sample cases examined in this chapter are the effects of self-regulation on the timing of retirement and the effects of self-regulation upon health-related behaviors in different ethnic communities and social classes.

We are grateful for the financial support of the conference provided by conference grant R13 AG 09787 from the National Institute on Aging that led to this volume, and for the additional support from the College of Health and Human Development of the Pennsylvania State University. We are also grateful to Chriss Schultz for handling the conference logistics, and to Jenifer Hoffman for coordinating the manuscript preparation and preparing the indexes.

K. Warner Schaie
January, 2006

REFERENCES

Bengtson, V. L., Schaie, K. W., & Burton, L. (Eds.). (1995). *Adult inter-generational relations: Effects of societal changes.* New York: Springer Publishing Co.

Charness, N., & Schaie, K. W. (Eds.). (2003). *Impact of technology on the aging individual.* New York: Springer Publishing Co.

Kertzer, D., & Schaie, K. W. (Eds.). (1989). *Age structuring in comparative perspective.* Hillsdale, NJ: Erlbaum.

Rodin, J., Schooler, C., & Schaie, K. W. (Eds.). (1991). *Self-directedness and efficacy: Causes and effects throughout the life course.* Hillsdale, NJ: Erlbaum.

Schaie, K. W., & Achenbaum, W. A. (Eds.). (1993). *Societal impact on aging: Historical perspectives.* New York: Springer Publishing Co.

Schaie, K. W., & Elder, G. H., Jr. (Eds.). (2005). *Historical influences on lives and aging.* New York: Springer Publishing Co.

Schaie, K. W., & Hendricks, J. (Eds.). (2000). *Evolution of the aging self: Societal impacts.* New York: Springer Publishing Co.

Schaie, K. W., House, J., & Blazer, D. (Eds.). (1992). *Aging, health behaviors, and health outcomes.* Hillsdale, NJ: Erlbaum.

Schaie, K. W., Krause, N., & Booth, A. (Eds.). (2004). *Religious influences on health and well-being in the elderly.* New York: Springer Publishing Co.

Schaie, K. W., Leventhal, H., & Willis, S. L. (Eds.). (2002). *Societal impacts on health behaviors in the elderly.* New York: Springer Publishing Co.

Schaie, K. W., & Pietrucha, M. (Eds.). (2000). *Mobility and transportation in the elderly.* New York: Springer Publishing Co.

Schaie, K. W., & Schooler, C. E. (Eds.). (1989). *Social structure and aging: Psychological processes.* Hillsdale, NJ: Erlbaum.

Schaie, K. W., & Schooler, C. E. (Eds.). (1998). *Impact of the work place on older persons.* New York: Springer Publishing Co.

Smyer, M., Schaie, K. W., & Kapp, M. B. (Eds.). (1996). *Older adults' decision-making and the law.* New York: Springer Publishing Co.

Willis, S. L., Schaie, K. W., & Hayward, M. (Eds.). (1997). *Impact of social structures on decision making in the elderly.* New York: Springer Publishing Co.

Zarit, S. H., Pearlin, L., & Schaie, K. W. (Eds.). (1993). *Social structure and caregiving: Family and cross-national perspectives.* Hillsdale, NJ: Erlbaum.

Zarit, S. H., Pearlin, L., & Schaie, K. W. (Eds.). (2002). *Mastery and control in the elderly.* New York: Springer Publishing Co.

1

Societal Influences That Affect Cognitive Functioning in Old Age

Selam Negash and Ronald C. Petersen

INTRODUCTION

With the increasing of the population of older adults, there is a growing interest in improving quality of life in old age, and in early detection and prevention of cognitive declines with aging. One important aspect of this endeavor pertains to achieving and maintaining cognitive vitality, which is shown to be essential to quality of life and survival in old age (Fillit et al., 2002). Although it is well documented that aging is accompanied by a decline in several domains of cognitive functions, studies have also shown that such a decline is not common to all older people, and that some older adults can in fact enjoy optimal aging without experiencing a significant cognitive impairment. For example, in successful aging, where individuals function effectively and successfully as they age, there is likely very little cognitive decline over the life span, and cognitive function can be preserved well into the 10th decade or beyond (Kaye et al., 1994). Further, even in typical aging, where individuals encounter co-morbidities such as hypertension and coronary artery disease as part of aging, it has generally been observed that some cognitive functions such as those involving crystallized knowledge (e.g., vocabulary) remain preserved or even improve with age (Lindenberger & Baltes, 1997).

Researchers over the past several decades have been investigating whether there are factors, intrinsic or extrinsic, that would allow some individuals to age successfully while others experience the consequences of normal aging or even pathological forms of aging such as Alzheimer's disease (AD). The literature in the field implicates an association between cognitive decline and factors such as educational and occupational attainment, cognitive and physical activity, and nutrition (Fratiglioni, Paillard-Borg, & Winblad, 2004). The present chapter discusses some of these lifestyle factors that are thought to influence cognitive vitality in normal aging and dementia, and also the mechanisms that are speculated to underlie this relationship.

Terminology

In discussing cognitive declines with aging, it is important to consider some of the terms that have been used over the years to describe the different degrees of cognitive impairment associated with aging. Historically, attempts at characterizing cognitive changes at the normal tail end of the continuum have produced several terms such as benign senescent forgetfulness (Kral, 1962), age-associated memory impairment (AAMI) (Crook et al., 1986), and age-associated cognitive decline (AACD) (Levy, 1994). These terms are meant to reflect the extremes of normal aging in general. Recently, increased attention is being given to the boundary between normal aging and very early AD, and this transitional zone has been termed mild cognitive impairment (MCI) (Petersen et al., 1999). MCI represents a condition where individuals show memory impairment greater than expected for their age, but otherwise are functioning well and do not meet the commonly accepted criteria for dementia. The construct of MCI has become recognized as a pathological condition rather than a manifestation of normal aging, and it has recently received a great deal of attention as a useful entity for possible therapeutic intervention.

The most typical scenario of MCI pertains to the amnestic subtype (a-MCI), where individuals show impairment in a single domain of memory with other cognitive domains remaining relatively intact. More recently, as the field of MCI has advanced, it has become apparent that other clinical subtypes exist as well (Petersen, 2003). *Multiple domain amnestic MCI* pertains to individuals who, in addition to memory deficit, also have impairments in at least one other cognitive domain such as language, executive function, or visuospatial skills. *Multiple domain non-amnestic MCI,* on the other hand, pertains to individuals who have impairments in multiple cognitive domains, but not including memory. *Single domain non-amnestic MCI,* which is the least common subtype, pertains to individuals with impairment in a single non-memory domain of language, executive function, or visuospatial skills. Other cognitive domains, including memory, are essentially normal. Individuals in this subtype likely have a different outcome from those with memory impairment. It is also imperative that individuals in all of these subtypes of MCI have minimal impairments in functional activities that do not represent a significant change in function from a prior level, and also do not meet the criteria for dementia. Clinical subtypes of MCI have been proposed to broaden the concept and include prodromal forms of a variety of dementias. As the field matures, and as we learn more about the various subtypes of MCI and their ability to predict various forms of cognitive impairment, these could lay the groundwork for therapeutic interventions that are tailored for specific prodromal forms of dementia.

LIFESTYLE FACTORS

In the following section, we summarize the main findings from studies that have examined the associations between cognitive functioning in old age and lifestyle factors, such as attainment level, cognitive and physical activity, and nutrition. The link between these factors and the risk for dementia will also be briefly discussed.

Educational and Occupational Attainment

Several studies have reported an association between cognitive decline late in life and educational and occupational attainment. Cross-sectional and longitudinal data show that individuals with low levels of education perform poorly on tests of cognitive function and exhibit greater decline over time compared to those with higher education levels (Evans et al., 1993; Farmer, Kittner, Rae, Bartko, & Regier, 1995). Low levels of educational attainment have also been linked to increased risk of dementia. Prevalence studies conducted in various parts of the world have shown that the incidence and prevalence of AD was higher in individuals with low levels of education (Katzman, 1993; Stern et al., 1994; Zhang et al., 1990; Callahan et al., 1996). There is also evidence that education modifies the relation of AD pathology to cognitive functions; the relation of senile plaques and level of cognitive function has been shown to differ by years of education

(Bennett et al., 2003). Similarly, data derived from autobiographies of sisters participating in the Nun Study have shown that poor linguistic ability (as measured by idea density and grammatical complexity) in early life was a strong predictor of poor cognitive function and AD in late life (Snowdon et al., 1996).

The link between occupational attainment and AD has also been documented. Many studies have shown that the incidence of AD was higher in individuals with low levels of occupational attainment (Callahan et al., 1996; Dartigues et al., 1992), although there have been some exceptions (Beard, Kokmen, Offord, & Kurland, 1992). Studies have also found a relationship between occupational demands and cognitive decline, where individuals in occupations involving lower mental demands and greater use of manual skills showed poor cognitive performance and higher prevalence of dementia (Jorm et al., 1998). Similarly, AD patients have been shown to engage in significantly lower mental occupational demands and significantly higher physical occupational demands compared to control participants (Smyth et al., 2004).

The mechanisms underlying the above associations, however, are not fully understood. Nevertheless, some plausible explanations have been put forth by several studies. Katzman (1993) has proposed that the protective effect of education against cognitive decline is due to a neuronal reserve, where higher educational attainment increases synaptic density, allowing individuals to delay the onset of symptoms of cognitive impairment. The extensive work in animal studies also appears to support this hypothesis in that it shows brain weight and numbers of neuronal processes in rodents are related to environmental stimulation (Kempermann, Kuhn, & Gage, 1998; Sirevaag, Black, Shafron, & Greenough, 1998). However, the extent to which such findings can be extrapolated to humans is unclear. Another support for this view comes from imaging studies, which have shown prominent regional cerebral blood flow deficits, suggestive of more advanced pathology, in AD patients with higher educational and occupational attainment (Stern, Alexander, Prohovnik, & Mayeux, 1992; Stern et al., 1995). The authors in these studies concluded that individuals with more reserve are able to tolerate more AD pathology, and that at any level of clinical severity, the underlying pathology is more advanced in patients with higher levels of attainment. Consistently, they have proposed that increased educational and occupational attainment may reduce the risk of AD, either by decreasing ease of clinical detection or by supplying a reserve that allows individuals to cope longer before AD is clinically expressed. However, as proponents of the above view also note, the concept of a reserve must be weighted against the alternate explanation of a detection bias. That is, it is possible that low educational or occupational attainment enables the clinician to diagnose dementia at an earlier point in time, in which case the attainment effect would confound the diagnostic criteria (Katzman, 1993). Although this remains a possibility, the above findings have also been replicated in cases involving a more careful application of the diagnostic criteria in order to reduce the likelihood of a spurious effect attainment level, thus suggesting that links between higher incidence of AD and low levels of educational or occupational attainment are not simply a result of detection bias (Stern et al., 1994). In general, then, the protective effects of educational and occupational attainment against cognitive decline late in life appear to be supported by the literature.

Cognitive Activity

Recent research indicates that frequent participation in cognitively stimulating activities may also protect against cognitive decline and reduce the risk of AD (Hultsch, Hertzog, Small, & Dixon, 1999; Wilson et al., 2002). The construct of cognitive activity is generally operationalized in the literature through use of a number of scales that measure frequency of cognitive activities that are judged to primarily involve seeing or processing information (Wilson & Bennett, 2003). These may include reading a book, playing a game such as chess or crosswords, or listening to a radio program. Studies that have examined the relationship between cognitive activity and cognitive decline in old age have found that individuals who participate in cognitive activity and are engaged in their environment show the least decline in cognitive function compared to those with disengaged lifestyles (Hultsch et al., 1999; Schaie, 1984). Engaging in cognitively stimulating activities during childhood has also been associated with a higher cognitive function in old age (Everson-Rose, Mendes de Leon, Bienias, Wilson, & Evans, 2003). In addition, cognitive activity has been hypothesized to be associated with incidence of AD. Several studies have found that individuals who reported lower participation in cognitively stimulating activities were at a higher risk of developing AD compared to those reporting frequent cognitive activity

(Scarmeas, Levy, Tang, Manly, & Stern, 2001; Wang, Karp, Winblad, & Fratiglioni, 2002; Wilson et al., 2002).

The mechanisms that might account for the association between cognitive activity and risk of AD are also unknown. One hypothesis, similar to that mentioned previously for the attainment level, is that cognitive activity contributes to the development and maintenance of neural systems that underlie cognitive processes, thereby requiring more AD pathology before these processes are disrupted and the disease is expressed clinically (Wilson & Bennett, 2003). The considerable data from animal studies appear to be consistent with this view, and indicate that environmental enrichments influence increased neurons, synapses, and dendritic arbors in several brain regions including the hippocampus and cerebellum (Kempermann, Kuhn, & Gage, 1997; Kleim, Vij, Ballard, & Greenough, 1997).

Physical Activity and Nutrition

There is also evidence that cognitive function in old age is associated with physical exercise and nutrition. For example, animal model studies have demonstrated that physical exercise, such as access to a running wheel, enhanced neurogenesis and improved performance on learning and memory tasks in adult mice (Praag, Kempermann, & Gage, 1999). The results from human studies, on the other hand, have been mixed. While several studies report exercise-related benefits such as improvements in cognitive function (Weuve et al., 2004) and reduced risk of dementia (Abbott et al., 2004), others studies have not. For example, cross-sectional data have shown that individuals who had engaged in aerobic exercise performed better than non-exercisers on several tasks, such as reasoning, working memory, and vigilance monitoring (Bunce, Barrowclough, & Morris, 1996; Powell & Pohndorf, 1971). Other studies, however, have not found such association (Madden, Blumenthal, Allen, & Emery, 1989). Some epidemiological studies have also reported a link between physical exercise and reduced risk of dementia (Abbott et al., 2004; Laurin, Verreault, Lindsay, MacPherson, & Rockwood, 2001), while others have not (Wilson et al., 2002). The inconsistent findings among these studies may have resulted from several factors such as differences in the types of exercise and aspects of cognition examined by the different studies. Nonetheless, it appears generally that the animal and human data support some beneficial effect of physical activity on cognitive functioning in old age.

Likewise, the relationship between nutrition and cognitive function late in life has been investigated by various studies in several research areas. Some animal studies have found that caloric restriction may have beneficial effects on cognition in old age (Mattson, Duan, Lee, & Guo, 2001). Other studies, however, have not found an association (Bellush, Wright, Walker, Kopchick, & Colvin, 1996), and as such, the results with regards to caloric restriction have been mixed. Further, caloric restriction is not generally recommended in older adults because it may promote malnutrition, which could cause long-term cognitive impairments. Studies have also examined the relationship between dietary fat consumption and cognitive decline, and have found that high consumption of total fats, saturated fatty acids, and cholesterol was associated with cognitive decline in elderly people (Ortega et al., 1996), while consumption of fish and n-3 fatty acids correlated with reduced risk of AD (Morris et al., 2003). Further, some studies have also reported an association between higher serum levels of cholesterol and increased risk of dementia (Notkola et al., 1998), although others have not (Engelhart et al., 2002). More research is needed in this area to understand the relationship between diet and risk of dementia.

Another area of investigation that has gained increased interest, especially in recent years as the focus of AD research moves toward prevention, is the effect antioxidants may have against cognitive decline in aging. Antioxidants such as Vitamins E and C help neutralize free radicals that can cause oxidant injury, and they have been associated with various benefits such as promoting cardiovascular health (Frei, 1995). Vitamin E has also recently gained attention in the clinical trials for MCI. A recent study involving Vitamin E and donepezil, however, has indicated no therapeutic effect for Vitamin E while donepezil reduced the risk of progressing to AD for the first 12 months of the trial (Petersen et al., 2005). Further investigation is needed in this area, and additional work is likely to continue.

SUMMARY

In general, then, the literature indicates a strong association between various lifestyle factors and cognitive functioning late in life, although some studies have not found such associations. Some of this variability may be the result of several factors, including differences in the design of studies (e.g., longitudinal versus cross-sectional), the operational definitions of variables under consideration, and the types of assessments of cognitive performance (Fratiglioni et al., 2004). Nonetheless, despite such limitations, the literature provides enough evidence to support the hypothesis that an active and socially integrated lifestyle influences cognitive vitality in old age. A lifestyle such as this may also serve to buffer against cognitive decline and perhaps aid in delaying the diagnosis of dementia. It remains unclear, however, what mechanisms underlie these associations, and whether this effect can be causal. It is possible that the aforementioned associations are markers of innate characteristics such as genetic background. Indeed, the link between genetic markers such as apolipoprotein E (apoE) and risk of dementia has been established, in that individuals with an E4 allele were found to be at increased risk for AD (Corder et al., 1993; Strittmatter et al., 1993). The presence of an E4 allele in MCI patients as a predictor of progression to AD has also been reported (Petersen et al., 1995). However, not all persons with the E4 allele develop dementia, and this underscores the likelihood that the E4 allele is a risk factor that interacts with other factors to cause dementia. As such, these observations stress the importance of genetic and environmental interactions in influencing cognitive vitality late in life, and highlight the importance of gaining an understanding of these interactions for early detection and prevention of cognitive decline and dementia.

ACKNOWLEDGMENTS

Supported by the National Institute of Aging Alzheimer's Disease Patient Registry, AG 06576 and Alzheimer's Disease Research Center, AG 16574.

Commentary: Societal Factors in Cognitive Aging: One Eye Wide Shut?

Naftali Raz

The process of aging is marked by significant individual variability, the sources of which are multiple and, by and large, ill-defined. Nonetheless, as longitudinal studies of brain and cognition show, individual differences may be quite stable and are transferred reliably along the path of late life development (Deary et al., 2004; Hertzog & Schaie, 1986; Raz et al., 2005). In an attempt to explicate some reasons for variability in trajectories of aging, Negash and Petersen turn their attention to the factors that until recently have been underestimated in biomedical and cognitive gerontology. Specifically, they present a brief review of the evidence pertaining to the role of educational and occupational attainment, cognitive and physical activity, and nutrition in cognitive decline and stability. They conclude, on the balance of the surveyed evidence, that all of the listed factors exert significant influence on the individual paths of aging and affect the likelihood of crossing a diagnostic line between normal aging and dementia. Although they mention the role of a specific genotypic variation (ApoE-E4 allele) in cognitive decline, the authors assume that all of the factors considered in their brief survey are societal in nature.

On the surface this seems true. However, there may be valid reasons to doubt the exclusivity and even the primacy of society in the influences discussed by Negash and Petersen. The aim of the following brief commentary is to broaden the Negash and Petersen argument for paying attention to the aforementioned so-called societal factors by highlighting the non-societal aspects that fall beyond the scope of their review. More specifically, I will argue that social and cultural influences notwithstanding, a significant portion of the variance in the modifiers of cognitive aging identified by the authors can be attributed to genetic sources that reside outside the realm of society and family environment, and need to be taken into account in determining the mechanisms of cognitive aging.

Education is the first of the societal factors Negash and Petersen mention. Indeed, an institutionalized education process is implemented within the confines of culture and society and is therefore a good candidate for a non-biological modifier of aging. However, population genetics studies present evidence that complicates that expectation. A significant genetic component for educational achievement was found in large European cohorts (Bartels, Rietreld, Van Baal, & Boomsma, 2002; Heath et al., 1985). Research of the past several decades has established that whatever intelligence quotient (IQ) may reflect, and no matter how malleable it may appear, educational achievement is heritable to a substantial degree (Bouchard, Lykken, McGue, Segal, & Tellegen, 1990). Regardless to the discussion of causality, educational attainment is linked to IQ and cognitive performance in the general population and in older adults (Pedersen, Plomin, Nesselroade, & McClearn, 1992; Pedersen, Reynolds, & Gatz, 1996). Moreover, the association between achievement and IQ is also influenced by genotype (Bartels et al., 2002; Heath et al., 1985), and age-related changes in heritability of cognitive traits are unlikely to be large (McArdle & Hamagami, 2003). Notably, in genetically related individuals, education does not predict incidence of pathological cognitive decline (Gatz et al., 2001). Thus, if education has any effect on how we age, it is likely to act as an expression of genetic endowment and early experiences, including, and maybe especially, biological events of embryogenesis rather than societal events of adulthood.

Recent studies of a well-documented Scottish cohort support the hypothesis that cognitive skills measured at age 11 determine to a large extent cognitive performance at age 79 (Deary et al., 2004). The Nun Study (Snowdon et al., 1996) cited by Negash and Petersen in support of societal influences on cognitive aging, can actually provide the evidence against them. As the lifestyle within religious order is tightly controlled and societal influences are minimized, the variability in age trajectories of cognitive performance is probably determined by non-societal, mainly biological, factors, many of which are inherited. The findings that persons engaged in occupations with reduced mental demands evidence "poor cognitive performance and higher prevalence of dementia" can be just as parsimoniously explained by variation in levels of cognitive prowess registered before entering a specific occupation.

The next societal factor considered by Negash and Petersen is enriched cognitive activity. They conclude that "individuals who reported lower participation in cognitively stimulating activities were at a higher risk of developing AD compared to those reporting frequent cognitive activity." The problem with this argument is twofold. First, cognitive activity is not independent of general cognitive abilities and skills, thus referring this proposition to the previously discussed role of premorbid and inherited cognitive abilities. Second, propensity for cognitive activity and other recreational interests show a reasonably high level of heritability (Lykken, Bouchard, McGue, & Tellegen, 1993). Thus, "active lifestyles" are not assigned to individuals at random, but may be predicated on interaction between their genetic endowment and their early life history, not current societal influences.

Vascular risk factors exert negative influence on brain and cognitive aging even at the levels that used to be considered benign (e.g., Raz, Rodrigue, & Acker, 2003). The authors consider the effects of potential positive modifiers of vascular risk, such as physical activity and nutrition on cognitive aging. Indeed there is growing evidence of beneficial effects of exercise on the brain and behavior of older adults (e.g., Colcombe et al, 2003). However, activity levels and propensity to engage in exercise and sports (An et al., 2003; Maes et al., 1996), as well as important biological determinants of tolerance to high levels of exercise (VO_{2max}), are heritable (De Geus, Boomsma, & Snieder, 2003). Moreover, although exercise is a reasonable way to reduce blood pressure (Bassuk & Manson, 2005), the response of blood pressure to behavioral interventions is heritable to a significant degree (Rice et al., 2002). As for nutrition, genetic factors also play a significant role in shaping the extent of risk and the risk-enhancing interactions with the environment, with high heritability observed for such indices of obesity as body mass index (Speakman, 2004). Significant heritability has been found for the daily amount of food, alcohol, and water consumption, especially for the meal portion size, whereas the familial environment effect on those indices is negligible de Castro, 1993). The response to reactive oxygen species (free radicals) that are linked to nutrition and play a role in emergence of vascular disease may also depend on specific genes (Kachiwala et al., 2005). Thus, societal modifications of exercise and nutrition conducted in an attempt to introduce healthier lifestyles are constrained to a significant extent by genetic factors.

In conclusion, Negash and Petersen's attention to the relatively neglected and potentially powerful influences on cognitive aging is welcome and commendable. However, the term societal when applied to education, occupation, nutrition, mental engagement, and physical activity may be a misnomer. Although we need to learn more about how the genetic variability and societal influences contribute to cognitive aging, more important may be to understand how the heritable complex traits interact with societal constraints in shaping the patterns of cognitive stability and declines observed in older adults. It may be surprising, but this conclusion, derived from a different platform, is not fundamentally at odds with that of the authors, who issue a broad appeal for understanding the "importance of genetic and environmental interactions in influencing cognitive vitality." However, such understanding will necessitate an understanding of the genetics of cognitive aging beyond ApoE, and an acknowledgement that all behavioral and social traits are shaped by the workings of the genes in the complex environment, and not by gene-free societal forces.

ACKNOWLEDGMENT

The author is supported by the grant 2R37AG011230 from the National Institutes of Health.

Commentary: Societal Influences on Cognition in Historical Context

K. Warner Schaie

INTRODUCTION

Negash and Petersen have identified and discussed a number of societal influences and lifestyle factors that mediate or moderate the path from normal cognitive functioning, through mild cognitive impairment, to the diagnosis of full-blown dementia. In this commentary, I will first describe the different forms of cognitive aging as characterized by differences in level and slope of cognitive trajectories across the adult years. I will then comment on the various risks and protective factors inherent in differential social status characteristics and lifestyles, and indicate how the role of these factors is modified by changes in historical context. Finally, I will provide some illustrations of these changes with data from the Seattle Longitudinal Study (SLS).

FORMS OF COGNITIVE AGING

It is readily apparent that there are vast individual differences in patterns of cognitive change across adulthood. Scrutiny of a variety of longitudinal studies of cognition (cf., Schaie & Hofer, 2001) suggest that four major patterns will describe most of the observed differences, although further subtypes could, of course, be considered. These patterns would classify individuals into those who age normally, those who age successfully (the super-normals), those who develop mild cognitive impairment, and finally those who become clinically diagnosable as suffering from dementia. Figure 1.1 shows commonly found cognitive trajectories as reported in the SLS (Schaie, 2005), separately from young adulthood through midlife, and from midlife to advanced old age.

The most common pattern is what we could denote as the *normal aging* of cognitive abilities. This pattern is characterized by most individuals

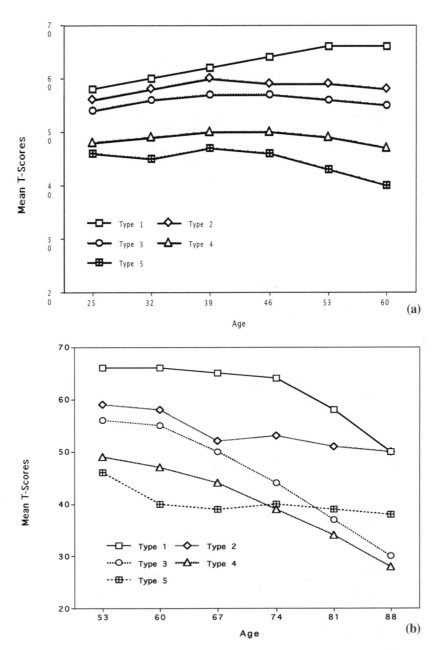

FIGURE 1.1   Alternate cognitive trajectories from young adulthood to midlife (a), and from midlife to advanced old age (b).

reaching an asymptote in early midlife, maintaining a plateau until the late 50s or early 60s, and then showing modest decline on most abilities through the early 80s, with more marked decline in the years prior to death (cf., Bosworth & Schaie, 1999). Among those whose cognitive aging can be described as normal, we can distinguish two subgroups. The first includes those individuals who reach a relatively high level of cognitive functioning who can remain independent until close to their demise even if they become physically frail. On the other hand, the second group includes those who only reach a modest asymptote in cognitive development, and may require greater support and be more likely to experience a period of institutional care in old age.

A small subgroup of adults experience what is often described as *successful aging* (Fillit et al., 2002; Rowe & Kahn, 1987). Members of this group are often genetically and socioeconomically advantaged, and tend to continue cognitive development later than most, typically reaching their cognitive asymptotes in late midlife. While they too show some very modest decline on highly speeded tasks, they are likely to maintain their overall level of cognitive functioning until shortly before their demise. These are the fortunate individuals for whom the mortality curve has been virtually squared and whose active life expectancy comes very close to their actual life expectancy.

The third pattern, *mild cognitive impairment* (MCI), includes that group of individuals who typically experience greater than normative cognitive declines in early old age (Petersen et al., 1999). Various definitions, mostly statistical, have been advanced to assign membership to this group. Some have argued for a criterion of 1 *SD* of performance compared to the young adult average, while others have proposed a rating of 0.5 on a clinical dementia rating scale, where 0 is normal and 1.0 is probable dementia. Previously the identification of MCI required the presence of memory loss, in particular. However, more recently the diagnosis has been extended to include decline in other cognitive abilities. There has also been controversy surrounding the question of whether individuals with the diagnosis of MCI inevitably progress to dementia, or whether this group of individuals represents a unique entity; which could perhaps be described as experiencing *unsuccessful aging* (cf., Petersen, 2003).

The final pattern includes those individuals who are diagnosed with *dementia* in early or advanced old age. Regardless of the specific cause of the dementia, what these individuals have in common is dramatic impairment in cognitive functioning. However, the pattern of cognitive change, particularly in those whose diagnosis at postmortem turns out to be Alzheimer's disease, is very different from those experiencing normal aging. When followed longitudinally, at least some of these individuals show earlier decline, perhaps starting in midlife. Figure 1.2 shows the longitudinal ability patterns over a 35-year period prior to death for two women, one who was diagnosed with Alzheimer's disease, and another who died from a Cerebral Vascular Accident (CVA) and presented a virtually so-called clean cortex.

SOCIETAL INFLUENCES THAT MEDIATE OR MODERATE COGNITIVE CHANGE WITH AGE

Of the whole array of societal structures that can influence cognitive change in cognitive functioning across adulthood (cf., Nagesh & Petersen, this volume), the most thoroughly documented ones appear to be educational and occupational attainment. Although there are differences among the studies cited by Nagesh and Petersen, their sum total suggests that educational attainment in particular may have some protective value or at least postpone the onset of dementia (e.g., Katzman, 1990). It should be immediately noted that these influences are not constant, but vary across changing historical contexts (cf., Schaie & Elder, 2005; Schaie, Willis, & Pennak, 2005).

Educational Attainment

There has been a dramatic increase in educational attainment in the United States over the past century. One of the major historical events that particularly contributed to the increase of educational attainment in men was the GI Bill, which was originally designed to reduce potential veteran unemployment after the end of World War II (cf., Laub & Sampson, 2005). Disregarding changes in quality of education, the fact remains that the duration of the educational exposure has increased markedly. Data from the SLS suggest that there has been an average increase of approximately 5 ½ years of educational exposure over a 70-year period (see Figure 1.3).

Not only have there been dramatic increases in educational exposure, but there have also been dramatic changes in educational practice that have

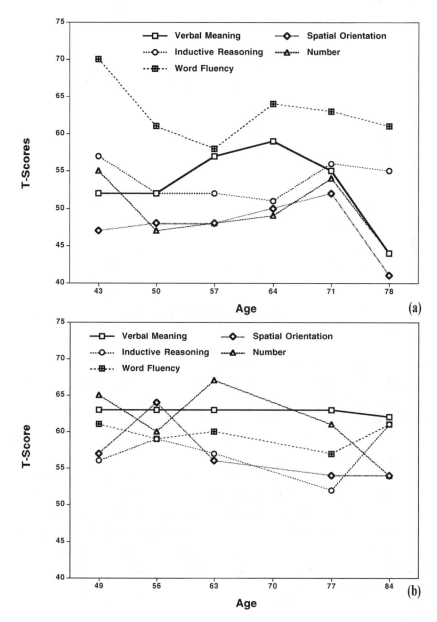

FIGURE 1.2   Longitudinal cognitive profiles over 35 years prior to death of two women, one diagnosed with Alzheimer's disease (a) and the other with no cerebral abnormalities (b) upon post mortem.

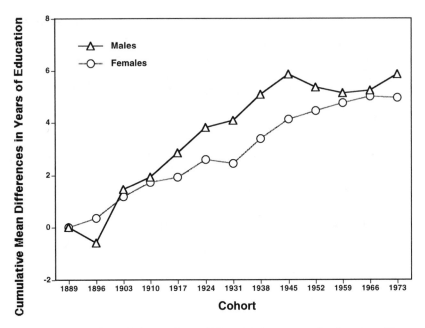

FIGURE 1.3   Cumulative cohort difference in years of education (from Schaie, 2005).

markedly affected performance on mental abilities. Some of these changes in practice have been positive, such as the increased emphasis on problem solving skills, supporting gains in executive function for many. The basic abilities affected are, in particular, Verbal Ability (due to increased educational exposure) and Inductive Reasoning (due to increased *emphasis* on discovery methods in problem solving).

Evidence for these effects has been found in the SLS (Schaie, 2005). The association between educational exposure and Verbal Ability is particularly striking. Figure 1.4 shows a lifelong advantage for the well-educated, in that the verbal ability of the average 80-year-old with post-college education remains at the level of the average 25-year-old grade school graduate. Similar findings are also shown for the association of educational attainment and Reasoning Ability.

Occupational Status

Over the past century there have been dramatic changes in the workplace. Nevertheless, it remains true that the workplace characteristics that are most likely to affect maintenance of high levels of cognitive

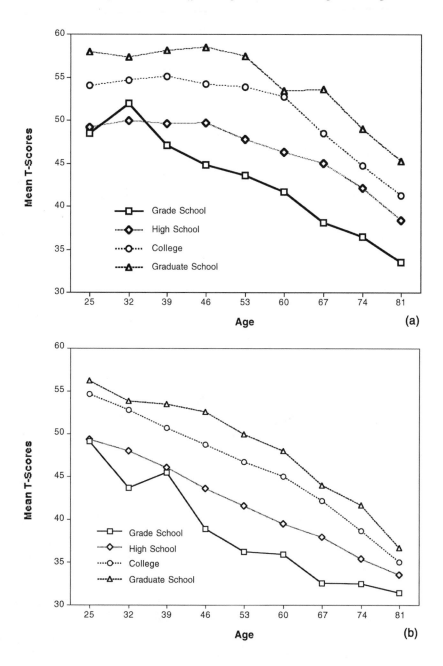

FIGURE 1.4   Association between level of educational attainment and performance on tests of Verbal Ability (a) and Inductive Reasoning (b).

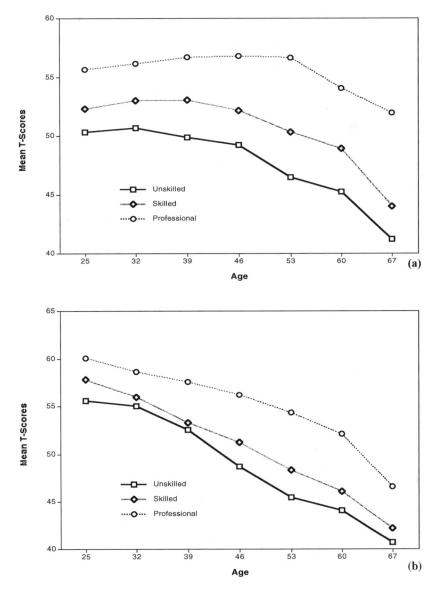

FIGURE 1.5   Association between occupational status and performance on tests of Verbal Ability (a) and Inductive Reasoning (b).

functioning are the extent to which the worker/employee is in control of his time, engages in non-routine work activities, and engages in inter-personally challenging work pursuits (cf., Schooler, Mulatu, & Oates, 2004).

Similar to the relationship with education, striking differences in longitudinal patterns of cognitive abilities for different occupational levels can also be found. When study participants are classified into unskilled, skilled, and professional workers, at the end of their work life, those termed professional still outperform skilled or unskilled workers at any life stage on Verbal Ability, and remain at an advantage on Reasoning Ability throughout life (see Figure 1.5).

LIFESTYLE FACTORS THAT AFFECT COGNITIVE FUNCTION THROUGHOUT ADULTHOOD

The most thoroughly investigated lifestyle influences that appear to affect cognitive functioning throughout adulthood appear to be nutrition, exercise, and intellectually stimulating activities. All of these factors have been subject to dramatic historical changes that seem to put cohorts born in later generations at a great advantage in comparison to cohorts at similar ages born in earlier generations. These factors include not only the increase in educational exposure discussed earlier, but also changes in educational practice that may positively or negatively affect performance on cognitive abilities (see below; Schaie et al., 2005). Marked changes have also occurred in occupational distribution. Over the past century, following a shift from agriculture to manufacturing as the principal source of employment, there was a shift to a service economy that has demanded the acquisition of computer skills and other more specialized competencies.

Although the evidence on the impact of changes in lifestyles on maintenance of cognitive functions into old age is still limited, generational differences in the practice of exercise, dietary restraint, and the utilization of preventive health care are substantial (cf., Zanjani, 2004). Also impressive is the increase in the availability of cognitively stimulating activities known to have protective effects against cognitive decline (cf., Wilson et al., 2002).

CUMULATIVE COHORT DIFFERENCES IN COGNITIVE ABILITIES

The historical changes described above have had significant impact on levels of performance on cognitive abilities. Figure 1.6 provides evidence of cumulative cohort differences measured in the SLS by obtaining averages between successive cohorts over all available ages. Over the 84-year

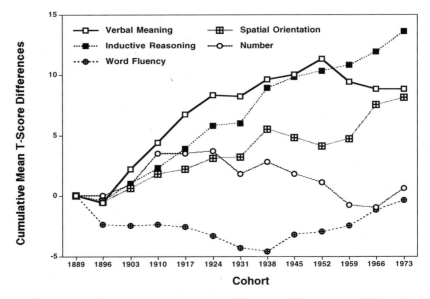

FIGURE 1.6   Cumulative generational difference of five mental abilities for birth cohorts in seven-year intervals from 1889–1973.

Source: Schaie, K. W. (2005). *Developmental influences on adult intelligence: The Seattle Longitudinal Study.* New York: Oxford University Press, p. 137. Reproduced by permission of the publisher.

period for which data is available, it will be noted that there is a positive cohort gradient for those abilities most directly impacted by educational and occupational changes in our society: Inductive Reasoning, Verbal Ability, and Spatial Ability. Numeric ability reached an asymptote early in the 20th century and has been steadily declining, while Word Fluency declined until the 1930s and then started returning to the level observed in our oldest study participants, those born in the late 19th century.

To illustrate differences of within-cohort trajectories of mental abilities across age, we selected three cohorts who, among them, in our study, cover the age range from 25–81 years of age and who overlap each other at least at three ages. The cohorts chosen are cohort 2 (born 1893–1899), cohort 6 (born 1921–1927), and cohort 10 (born 1949–1955). We are thus comparing baby boomers with the generations of their parents and grandparents. Figure 1.7 again focuses on the abilities of Verbal Ability and Inductive Reasoning. Note that the within-cohort slopes for Verbal Meaning differ primarily in old age, while the slopes for Inductive Reasoning differ significantly at all ages covered.

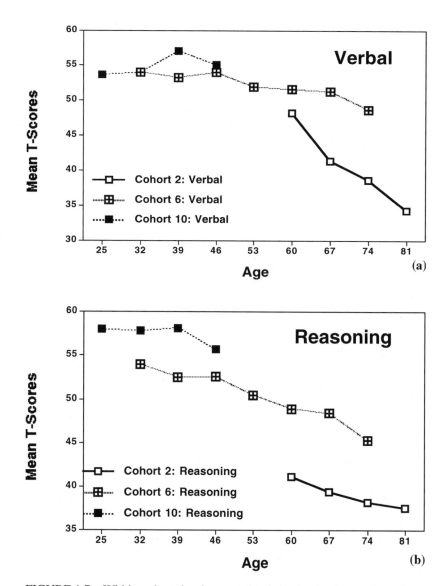

FIGURE 1.7   Within-cohort developmental trajectories for three cohorts born 28 years apart on tests of Verbal Ability (a) and Inductive Reasoning (b).

CONCLUSIONS

My interpretation of the review offered by Negash and Petersen and the data I have presented from mine and my colleagues' work in the SLS lead me to five major conclusions about the role of societal influences on cognition over the adult life course:

First, it is clear that societal influences ensure that there is no single uniform pattern of cognitive aging. Hence, there is need to discover the different types of individual trajectories that characterize different forms of cognitive aging. Second, there is conclusive evidence of generational differences in cognitive trajectories. That is, successive generations age differently. Third, it follows that historical changes in societal practices and allocation of resources will affect both individual cognitive trajectories as well as the prevalence of differential trajectories. Fourth, given the currently observable pattern of generational succession in cognitive level and rate of decline, it is most likely that future generations will have greater prevalence of more positive cognitive trajectories. Fifth, and finally, it is likely that the greater availability of societal resources that serve as protective factors against cognitive decline will serve to compensate for the impact of many cognitive risks now leading to unfavorable cognitive trajectories in late life.

REFERENCES

Abbott, R. D., White, L. R., Ross, G. W., Masaki, K. H., Curb, J. D., & Petrovitch, H. (2004). Walking and dementia in physically capable elderly men. *Journal of the American Medical Association, 292,* 1447–1453.

An, P., Perusse, L., Rankinen, T., Borecki, I. B., Gagnon, J., Leon, A. S., et al. (2003). Familial aggregation of exercise heart rate and blood pressure in response to 20 weeks of endurance training: The HERITAGE family study. *International Journal of Sports Medicine, 24,* 57–62.

Bartels, M., Rietveld, M. J., Van Baal, G. C., & Boomsma, D. I. (2002). Heritability of educational achievement in 12-year-olds and the overlap with cognitive ability. *Twin Research, 5,* 544–553.

Bassuk, S. S., & Manson, J. E. (2005). Epidemiological evidence for the role of physical activity in reducing risk of type 2 diabetes and cardiovascular disease. *Journal of Applied Physiology, 99,* 1193–1204.

Beard, C. M., Kokmen, E., Offord, K. P., & Kurland, L. T. (1992). Lack of association between Alzheimer's disease and education, occupation, marital status, or living arrangement. *Neurology, 42,* 2063–2068.

Bellush, L. L., Wright, A. M., Walker, J. P., Kopchick, J., & Colvin, R. A. (1996). Caloric restriction and spatial learning in old mice. *Physiology and Behavior, 60,* 541–547.

Bennett, D. A., Wilson, R. S., Schneider, J. A., Evans, D. A., Mendes de Leon, C. F., Arnold, S. E., et al. (2003). Education modifies the relation of AD pathology to level of cognitive function in older persons. *Neurology, 60,*1909–1915.

Bosworth, H. B., & Schaie, K. W. (1999). Survival effects in cognitive function, cognitive style, and sociodemographic variables in the Seattle longitudinal Study. *Experimental Aging Research, 25,* 121–139.

Bouchard, T. J., Lykken, D. T., McGue, M., Segal, N. L., & Tellegen, A. (1990). Sources of human psychological differences: The Minnesota study of twins reared apart. *Science, 250,* 223–228.

Bunce, D. J., Barrowclough, A., & Morris, I. (1996). The moderating influence of physical fitness on age gradients in vigilance and serial choice responding tasks. *Psychology and Aging, 11,* 671–682.

Callahan, C. M., Hall, K. S., Hui, S. L., Musick, B. S., Unverzagt, F. W., & Hendrie, H. C. (1996). Relationship of age, education, and occupation with dementia among a community-based sample of African Americans. *Archives of Neurology, 53,* 134–140.

Colcombe, S., Erickson, K. I., Raz, N., Webb, A. G., Cohen, N. J., McAuley, E. & Kramer, A. (2003). Aerobic fitness reduces brain tissue loss in aging humans. *Journal o fGerontology, 58A,* 176–180.

Corder, E. H., Saunders, A. M., Strittmatter, W. J., Schmechel, D., Gaskell, P., Small, W., et al. (1993). Gene dose of apolipoprotein E type 4 allele and the risk of Alzheimer's disease in late onset families. *Science, 261,* 921–923.

Crook, T., Bartus, R. T., Ferris, S. H., Whitehouse, P., Cohen, G. D., & Gershon, S. (1986). Age-associated memory impairment: Proposed diagnostic criteria and measures of clinical change—Report of a National Institute of Mental Health Work Group. *Developmental Neuropsychology, 2,* 261–267.

Dartigues, J. F., Gagnon, M., Letenneur, L., Barberger-Gateau, P., Commenges, D., Evaldre, M., et al. (1992). Principal lifetime occupation and cognitive impairment in a French elderly cohort (Paquid). *American Journal of Epidemiology, 135,* 981–988.

Deary, I. J., Whiteman, M. C., Starr, J. M., Whalley, L. J., & Fox, H. C. (2004). The impact of childhood intelligence on later life: Following up the Scottish mental surveys of 1932 and 1947. *Journal of Personality and Social Psychology, 86,* 130–147.

de Castro, J. M. (1993). Genetic influences on daily intake and meal patterns of humans. *Physiology and Behavior, 53,* 777–782.

De Geus, E. J., Boomsma, D. I., & Snieder, H. (2003). Genetic correlation of exercise with heart rate and respiratory sinus arrhythmia. *Medicine and Science in Sports and Exercise, 35,* 1287–1295.

Engelhart, M. J., Geerlings, M. I., Ruitenberg, A., Swieten, J. C., van Hofman, A., Witteman, J.C.M., et al. (2002). Diet and risk of dementia: Does fat matter? The Rotterdam Study. *Neurology, 59,* 1915–1921.

Evans, D. A., Beckett, L. A., Albert, M. S., Hebert, L. E., Scherr, P. A., Funkenstein, H. H., et al. (1993). Level of education and change in cognitive function in a community population of older persons. *Annals of Epidemiology, 3,* 71–77.

Everson-Rose, S. A., Mendes de Leon, C. F., Bienias, J. L., Wilson, R. S., & Evans, D. A. (2003). Early life conditions and cognitive functioning in later life. *American Journal of Epidemiology, 158,* 1083–1089.

Farmer, M. E., Kittner, S. J., Rae, D. S., Bartko, J. J., & Regier, D. A. (1995). Education and change in cognitive function. The Epidemiologic Catchment Area Study. *Annals of Epidemiology, 5,* 1–7.

Fillit, H. M., Butler, R. N., O'Connell, A. W., Albert, M. S., Birren, J. E., Cotman, C. W., et al. (2002). Achieving and maintaining cognitive vitality with aging. *Mayo Clinic Proceedings, 77,* 681–696.

Fratiglioni, L., Paillard-Borg, S., & Winblad, B. (2004). An active and socially integrated lifestyle in late life might protect against dementia. *Lancet Neurology, 3,* 343–353.

Frei, B. (1995) Cardiovascular disease and nutrient antioxidants: Role of low-density lipoprotein oxidation. *Critical Reviews in Food Science and Nutrition, 35,* 83–98.

Gatz, M., Svedberg, P., Pedersen, N. L., Mortimer, J. A., Berg, S., & Johansson, B. (2001). Education and the risk of Alzheimer's disease: Findings from the study of dementia in Swedish twins. *The Journals of Gerontology. Series B, Psychological Sciences and Social Sciences, 56,* 292–300.

Heath, A. C., Berg, K., Eaves, L. J., Solaas, M. H., Corey, L. A., & Sundet, J., et al. (1985). Education policy and the heritability of educational attainment. *Nature, 314,* 734–736.

Hertzog, C., & Schaie, K. W. (1986). Stability and change in adult intelligence: 1. Analysis of longitudinal covariance structures. *Psychology and Aging, 1,* 159–171.

Hultsch, D. F., Hertzog, C., Small, B. J., & Dixon, R. A. (1999). Use it or lose it: Engaged lifestyle as a buffer of cognitive decline in aging? *Psychology and Aging, 14,* 245–263.

Jorm, A. F., Rodgers, B., Henderson, A. S., Korten, A. E., Jacomb, P. A., Christensen, H., et al. (1998). Occupation type as a predictor of cognitive decline and dementia in old age. *Age and Aging, 27,* 477–483.

Kachiwala, S. J., Harris, S. E., Wright, A. F., Hayward, C., Starr, J. M., Whalley, L. J., et al. (2005). Genetic influences on oxidative stress and their association with normal cognitive aging. *Neuroscience Letters, 386,* 116–120.

Katzman, R. (1993). Education and the prevalence of dementia and Alzheimer's disease. *Neurology, 43,* 13–20.

Kaye, J. A., Oken, B. S., Howieson, D. B., Howieson, J., Holm, L. A., & Dennison, K. (1994). Neurologic evaluation of the optimally healthy oldest old. *Archives of Neurology, 51,* 1205–1211.

Kempermann, G., Kuhn, H. G., & Gage, F. H. (1997). More hippocampal neurons in adult mice living in an enriched environment. *Nature, 386,* 493–495.

Kempermann, G., Kuhn, H. G., & Gage, F. H. (1998). Experience-induced neurogenesis in the senescent dentate gyrus. *The Journal of Neuroscience, 18,* 3206–3212.

Kleim, J. A., Vij, K., Ballard, D. H., & Greenough, W. T. (1997). Learning-dependent synaptic modifications in the cerebellar cortex of the adult rat persist for at least four weeks. *The Journal of Neuroscience, 17,* 717–721.

Kral, V. A. (1962). Senescent forgetfulness: Benign and malignant. *Canadian Medical Association Journal, 86,* 257–260.

Laub, J. H., & Sampson, R. J. (2005). Coming of age in wartime: How World War II and the Korean War changed lives. In K. W. Schaie & G. H. Elder, Jr. (Eds.), *Historical influences on lives and aging* (pp. 208–228). New York: Springer Publishing Co.

Laurin, D., Verreault, R., Lindsay, J., MacPherson, K., & Rockwood, K. (2001). Physical activity and risk of cognitive impairment and dementia in elderly persons. *Archives of Neurology, 58,* 498–504.

Levy, R. (1994). Aging-associated cognitive decline. *International Psychogeriatrics, 6,* 63–68.

Lindenberger, U., & Baltes, P. B. (1997). Intellectual functioning in old and very old age: Cross-sectional results from the Berlin Aging Study. *Psychology and Aging, 12,* 410–432.

Lykken, D. T., Bouchard, T. J., Jr., McGue, M., & Tellegen, A. (1993). Heritability of interests: A twin study. *Journal of Applied Psychology, 78,* 649–661.

Madden, D. J., Blumenthal, J. A., Allen, P. A., & Emery, C. F. (1989). Improving aerobic capacity in healthy older adults does not necessarily lead to improved cognitive performance. *Psychology and Aging, 4,* 307–320.

Maes, H. H., Beunen, G. P., Vlietinck, R. F., Neale, M. C., Thomis, M., Vanden Eynde, B., et al. (1996). Inheritance of physical fitness in 10-yr-old twins and their parents. *Medicine and Science in Sports and Exercise, 28,* 1479–1491.

Mattson, M. P., Duan, W., Lee, J., & Guo, Z. (2001). Suppression of brain aging and neurodegenerative disorders by dietary restriction and environmental enrichment: Molecular mechanisms. *Mechanisms of Aging and Development, 122,* 757–778.

McArdle, J. J., Hamagami, F. (2003). Structural equation models for evaluating dynamic concepts within longitudinal twin analyses. *Behavior Genetics, 33,* 127–159.

Morris, M. C., Evans, D. A., Bienias, J. L., Tangney, C. C., Bennett, D. A., Aggarwal, N., et al. (2003). Dietary fat and the risk of incident Alzheimer disease. *Archives of Neurology, 60,* 194–200.

Notkola, I. L., Sulkava, R., Pekkanen, J., Erkinjuntti, T., Ehnholm, C., Kivinen, P., et al. (1998). Serum total cholesterol, apolipoprotein E epsilon 4 allele, and Alzheimer's disease. *Neuroepidemiology, 17,* 14–20.

Ortega, R. M., Manas, L. R., Andres, P., Gaspar, M. J., Agudo, F. R., Jimenez, A., et al. (1996). Functional and psychic deterioration in elderly people may be aggravated by folate deficiency. *The Journal of Nutrition, 126,* 1992–1999.

Pedersen, N. L., Plomin, R., Nesselroade, J. T., & McClearn, G. E. (1992). A quantitative genetic analysis of cognitive abilities during the second half of the life span. *Psychological Science, 3,* 346–353.

Pedersen, N. L., Reynolds, C. A., & Gatz, M. (1996). Sources of covariation among Mini-Mental State Examination scores, education, and cognitive abilities. *The Journals of Gerontology. Series B, Psychological Sciences and Social Sciences, 51,* 55–63.

Petersen, R. C. (2003). Conceptual overview. In R. C. Petersen (Ed.), *Mild cognitive impairment: Aging to disease* (pp. 1–14). New York: Oxford University Press.

Petersen, R. C., Smith, G. E., Ivnik, R. J., Tangalos, E. G., Schaid, D. I., Thibodeau, S., et al. (1995). Apolipoprotein E status as a predictor of the development of Alzheimer's disease in memory-impaired individuals. *Journal of the American Medical Association, 273,* 1274–1278.

Petersen, R. C., Smith, G. E., Waring, S. C., Ivnik, R. J., Tangalos, E. G., & Kokmen, E. (1999). Mild cognitive impairment: Clinical characterization and outcome. *Archives of Neurology, 56,* 303–308.

Petersen, R. C., Thomas, R. G., Grundman, M., Bennett, D., Doody, R., Ferris, S., et al. (2005). Vitamin E and donepezil for the treatment of mild cognitive impairment. *New England Journal of Medicine, 352*(23), 2379–2388.

Powell, R. R., & Pohndorf, R. H. (1971). Comparison of adult exercisers and nonexercisers on fluid intelligence and selected physiological variables. *Research Quarterly, 42,* 70–77.

Praag, H., van Kempermann, G., & Gage, F. H. (1999). Running increases cell proliferation and neurogenesis in the adult mouse dentate gyrus. *Nature Neuroscience, 2,* 266–270.

Raz, N., Rodrigue, K.M., & Acker, J.D. (2003). Hypertension and the brain: Vulnerability of the prefrontal regions and executive functions. *Behavioral Neuroscience, 17,* 1169–1180.

Raz, N., Lindenberger, U., Rodrigue, K. M., Kennedy, K. M., Head, D., Williamson, et al. (2005). Regional brain changes in aging healthy adults: General trends, individual differences, and modifiers. *Cerebral Cortex, 15,* 1676–1689.

Rice, T., An, P., Gagnon, J., Leon, A. S., Skinner, J. S., Wilmore, J. H., et al. (2002). Heritability of HR and BP response to exercise training in the HERITAGE Family Study. *Medicine and Science in Sports and Exercise, 34,* 972–979.

Rowe, J. W., & Kahn, R. L. (1987). Human aging: Usual and successful. *Science, 237,* 143–149.

Scarmeas, N., Levy, G., Tang, M. X., Manly, J., & Stern, Y. (2001). Influence of leisure activity on the incidence of Alzheimer's disease. *Neurology, 57,* 2236–2242.

Schaie, K. W. (1984). Midlife influences upon intellectual functioning in old age. *International Journal of Behavioral Development, 7,* 463–478.

Schaie, K. W. (2005). *Developmental influences on adult intelligence: The Seattle Longitudinal Study.* New York: Oxford University Press.

Schaie, K. W., & Elder, G. H. Jr. (Eds.). (2005). *Historical influence on lives and aging.* New York: Springer Publishing Co.

Schaie, K. W., & Hofer, S. M. (2001). Longitudinal studies in research on aging. In J. E. Birren & K. W. Schaie (Eds.), *Handbook of the psychology of aging* (5th ed., pp. 55–77). San Diego, CA: Academic Press.

Schaie, K. W., Willis, S. L., & Pennak, S. (2005). A historical framework for cohort differences in intelligence. *Research in Human Development, 2,* 43–67.

Schooler, C., Mulatu, M. S., & Oates, G. (2004). Occupational self-direction, intellectual functioning, and self-directed orientation in old workers: Findings and implications for individuals and societies. *American Journal of Sociology, 110, 161–197.*

Sirevaag, A. M., Black, J. E., Shafron, D., & Greenough, W. T. (1998). Direct evidence that complex experience increases capillary branching and surface area in visual cortex of young rats. *Brain Research, 471,* 299–304.

Smyth, K. A., Fritsch, T., Cook, T. B., McClendon, M. J., Santillan, C. E., & Friedland, R. P. (2004). Worker functions and traits associated with occupations and the development of AD. *Neurology, 63,* 498–503.

Snowdon, D. A., Kemper, S. J., Mortimer, J. A., Greiner, L. H., Wekstein, D. R., & Markesbery, W. R. (1996). Linguistic ability in early life and cognitive function and Alzheimer's disease in late life: Findings from the Nun Study. *Journal of the American Medical Association, 275,* 528–532.

Speakman, J. R. (2004). Obesity: The integrated roles of environment and genetics. *Journal of Nutrition, 134,* 2090S-2105S.

Stern, Y., Alexander, G. E., Prohovnik, I., & Mayeux, R. (1992). Inverse relationship between education and parietotemporal perfusion deficit in Alzheimer's disease. *Annals of Neurology, 32,* 371–375.

Stern, Y., Alexander, G. E., Prohovnik, I., Stricks, L., Link, B., Lennon, M. C., et al. (1995). Relationship between lifetime occupation and parietal flow: Implications for a reserve against Alzheimer's disease pathology. *Neurology, 45,* 55–60.

Stern, Y., Gurland, B., Tatemichi, T. K., Tang, M. X., Wilder, D., & Mayeux, R. (1994). Influence of education and occupation on the incidence of Alzheimer's disease. *Journal of the American Medical Association, 271,*1004–1010.

Strittmatter, W. J., Saunders, A. M., Schmechel, D., Pericak-Vance, M., Enghild, J., Salvesen, G. S., et al. (1993). Apolipoprotein E: High avidity binding to -amyloid and increased frequency of type 4 allele in late-onset familial Alzheimer disease. *Proceedings of the National Academy of Science, 90,* 1977–1981.

Wang, H. X., Karp, A., Winblad, B., & Fratiglioni, L. (2002). Late-life engagement in social and leisure activities is associated with a decreased risk of dementia: A longitudinal study from the Kungsholmen project. *American Journal of Epidemiology, 155,* 1081–1087.

Weuve, J., Kang, J. H., Manson, J. E., Breteler, M. M., Ware, J. H., & Grodstein, F. (2004). Physical activity, including walking, and cognitive function in older women. *Journal of the American Medical Association, 292,* 1454–1461.

Wilson, R. S., & Bennett, D. A. (2003). Cognitive activity and risk of Alzheimer's disease. *Current Directions in Psychological Science, 12,* 87–91.

Wilson, R. S., Mendes de Leon, C. F., Barnes, L. L., Schneider, J. A., Bienias, J. L., Evans, D. A., et al. (2002). Participation in cognitively stimulating activities and risk of incident Alzheimer disease. *Journal of the American Medical Association, 287,* 742–748.

Zanjani, F.A.K. (2004). *Developmental trajectory of health behaviors across the adult lifespan.* Unpublished doctoral dissertation, The Pennsylvania State University.

Zhang, M., Katzman, R., Salmon, D., Jin, H., Cai, G., Wang, Z., et al. (1990). The prevalence of dementia and Alzheimer's disease in Shanghai, China: Impact of age, gender, and education. *Annals of Neurology, 27,* 428–437.

2

Wisdom in Social Context

Ursula M. Staudinger, Eva-Marie Kessler, and Jessica Dörner

In this chapter, we discuss the social nature of wisdom. A social-contextual framework for the study of wisdom is indeed highly useful because wisdom is an inherently social phenomenon. A number of different facets of this social nature of wisdom can be distinguished: (a) its source (wisdom revolves around social conditions and their specific challenges and uncertainties); (b) its genesis (social interactions are an important antecedent and correlate in micro- and ontogenesis); (c) its recognition (wisdom is typically identified through consensus); and (d) its function (usually wisdom dilemmas have a social dimension). It is the central aim of this chapter to illustrate and elaborate these facets covering proximal social environments (including persons), as well as distal social contexts (e.g., societies and historical periods). In doing so, we focus on the Berlin wisdom paradigm as a particularly well-validated empirical approach that has assigned importance to the social nature of wisdom from its beginning in the 1980s (Baltes & Staudinger, 2000).

The chapter is divided into two main parts. In the first part, we describe our conceptualization of wisdom which distinguishes personal from general wisdom (see also Staudinger, Dörner, & Mickler, 2005b). Based on this theoretical background, we then explicate how wisdom is expressed in as well as influenced by social context ranging from the micro to the macro level. The second part is a detailed account of the different facets of the social nature of wisdom.

WISDOM IN SOCIAL CONTEXT: CONCEPTUALIZATION AND THEORETICAL CONSIDERATIONS

Defining Wisdom

Within the Berlin wisdom paradigm, wisdom is defined as the highest level of insight and judgment in the *fundamental pragmatics of life*. The fundamental pragmatics encompass knowledge and judgment about the essence of the human condition and the ways and means of planning, managing, and understanding a good life. Please note that this definition of wisdom focuses on insights into life *in general;* that is, the definition concentrates on insights that have been derived *from an observer's point of view* and that are applied to general and not personal problems in life. It has been proposed that in addition to this type of wisdom, which has been labeled *general* wisdom, there is another kind of wisdom called *personal* wisdom (Staudinger, 1999b, 2005; Staudinger et al., 2005b). This distinction is loosely related to the philosophical separation between the ontology of the first and the third person (Searle, 1992). The ontology of the first person indicates insight into life based on personal experience. In contrast, the ontology of the third person refers to the view of life based on an observer's perspective. In loose analogy to Searle's first-person perspective, we maintain that personal wisdom refers to a person's insight into his or her own life: What does a person know about himself/herself, his/her life? Analogous to the third-person perspective as mentioned above, general wisdom is concerned with general insights about life. We would like to suggest that this distinction between personal and general wisdom might be helpful when trying to settle some of the ongoing debates in the field of wisdom research. We believe that it is an empirical question whether or not both types of wisdom always coincide in a person. A person can be wise about life and the problems of other people, and can be sought out for advice from others because of his or her wisdom, but the very same person does not necessarily have to be wise about his or her own life and problems (see Table 2.1). This question can only be answered, however, if the two types of wisdom are conceptualized and measured independently of each other.

The two types of wisdom are related to different research traditions. The approaches primarily geared towards personal wisdom usually originate

TABLE 2.1 Theoretical Dimensions to be Considered When Studying Wisdom

Level of performance	Life Experience: Personal		Life Experience: General	
	Judgment	Action	Judgment	Action
Normal	Self-Insight	Life Management	Life Insight	Advice Giving
Top	Personal Wisdom		General Wisdom	
		Wisdom		

out of personality research and personality development. Wisdom in this perspective describes the mature personality or the endpoint of personality growth (e.g., Erikson, 1959; Helson & Srivastava, 2001; Helson & Wink, 1987). When thinking about wisdom from this vantage point, clearly there are close links to research on coping (e.g., Aldwin & Sutton, 1998; Vaillant, 1993). In comparison, the approaches primarily oriented towards investigating general wisdom typically have a stronger connection with the historical wisdom literature and an expertise approach to the study of wisdom (e.g., Aldwin & Sutton, 1998; Baltes, Smith, & Staudinger, 1992; Sternberg, 1998; Vaillant, 1993).

General and Personal Wisdom: The Assessment Paradigm

In the Berlin Model, five criteria have been developed to index general wisdom (Baltes et al., 1992) and another five criteria to index personal wisdom (Staudinger et al., 2005b) considered as crucial in order to judge wisdom-related action or thoughts (Baltes et al., 1992). We will first describe the criteria used to evaluate accomplishments with regard to general wisdom, and subsequently summarize the ones related to personal wisdom.

The first criterion used to evaluate general wisdom-related performance, *factual knowledge,* concerns insights into domains such as human nature, lifespan development, variations in developmental processes and outcomes, interpersonal relations, and social norms and their limitations. A second criterion, *procedural knowledge,* involves insight into the strategies and heuristics for dealing with the meaning and conduct of life, for example, heuristics for giving advice and ways to handle conflicts. Additionally, a wise person should show *lifespan contextualism;* that is, consider life problems in relation to the domains of life (e.g., education, family, work, friends, leisure, the public good of society, etc.), their interrelations, and to put these in a lifetime perspective (i.e., past, present, future). *Relativism of values and life priorities* is another criterion of wisdom. It means to acknowledge and tolerate interindividual differences in values, as long as they are geared towards optimizing and balancing the individual and the common good. Finally, the last criterion, the *recognition and management of uncertainty,* is based on the idea that human beings can never know everything that is necessary to determine the best decision in the present, to predict the future perfectly, or to be 100% sure about why things happened the way they did in the past. A wise person is aware of this uncertainty and has developed ways to manage it.

Five criteria have been defined to index personal wisdom based on the literature about personality development (Mickler & Staudinger, 2006; Staudinger et al., 2005b): The first criterion is *rich self-insight,* that is, deep insight into oneself. A self-wise person should be aware of his or her own competencies, emotions, and goals, and have a sense of meaning in life. The second criterion requires a self-wise person to have available *heuristics for growth and self-regulation,* such as how to express and regulate emotions or how to develop and maintain deep social relations. *Interrelating the self,* the third criterion, refers to the ability to reflect on and have insight into the possible causes of one's behavior and/or feelings. Such causes can be age-related, situational, or linked to personal characteristics. Interrelating the self also implies that there is awareness about one's own dependency on others. The fourth criterion is called *self-relativism.* People high in self-relativism are able to evaluate themselves as well as others from a distance. They critically appraise their own behavior, but at the same time display a basic acceptance of themselves. They also show tolerance for others' values and lifestyles—as long as they are not damaging to self or others. Finally, *tolerance of ambiguity* involves the ability to recognize and manage the uncertainties in one's own life and one's own development. It is reflected in the awareness that life is full of uncontrollable and unpredictable events, including death and illness. At the same time, tolerance for ambiguity includes the availability of strategies to manage this uncertainty through openness to experience, basic trust, and the development of flexible solutions.

In theory, the criteria indexing general wisdom can be used to evaluate any outcome, be it by individuals, groups, or even entire societies. Within empirical studies, so far the criteria have primarily been used to judge the performance of individuals. An individual's wisdom-related performance in terms of general wisdom is assessed by presenting individuals with fictitious life dilemmas such as the following: "Someone receives a telephone call from a good friend who says that he or she cannot go on like this and has decided to commit suicide. What might one/the person take into consideration and do in such a situation?" Likewise, in order to measure personal wisdom, individuals are required to answer such questions as, "How are you as a friend/in friendships? What comes to mind when you think about this question?" Participants are then asked to think aloud about the task.

The responses are recorded on tape, transcribed, and subsequently rated by a panel of 10 judges in the light of the five criteria (two raters evaluate the same criterion).

Table 2.1 shows that yet another distinction seems relevant when investigating wisdom. It is the distinction between normal levels of functioning and highest levels of functioning. By definition, wisdom is reserved to denote highest levels or ideal forms of functioning (e.g., Baltes, 1993). It may be confusing to also denote lower or average levels of functioning as wisdom (although it is often done in the literature). It is therefore suggested to choose a different term for levels of functioning below the highest level. One may either call them wisdom-related (e.g., Staudinger, Smith, & Baltes, 1994), or even use a completely different term such as "insight," as suggested in Table 2.1. Wisdom is called *self-insight* when the focus is on personal wisdom and *life-insight* whenever forms of general wisdom are concerned. The relationship with predictors such as personality may differ depending on whether average or highest levels of functioning are concerned. Very rarely, however, is the relation between wisdom and personality tested for non-linear trends (for exception see Staudinger, Lopez, & Baltes, 1997; Staudinger & Pasupathi, 2003).

As will be discussed later, there is a third dimension that should be considered, namely wisdom referring to judgment and wisdom referring to action. Mostly wisdom research has focused on judgment. Only a few studies have started to examine the action side of wisdom (eg., Bluck, 2004; Oser, Schenker & Spychinger, 1999). One kind of wise action in the realm of general wisdom is certainly advice giving. With regard to personal wisdom it is *life-management* that represents the action side of wisdom.

THE SOCIAL NATURE OF WISDOM

Since the beginning of research within the Berlin wisdom paradigm, the social nature of wisdom has been given credit. But with regard to the assessment paradigm described above, a person-centered approach was still predominant (Baltes et al., 1992). Over the years, a social perspective on wisdom became more and more elaborated on, both theoretically and empirically (Staudinger, 1996; Staudinger & Baltes, 1996). At the center of this perspective is the four-fold social nature of wisdom. Wisdom is social with regard to (a) its source, (b) its acquisition/activation, (c) its function, as well as (d) its recognition.

First, as mentioned above, wisdom addresses questions concerning important and difficult life problems about the conduct and meaning of life. As life problems are mostly of a social nature (Berg, Strough, Calderone, Sansone, & Weir, 1998; Meegan & Berg, 2002; Strough, Berg, & Sansone, 1996), social contexts with their specific and interconnected challenges and uncertainties can be regarded *as a fundamental source of wisdom*—both in the course of cultural evolution as well as ontogenesis. Second, wisdom— as any kind of human knowledge—is mostly *acquired* in social contexts (Baltes & Smith, 1990; Staudinger, 1996). A wise Kaspar Hauser is difficult to imagine; the Buddhist monk who is meditating in a monastery without communicative contact over weeks cannot be assumed to have acquired his insights without former social interaction (including interaction with social artifacts such as religious texts, law compendiums, novels). These very examples illustrate that social contexts are *conditiones sine qua non* when it comes to the evolution and ontogenesis of wisdom. However, we will argue later that when it comes to the activation (microgenesis) of wisdom in a given situation, social contexts are not only constitutive of—at least in the case of general wisdom—but also facilitative for wisdom-related performance (Staudinger & Baltes, 1996). Third, in philosophical, cultural-historical, psychological, and lay theories of wisdom, wisdom implies a very strong orientation towards the social context. Striving towards an equilibrium between self-interests and interests of others and seeking a common good is what characterizes wisdom across many theories (e.g., Baltes & Staudinger, 2000; Sternberg, 1998). General wisdom also includes good advice giving (see Table 2.1). Wisdom, thus, has a strong *social function*. Fourth, the *recognition of wisdom* requires social consensus (Staudinger, 1996). A so-called wise person does not attribute wisdom to him- or herself; rather, wisdom is attributed to her or him by others based on characteristics that are usually agreed upon by observers (Meacham, 1983).

Before we start to elaborate on these considerations about the social foundation of wisdom, we would like to spend some time clarifying the rather vague notion of social contexts (Staudinger, 1996). First of all, social contexts need to be differentiated according to their degree of proximity. To do this, we refer to one of the most prominent systematizations of the human ecology, proposed by Bronfenbrenner (1979). He distinguishes four levels of contexts within the ecology of human development, which he calls systems. These four levels are described here by focusing on social contexts in particular (see also Kessler & Staudinger, 2006): (a) The microsystem that is composed of immediate settings (including the person), such as the relationship of an individual to his/her parents; (b) the mesosystem that contains all the microsystems of a person and their interrelations, such as the relationship between a person's family and workplace; (c) the exosystem that does not contain the developing person but impinges upon or encompasses the immediate settings in which the person is living and thereby influences a person's life (e.g., the school of one's children); and (d) the macrosystem that comprises historical events (wars, etc.) as well as cultural values and artifacts that affect all other ecological systems.

Note that our considerations about the four-fold social nature of wisdom can be applied to all four social levels. Specifically, we assume that all four social levels play a role with regard to the source, the acquisition/activation, the function, as well as the recognition of wisdom. Two theoretical consequences are of particular importance here. Wisdom is expressed in as well as influenced by social contexts ranging in level from the micro to the macro. On one hand, individuals, groups of individuals, or the society at large can be agents of wisdom. This implies that we can differentiate between personalized and rather depersonalized (e.g., sociocultural products such as tales or proverbs) carriers of wisdom. Based on the extremely high demands that the elicitation of wisdom puts on knowledge and skills, it is even argued that wisdom, by definition, will hardly ever be found in an individual, but rather in cultural- or social-interactive products like human rights, proverbs, sayings, or tales (Baltes & Smith, 1990; Staudinger, 1996).

On the other hand, social factors that influence the activation and acquisition (as well as maintenance) of wisdom can be immediate or aggregated over individuals and over time—ranging from direct face-to-face interactions between two or more individuals, to interactions with cultural artifacts of any kind (Staudinger, 1996). In accordance with the propositions of lifespan psychology (Baltes, Lindenberger, & Staudinger, 1998, in press), we do not assume that carriers of wisdom are passively exposed to these different types of social contexts. Rather, as people are active contributors to their development (e.g., Brandtstädter, 1984; Kaufmann & Busch-Rossnagel, 1981) transactions (Sameroff, 1975) or dynamic interactions (Lerner, 1984) between social contexts of any level and agents of wisdom need to be taken into account. Note, however, that social contexts do not necessarily contribute to gains in wisdom-related performance. In accordance with lifespan contextualism, we assume that social contexts may be facilitative as well as constraining with regard to the acquisition of wisdom—just as it is the case for any other aspect of cognitive performance (Kessler & Staudinger, 2006; Staudinger & Lindenberger, 2003). For the micro-level perspective, the social-psychological literature on group problem solving has demonstrated most convincingly that two heads are not necessarily better than one (see Staudinger, 1996, for an overview). It has been shown in numerous studies that on the socio-emotional and motivational level, the presence of a group increases arousal, alertness, and perseverance, but also social loafing, free riding, and aggression. On the cognitive level, it has been shown that processes of knowledge activation, modification, and innovation become operative as a consequence of taking part in social interaction, but also so-called coordination losses such as blocking or interference take place.

FACETS OF THE SOCIAL NATURE OF WISDOM

In the next section, we will provide illustrations of the social nature of wisdom as it becomes manifest in cultural evolution, human ontogenesis, and microgenesis. Beyond this developmental perspective, the social nature of wisdom also extends to its function and recognition.

The Social Sources of Wisdom

According to cultural anthropology, whenever human beings form a community, bodies of knowledge dealing with the conduct, interpretation, and meaning of life are constructed that in their highest elaboration are then called wisdom (Cole, 1990, 1996; D'Andrade, 1995). Such knowledge is regarded as one of the first bodies of knowledge to develop in any community of interacting human beings, and is a sign of cultural evolution in process (e.g., Assmann, 1994; Baltes, 1995; Rudolph, 1987). In turn, complex social contexts are a necessary condition for the cultural evolution of wisdom. The body of knowledge and heuristics indexed as wisdom can only develop if and when people intensively and frequently think and act together over time. In this vein, wisdom can be regarded as an indicator as well as a coproduct of sociocultural evolution. The study of proverbs exemplifies the collective nature of the evolution of wisdom-related insight and judgment. Proverbs as "a truth based on common sense or the practical experience of mankind" (*Oxford Dictionary of the English Language,* 1933, p. 165) can be regarded as prototypical products of crystallized social insight (Staudinger, 1996). With increasing size and complexity of human community, the number of proverbs increases, too. An evolutionary approach to the collective manifestation and development of wisdom suggests that wisdom-related insight and judgment increases the likelihood of survival. As bodies of knowledge and skills, they contribute to successful solutions to life problems of a community and thus have adaptive value for humankind. In this vein, Csikszentmihalyi and Rathunde (1990) argue that concepts such as wisdom, which have been used for many centuries under very different social and historical conditions to evaluate human behavior, are most likely to have adaptive value for humankind.

The Ontogenesis of Wisdom

The ways in which specific social contexts facilitate or constrain the development of wisdom will now be illustrated. We have selected three kinds of social contexts that have been studied empirically, namely age, historical background, and profession.[1]

Wisdom and Age

The reader may wonder what is social about age. It is often regarded as a proxy of the experiences made and the number of contexts one has been exposed to. Thus, the question is whether it is enough to grow older in order to become wiser. The answer is a clear no. In contrast to the clichés transported by fairytales and proverbs, empirical studies have consistently failed to corroborate a normative linkage between wisdom and age during adulthood (for a review, see Staudinger, 1999a). For instance, four studies assessing general wisdom by using the Berlin wisdom paradigm with a

---

1. The common core of wisdom can be described as follows (Baltes, 1993): (a) Wisdom represents a truly superior level of knowledge, judgment, and advice; (b) wisdom addresses important and difficult questions and strategies about the conduct and meaning of life; (c) wisdom includes knowledge about the limits of knowledge and the uncertainties of the world; (d) wisdom constitutes knowledge with extraordinary scope, depth, measure, and balance; (e) wisdom involves a perfect synergy of mind and character; (f) wisdom represents knowledge used for the good or well-being of oneself and that of others; and (g) wisdom, although difficult to achieve and to specify, is easily recognized when manifested.

total of 533 participants ranging from 20 to 83 years of age unanimously yielded a nonsignificant correlation between wisdom-related performance and chronological age. (Staudinger & Baltes, 1996). According to these results, even a slight negative trend emerges after age 80. This latter finding seems to confirm the notion that wisdom-related performance requires a certain level of cognitive functioning; once this minimum level of functioning is lost in the wake of the general age-graded decrease in cognitive resources in old age, individuals seem to also have difficulty maintaining their level of wisdom-related performance. So far, however, the number of participants above 80 has been too small to confirm this explanation.

In a study with adolescents (14–19 years of age), it has been shown that age *does* play a significant role for general wisdom-related performance when it comes to younger age groups (Pasupathi, Staudinger, & Baltes, 2001): The relationship between age and wisdom-related performance in adolescence is $r = .46$ (even after controlling for fluid intelligence). Taken together, the results concerning the relation between chronological age and general wisdom suggest that (a) a certain minimum age is necessary to acquire a solid basis of wisdom-related insight and judgment; and (b) further development of wisdom, however, seems to depend on a more complicated pattern of influences than passing time or number of experiences.

With regard to personal wisdom, it was shown that there were even significant negative differences between younger adults (20–40 years of age) and older adults (60–80 years of age). Older people scored significantly lower on the personal wisdom task (Mickler & Staudinger, 2006). This negative difference was amended, however, when controlling for self-disclosure and length of protocol. Nevertheless, it seems that assessing the relationship between age and personal wisdom may pose an even stronger challenge than for general wisdom because it requires self-regulation in addition to deep insight.

We must take into account yet a further qualification about the effect of age on general wisdom, at least. It was shown that it is not the length of exposure to social contexts by itself that fosters wisdom, but rather the salience of the life problem at hand for the participant's current life context that is decisive for the quality of the response. Replicated across four studies was the finding that the quality of performance of a certain age group depended on the age of the fictitious character described in the task: In general, the smaller the age difference between the fictitious character and participant, the better the performance. This phenomenon was called the *age-match effect*

(Smith & Baltes, 1990; Smith, Staudinger, & Baltes, 1994; Staudinger, 1989; Staudinger, Smith, & Baltes, 1992). The age-match effect suggests that, in accordance with the notion of developmental tasks, each life phase is characterized by its own unique tasks and challenges. According to this view, while certain bodies of knowledge get lost or transformed because they are no longer needed at a certain stage in life, other bodies of knowledge are newly acquired in response to the necessities of a new phase in life. As a consequence, one possible way of avoiding this fading of knowledge and of fostering the updating of knowledge related to earlier life phases may be the exposure to age-heterogeneous contexts. On the one hand, this allows anticipatory socialization for younger generations, and on the other hand, it allows older individuals to stay in contact with the tasks of earlier life phases under changed cultural-historical circumstances. With regard to personal wisdom, no such studies are available yet, but it is assumed that the effect may play out in a complementary fashion. We hypothesize that personal life problems of earlier phases in one's life may be approached with greater personal wisdom than currently pressing personal problems.

Historical Contexts

Historical circumstances such as wars or economic crises represent another kind of social context that influences the acquisition of wisdom. This is a field of study that is closely linked with the work of Glen Elder (e.g., 1998). Even though Elder's work has not yet explicitly addressed questions of the ontogenesis of wisdom, his studies of the effects of combat experiences, be it in World War II or the Vietnam War, indirectly bear some relevance. There he found that such stressful and traumatic war events not always impaired, but under certain circumstances, actually enhanced personal growth trajectories (Clipp & Elder, 1996). Thus, he provides some evidence that historical circumstances such as wars may be promoters of the development of personal and possibly also general wisdom.

One study that supports the argument of the relevance of historical circumstances for wisdom development conducted under the Berlin wisdom work is the wisdom nominee study (Baltes, Staudinger, Maercker, & Smith, 1995). The participants in this study had been nominated as wise independently of the Berlin definition of wisdom. In order to avoid the ethical problems related to nominations procedures, public figures in Berlin were selected as a pool for potential nominees. As nominators,

Berlin journalists working on features articles about people were selected to make sure that they had a satisfactory knowledge base for the nomination process. Following a Delphi procedure, each journalist first generated a list of persons whom he or she considered to be wise according to his or her own definition. In a second round, the initial number of 156 wisdom nominees was reduced to a final sample of 16 based on an algorithm asking for high consensus and no veto. Although the age range covered by the wisdom nominees was relatively broad (41–88 years of age), the majority were older adults ($M = 68$ years). This first finding restates the paradoxical relation between wisdom and age addressed earlier—even though wisdom does not automatically come with age, there seems to be a higher likelihood that wise persons are old. By examining the biographical characteristics of this sample, we may be able to get a first impression of who is perceived as wise, and how the specific historical background experienced by these individuals may have shaped their accumulation of life insight.

All public spheres of life such as culture, theology, politics, sciences, and media were represented. Almost two-thirds of participants held a top position in public life, and 44% of them had published their biographies. Especially meaningful is the fact that during World War II, one-third of them had either emigrated from Germany or had been an active member of the resistance movement against the Nazi regime. When investigating their biographies more closely, it turned out that most of the nominees had biographies characterized by different kinds of *Grenzerfahrungen* related to Hitler's dictatorship.

This admittedly indirect evidence nevertheless conveys a first idea of how historical circumstances can be relevant for the accumulation of wisdom. Depending on historical times, our bodily existence may be threatened or our worldviews may be challenged. When mastered successfully, such experiences seem to contribute to gaining insight and making progress on the road to wisdom.

Wisdom and Profession

Besides age and historical setting, professional contexts are also relevant social settings that may facilitate or hinder the accrual of wisdom. Three conditions have been specified as especially relevant for such settings: (a) extensive experience with a wide range of human conditions; (b) tutored or mentor-guided practice in dealing with difficult life problems; and (c) motivational dispositions, such as generativity, are especially relevant when it comes to the ontogenetic sources of wisdom (Staudinger et al., 1992). In line with this framework, we sought to investigate in one study whether professional experience in a human-service profession (e.g., clinical psychologist) was conducive to the acquisition of wisdom-related knowledge and judgment. We assumed that certain characteristics of the profession of clinical psychologists, such as being concerned with the conduct and interpretation of life, and continuous training in dealing with difficult life problems as well as with giving advice in difficult and uncertain matters of life, would contribute to higher levels of general wisdom-related insight and judgment. According to our assumptions, clinical psychologists should therefore perform better on a wisdom-related task than a matched control group. The analysis of the results indeed indicated a clear effect for type of professional specialization: the group of clinical psychologists was rated significantly higher than the control group (i.e., professionals from non-human service professions but of comparative educational level and social standing). The factor type of professional specialization accounted for a sizeable 49% of the variance of the linear combination of the wisdom-related performance. Note, however, that although clinical psychologists outperformed the control group, they did not perform at a level that would be characterized as "wise." In fact, as a group, the clinical psychologists obtained only average scores on wisdom-related criteria. Such studies about the effect of professional contexts, however, bear the problem that effects of selection into a certain profession are difficult to separate from experimental effects (see Staudinger, Maciel, Smith & Baltes, 1998).

WISDOM AND MICROGENESIS

So far, we have discussed the effects of different kinds of social contexts on the ontogenesis of wisdom. Now, we will summarize evidence concerning the significance of social contexts for the very process of creating a wise outcome (such as thoughts and actions).

First of all, as mentioned previously, it is important to note that the most difficult problems are frequently of a social nature (Berg et al., 1998; Meegan & Berg, 2002; Strough, Berg, & Sansone, 1996). In turn, it seems only reasonable that the solution for problems of a social nature ideally requires more than one person. In fact, it might be fair to say that whenever a situation calls for wisdom, most often more than one person is involved. Thus, wisdom very often is activated in situations of advice seeking or giving when faced with a difficult life problem. For example, when we consider how people deal with existential life problems, we find that very often they do consult with others, or perhaps also with books, before making a decision or coming up with a proper interpretation of events.

This general observation is supported by the results of a survey where we asked people how they usually went about solving fundamental life problems. Specifically, a sample ($N = 140$) of differing social background ranging in age from 19–80 years was asked to which degree they dealt with life problems by (a) thinking about them by themselves; (b) "consulting" books or other media; (c) thinking what other people might say to the problem at hand; or (d) actually consulting with other people (Staudinger, 1996). Overall, participants reported the highest degree of endorsement for the option of consulting with others. Significantly lower in rank were both the option of thinking about the problem by oneself and the option of taking into account what other people might say to this problem. In sum, this finding seems to suggest that on average, people do indeed highly value others' perspectives and advice when trying to solve fundamental life problems.

When considering the effects of social interaction (in a proximal sense) on the microgenesis of wisdom-related performance, it is first of all useful to differentiate on the one hand between task-related cognitive gains and losses, and socioemotional and motivational interactive gains and losses on the other (Bales & Strodtbeck, 1951). With regard to general wisdom, task-related or cognitive effects might be of primary importance. We would like to propose that there are at least three different positive task-related or cognitive effects of social interaction on wisdom-related performance (Staudinger, 1996). First, others might compensate for blind spots that people might be unable or unwilling to see themselves. Using the language of a semantic network view of the mind, one could say that inactive nodes are reactivated by interaction partners. Thus, others can help to retrieve knowledge, and thereby enable a more comprehensive view. Additionally, because different individuals have different strengths, they can compensate for each other's weaknesses when it comes to solving a certain task. Second, others can modify our views. Numerous empirical studies have documented how strongly we are influenced by the feedback from others, be it with regard to our attitudes, our actions, or thoughts. In the language of semantic networks, this would imply that existing relationships between nodes are revised. Finally, a third wisdom-fostering feature of social interaction is that others enable innovation by providing us with new ideas, resulting in the emergence of new linkages between nodes. Not only can a participant reveal his or her ideas to another person, but during the conversation, new ideas might emerge that had not previously occurred to any of the participants, implying that nodes are added to the mental network. However, it should not be forgotten that social interaction can entail negative effects as well. Other people's stream of thoughts can interfere with those of an individual, they can distract the individual's attention from crucial points, and interaction partners might not be able to coordinate their thoughts with each other.

To examine the role of collaborative conditions, we conducted a study in which natural dyads responded to general wisdom tasks under varying conditions of social support and collaboration. Specifically, we compared participants who responded spontaneously and by themselves to a wisdom task with (a) those who discussed the problem with a significant other and had some time to think by themselves before responding individually; (b) those who engaged in a virtual internal dialogue about the wisdom problem with a person of their choice; (c) those who discussed the problem with a significant other but had no time to think about it on their own before responding; and (d) a group who had time to think about the problem by themselves and did not receive any further instruction before responding (Staudinger, 1996; Staudinger & Baltes, 1996).

The outcome was fully supportive of the view that social collaboration, whether internal or external, facilitates wisdom-related performance if there was enough time to integrate the materials and ideas activated during the conversation before responding. Social facilitation was also found for the condition that involved discourse with an inner rather than a real voice. The increase in performance was close to one standard deviation. In line with the social-context approach to wisdom was the finding that combining individual thinking time with a collaborative condition was the most successful to enhance wisdom-related performance. A possibly surprising finding was that symbolically mediated interaction was as facilitative as real interaction. We assume that this is due to the fact that it provides for more individual freedom in terms of when to access another person's knowledge system. Thus, interactional losses due to a lack of coordination or to socio-emotional discordances are minimized.

Recently, we also investigated the effects that social interaction has on performance in relation to personal wisdom. Because of the different nature of the tasks as well as the construct itself, we assumed we would see different effects of social interaction than in the case of general wisdom. In particular, whereas the effects of compensation, modification, and innovation should still be operating in a beneficial way when it comes to personal wisdom, some detrimental social effects may gain importance. Since personal wisdom is, among other aspects, related to reflecting about oneself in a critical and open manner, it seems crucial that the interaction partner is trustworthy and benevolent but also candid and outspoken. The dialogue is potentially threatening for the self-esteem of the target person and may therefore not be used to its fullest potential. Certainly, partners brought to the lab also differ in the degree to which they are willing and able to communicate frankly and constructively with the target person. Therefore, we expected the effect of the dyadic interaction to show greater interindividual differences in terms of personal wisdom-related performance than that of general. Furthermore, the closeness of the relationship between the interaction partners most likely plays an important role: With increasing closeness (in particular, length) of a relationship, there is a tendency to have established attitudes and views about the partner and also fixed communicative rituals that may not be conducive to change in mutual perceptions. Thus, even though we assumed that social interaction can have facilitative effects for personal wisdom performance, we also had to take into account these detrimental effects and assume that (a) difference between those experimental conditions that did involve social interaction and those that did not for personal than for general wisdom; and that (b) duration of the relationship between interaction partners would show a curvilinear relationship in the sense that a medium length relationship would be most facilitative to personal wisdom performance.

Besides the effect of social context, we examined the effect of different types of thinking about oneself (Staudinger, Dörner, & Mickler, 2005a). Namely, we were interested in whether training in structured life-reflection would facilitate the performance of personal wisdom more so than reminiscing about oneself or thinking about oneself without receiving any further instruction. The training in life-reflection was aimed at instructing participants to consider three elements when thinking about themselves: remembering, explaining, and evaluating (for a more detailed view, see Staudinger, 2001). With this approach we then investigated the following hypotheses:

1. Participants who received training in life-reflection should show higher personal wisdom performance than those who have not.
2. On average, dyadic life-reflection is not more facilitative than monadic.

But when considering closeness of relationships, it is relationships of medium closeness that are mostly conducive to increases in personal wisdom performance. Four experimental conditions were constructed to test these hypotheses: (a) a dialogue condition that involves structured self-reflection together with a familiar person before answering the task; (b) a monadic condition which included structured self-reflection done in private before answering; (c) a reminiscence condition where, before answering, participants were asked to remember events without having received training in structured life-reflection; and (d) a control condition where participants responded to the task right away, without having had time to reflect or having received training in life-reflection beforehand. One hundred sixty-nine persons took part in the experiment, half of them belonging to the group of younger adults (20–40 years of age), and the other half belonging to the group of older adults (60–80 years of age). Results demonstrated that training in structured life-review indeed enhanced personal wisdom performance; that is, participants in the dialogue and monadic condition yielded significantly higher scores on personal wisdom than participants of the other two conditions. Furthermore, in line with our hypothesis, dialogue and monadic condition did not differ significantly: This result seems to suggest that the potential beneficial effects of the social interaction in this experiment indeed were masked by inter-individual differences in the candidness of the social interaction. We also confirmed our hypothesis concerning the effect of the closeness of the relationship. Indeed it were those relationships of medium closeness that were most beneficial. In other words, a dialogue with one's best friends or one's spouse promoted personal wisdom performance less than talking to someone with whom one is quite familiar but less close (Staudinger et al., 2005).

When comparing results on the facilitative effect of contexts on general wisdom and personal wisdom, we gain the impression that it is easier to create social circumstances that promote general wisdom than those that facilitate personal wisdom. The potentially enlightening effect of social interaction is overshadowed by self-protective mechanisms utilized by both partners that aim to avoid threatening the self-esteem of the target person.

WISDOM AND CONSENSUAL RECOGNITION

A further facet of wisdom's social nature is that wisdom usually is recognized by consensus among members of a human community. There is no absolute standard according to which the quality of knowledge and judgment concerning the conduct and meaning of life can be evaluated. Rather, this kind of insight needs to be qualified by social consensus. In other words, bodies of knowledge only become wisdom by confirmation of recurrent action in a given community (Staudinger, 1996). Proverbs, such crystallizations of experience and insight, are a good example. They only crystallize and get put into use by recurrent agreement of a community of people on the basis of their experiences (Goodwin & Wenzel, 1981).

And indeed, studies on people's folk conceptions of wisdom suggest that people hold fairly clear-cut and consensual images about wisdom and wise people. Despite methodological differences, it is striking that all of the past studies in this area have uniformly shown that lay conceptions of wisdom entail social (e.g., empathy, the ability to give good advice), emotional (e.g., elaborate knowledge about other people's and one's own emotions), cognitive (e.g., intellectual abilities, exceptional levels of knowledge about the self and the world), and motivational (e.g., ability to pursue one's goals) capacities (e.g., Clayton & Birren, 1980; Holliday & Chandler, 1986; Orwoll & Perlmutter, 1990; Sternberg, 1985). Furthermore, subjective representations about the ontogenetic development of wisdom are widely shared. People show general beliefs that wisdom increases with age and that older people are more likely than young people to be nominated as wise (e.g., Sowarka, 1989). We also find a systematic overlap in conceptions of wisdom in cultural-historical and philosophical work. Baltes (1993) identified a common core of seven properties that represent wisdom.[2]

---

2. Mentorship in various social contexts, such as families, peer groups, or in professional socialization, is also regarded as another important factor in the acquisition of wisdom-related knowledge and judgment. However, as there are no studies with the framework of the Berlin wisdom paradigm that examine the effects of mentorship on the emergence of wisdom, this aspect is not discussed here (for a discussion, see Staudinger, 1996). At this point, we would only like to mention that only tailored forms of mentoring can be assumed to be beneficial in this process.

Thus, the concept of wisdom in its language-based representation and cultural-historical manifestation is widely shared.

These two aspects of consensual recognition (need for consensus, high empirical intersubjectivity) have been explicitly acknowledged in the Berlin wisdom paradigm. First, social consensus is part of the standard assessment paradigm (general and personal wisdom). The quality of participants' responses is evaluated via raters' judgments. The rating is done according to defined dimensions, but the rating procedure leaves room for the integration of the evaluative judgment in each rater's head. Nevertheless, we obtain reliabilities with this rating procedure that range between .7–.95 Cronbach's Alpha. Further, a rating of responses according to the raters' own conceptions of wisdom, without providing our definition, results in interrater consistencies of about .7 and a correlation of .7, with a wisdom rating obtained through the application of the five wisdom-related criteria (Staudinger et al., 1992). Also, in a study of people that were nominated as wise by a group of nominators (irrespective of our definition), high consensus was reached concerning the final group of nominees (Baltes et al., 1995).

WISDOM AND ITS SOCIAL FUNCTION

Finally, the social nature of wisdom is also expressed in the social function of wisdom. A core aspect of the definition of wisdom through cultures and historical times is its aim to further the well-being of oneself and others (Baltes & Staudinger, 2000.) Sternberg's (1998) balance theory of wisdom most explicitly takes this aspect into account. For him, wisdom by definition is practical intelligence that is oriented towards a balance between self-interest, the interests of others, and of other contextual interests. The term interest here encompasses multiple points of view that include cognitive, affective, and motivational divergences. By balancing intrapersonal, interpersonal, and extrapersonal cognitions, affects, and motivations, a common good is achieved.

The social function of wisdom is also contained in one of its central expressions, that is, wise advice. Take for example the famous judgment or advice of King Solomon that is often used as a prototypical example of wisdom. From early on, wisdom had the societal function of educating the youth (e.g., Assmann 1994; Rudolph, 1987). It is often argued, however, that exercise of power has been another social function of wisdom. Full access to this body of knowledge was confined to certain societal elites, enabling them to exercise power (Rudolph, 1987).

The social function of wisdom is also reflected in folk conceptions in which wise persons are described as being sensitive, sincere, fair, warm, and tolerant rather than being manipulative, irresponsible, calculating, or hostile (e.g., Clayton & Birren, 1980; Helson & Srivastava, 2002; Holliday & Chandler, 1986). These lay beliefs are perfectly matched by empirical findings emerging from the Berlin wisdom paradigm. For instance, it has been shown that individuals with higher scores on general wisdom-related performance report a preference for cooperative conflict strategies while expressing little preference for those strategies indicating dominance, submission, or avoidance (Kunzmann & Baltes, 2003). In the same study, general wisdom-related insight and judgment was positively related to other enhancing values such as values relating to the well-being of friends, societal engagement, and ecological protection, as well as self-enhancing values that are oriented toward self-actualization and insight into life in general. Similarly, in a recent study of personal wisdom, it was found that people with higher levels of personal wisdom performance also reported stronger endorsement of eudaimonic than hedonic values and interests (Mickler & Staudinger, 2006).

CONCLUSION

Dictionary definitions as well as implicit and explicit theories of wisdom speak to its social nature. Four facets have been distinguished and discussed: its source, its genesis, its recognition, and its function. This complex social nature suggests that even though wisdom is conceptualized as a body of superior insight and judgment, it is far more than "cold" cognitions of single individuals (as recently argued by Ardelt, 2004). Rather, wisdom—based on its social embeddedness and its underlying emotional and motivational factors—is a collectively anchored body of "hot" cognitions and judgments. We tried to illustrate this idea by highlighting the multiple social facets of wisdom in this chapter.

Using a social-contextual framework to investigate the concept of wisdom not only helps to grasp the different facets of the social nature of wisdom, but also to detect the uncharted territory in this field of research.

Particularly, we would like to mention three lacunae. First, the assessment of the social benevolence involved in wise judgments is usually based on self-report. However, it is one thing to report about behavior and values and another thing to actually realize them in actions. The degree to which such self-reported intentions generalize to the behavioral level is an exciting and challenging field of research to explore. Second, the interactive minds paradigm gives credit to the social-interactive nature of the activation of wisdom; however, general as well as personal wisdom are still assessed within the individual. Proceeding from the assumption that wisdom is a body of knowledge rather than a characteristic attributed to a person (Baltes & Staudinger, 1993), the empirical assessment should also be used beyond the "personological" approach to include the assessment of groups or of collective outcomes such as constitutional texts. The study of proverbs is a first step in this direction (e.g., Freund & Baltes, 2002). Third, extant research has focused almost exclusively on social contexts of the micro level as limiters or facilitators of wisdom. Investigating the role of social contexts of the macro level (ranging from specific events such as natural catastrophes and wars to educational systems and value systems prevailing at a given historical time) more closely may be a worthwhile undertaking. Cross-sequential longitudinal designs where multiple birth cohorts are followed over time would allow approaching the examination of the role of shifting cultural contexts in the development of wisdom in human ontogenesis as well as cultural evolution.

Commentary: The Dynamic Relationship Between Age Stereotypes and Wisdom in Old Age

Becca R. Levy and Corey Pilver

In their chapter "Wisdom in Social Context," Staudinger, Kessler, and Dörner (this volume) argue that wisdom, which they define as "the highest level of insight and judgment in the fundamental pragmatics of life" is the product of societal influences. Our comments will focus on: (a) the innovations of their presentation and the research it describes; (b) whether age stereotypes (defined as beliefs about old age) are an additional social factor, not considered in their chapter, that may influence and be influenced by wisdom; and (c) suggestions for future research prompted by their findings.

INNOVATIONS OF WISDOM IN SOCIAL CONTEXT

Previous empirical studies of wisdom have focused primarily on wisdom as a phenomenon rooted in the cognition of the individual, isolated from the social context. Staudinger and colleagues' point that wisdom is essentially social is well argued. They provide empirical evidence that wisdom is generated and enhanced through social interaction, is identified and defined by groups rather than individuals, and provides clear social functions, such as advice giving.

A strength of the wisdom research described in the chapter is that Staudinger and her colleagues found creative ways to operationalize wisdom as a social construct. For example, in one study, Staudinger and Baltes (1996) developed a method of assessing wisdom that requires participants to come to the laboratory with a friend. Then, using these naturally occurring dyads, participants are randomly assigned to one of five treatment conditions and asked to discuss two problem-solving tasks that focus on life problems that are embedded in social situations. Responses are then assessed by a panel of raters in order to mimic the social consensus that, the authors propose, is a part of recognizing wisdom.

Additionally, a strength of this chapter is that it places wisdom research into a greater social context by integrating the levels of wisdom operation with the various types of influence on them. The authors draw on the literatures of numerous disciplines, including cultural anthropology, history, personality psychology, and developmental psychology. For example, the authors explain how wisdom can be generated and influenced at each level of Broffenbroner's (1979) systems of social interaction.

AGE STEREOTYPES AND WISDOM

A paradox about the relationship between age and wisdom emerges from the important body of work described in the chapter. On the one hand, a number of studies, using a variety of methods, have found that a popular belief exists in many cultures that wisdom increases in old age (e.g., Baltes, et al., 1995; Heckhausen, Dixon, & Baltes, 1989). On the other hand, the authors point out that, "In contrast to the cliches transported by fairytales and proverbs, empirical studies have consistently failed to corroborate a normative linkage between wisdom and age during adulthood" (Staudinger et al., this volume p. 33). Indeed, one study described in the chapter found that older individuals had significantly lower scores on a personal wisdom tasks than younger individuals.

This contradiction was highlighted by a study that the authors describe in which Berlin journalists nominated individuals in public life that they considered "wise" and "life-experienced" (Baltes et al., 1995). It can be assumed that the journalists selecting the group of wisdom nominees were well informed about their choices since they all specialized in writing features articles about people. The mean age of the wisdom nominees was 64 years of age; with more than one-third of those initially identified as wise being over the age of 80. Yet the average level of wisdom performance among the wisdom nominees, and drawn from other sources, did not significantly increase with age, even though the final sample ranged from 25 to 80 years.

One way of resolving the apparent contradictory observations related to wisdom and age would be to expand the way wisdom is operationalized to also include agreement among members of a community that an individual is wise. This approach is consistent with defining wisdom as a social construct.

The divergence between the popular view that wisdom increases in old age and empirically-measured wisdom, that does not increase in old age, leads to a fundamental question: If, as the authors demonstrate, wisdom is a product of its social context, why is there a failure of societal expectations to result in greater wisdom among the old?

A potential explanation for this paradox can be found from drawing on a number of studies of how age stereotypes operate. We have previously shown that, for elders, societal expectations can be generated through images of aging, and that, in turn, these images can predict functioning over a 23-year period (Levy, Slade, & Kasl, 2002). These expectations seem to arise from two sources. First, there are the age stereotypes that become internalized during childhood and adulthood up until old age—before they become personally relevant to the individuals, so that there is no need to defend against the negative age stereotypes (Levy, Slade, Kunkel, & Kasl, 2003). Second, expectations result from elders' everyday life encounters, whether interpersonal or through the media (Donlon, Ashman, & Levy, 2005; Levy, 2003).

When images of aging take the form of self-stereotypes, we have found that they are capable of influencing cognitive functioning, a certain level of which Staudinger and her colleagues (this volume) state is necessary for wisdom performance. Specifically, we have found in our studies that positive and negative age stereotypes can have a positive and negative effect, respectively, on memory and mathematical performance (Levy, 1996; Levy, Hausdorff, Hecke, & Wei, 2000). In these studies, we subliminally primed elders with either positive or negative stereotype words (for a full description, see Levy, 1996). Among the positive age stereotype prime words was "wisdom."

Although both positive and negative age stereotype primes have been effective in eliciting predicted outcomes in controlled settings, outside the laboratory the negative age stereotypes tend to be more prevalent and salient (Butler, 2006). For example, Cohen (2000) argues, "Apart from exposure to grandparents, much of the earliest acquaintances of very young persons with older persons are through fairy tales, nursery rhymes, and children's stories . . . Portrayals of older persons are far too often negative or focused on the dark side of human nature. Central older figures in these tales are commonly depicted as wicked, weird, or weak" (p. 93). It appears that these negative images remain in old age as well. For example, in a survey of 717 individuals 70 years of age and older, we found that when we asked participants to generate five words or phrases they associate with elderly people, the majority (60%) of the associations were negative, whereas 17% were positive, and 23% were neutral. Thus, the stereotype that elders are most likely to encounter in everyday life is not that old age is a time of wisdom, but rather that old age is a time of physical and cognitive decline (Levy, 2003).

The adverse effect of negative age stereotypes on cognition may not be the only reason that they impede the ability of older individuals to engage in wisdom. Staudinger and her colleagues have stated that, "A core aspect of the definition of wisdom through cultures and historical times is its aim to further the well-being of oneself and others" (Staudinger et al., this volume, p. 33). We found that elders with negative age stereotypes were less likely than those with positive age stereotypes to support governmental programs designed to enhance the well-being of older individuals (Levy & Schlesinger, 2005). In contrast, the association between age stereotypes and support for age targeted programs was not found for the younger adults in the sample, for whom the age stereotypes were not personally relevant. It seems that those elders who held more negative age stereotypes viewed the old as undeserving of governmental programs. Thus, it may be that older individuals' wisdom scores are suppressed in part by the overriding influence of negative age stereotypes.

The possibility that wisdom may bolster positive age stereotypes is suggested by several studies that have shown wisdom performance can be increased in old age. For example, Staudinger and her colleagues have successfully enhanced wisdom by training different age groups in structured life-reflection (Staudinger et al., this volume). Perhaps improving wisdom performance would help to ameliorate the impact of negative age stereotypes by demonstrating that the expectation they generate of inevitable debilitation is not well-founded. Additionally, greater wisdom performance may instill a sense of self-efficacy which has been found to act as a mediator between positive age beliefs and their salutary influence (Levy et al., 2002).

SUGGESTIONS FOR FUTURE RESEARCH

One of the most intriguing findings presented by Staudinger and her colleagues is that when a person who had only relied upon an internal dialogue was chosen by the participants, performance on a wisdom task was enhanced to the same degree as when there was real interaction with another person (e.g., Staudinger & Baltes, 1996). This result can be seen as empirically confirming George Herbert Mead's conceptualization of the self as partly comprised of the attitudes held by others towards the individual (Mead, 1982). Not only does the finding by Staudinger and her colleagues speak to the generative and performance-enhancing power of social interaction, it suggests an area of cognition that is fertile ground for new research.

It would be useful to learn more about the identity of the virtual-internal dialogue partners. Does the richness of current or past social networks influence the number of available partners for virtual-internal dialogue? Do the virtual-internal dialogue partners change according to the nature of the wisdom tasks? Do different age groups tend to select different types of virtual-internal dialogue partners? Specifically, what determines the age of the virtual-internal dialogue partners? This last question may have particular relevance if it is found that a relationship exists between how much younger the virtual internal dialogue partners are than the participants and the negativity of the latters' age stereotypes. It has been found that elderly people, in contrast to members of other marginalized groups, tend to identify with out-group (i.e., the young) as strongly as the young themselves (Greenwald et al., 2002). It would be interesting to know whether this identification is partially a function of negative age stereotypes generating self-denigration, which then interferes with wisdom performance—as in the failure to support governmental programs for the old.

If it turns out that elders' age stereotypes are a factor in selecting the age of virtual-internal dialogue partners, this may suggest another link between these age stereotypes and wisdom performance. For in studies testing the age-match effect, it was found that wisdom performance was inversely related to the age difference between participants and the age of fictitious characters described in the task (e.g., Smith, Staudinger, & Baltes, 1994). The underlying assumption is that "each life phase is characterized by its own unique tasks and challenges" (Staudinger et al., this volume, p. 33). Presumably, then, when the symbolic dyad partners are close in age to the participant, wisdom performance would benefit.

The research reviewed in this chapter relies solely on verbal expressions of wisdom, as articulated by participants and judged by raters. The authors might consider the possibility of nonverbal expression as a means of displaying wisdom. For instance, participants could be asked to respond to the wisdom tasks through drawings. Although these tasks include complex scenarios, art might lend itself to the display of such complexity (Levy & Langer, 1999). Further, the creativity upon which art relies is not predicted by age (Simonton, 1998). Equally important, art operates as an indirect technique which may allow greater expression of the participants' implicit thought processes. As an example, it has been found that the operation of positive age stereotypes is facilitated on the implicit level (Levy & Banaji, 2002).

In conclusion, age stereotypes and their expectations are a product of elders' social context; insofar as these stereotypes are relevant to wisdom, they may add another dimension to wisdom's social context.

REFERENCES

Aldwin, C. M., & Sutton, K. J. (1998). A developmental perspective on post-traumatic growth. In R. G. Tedeschi & C. L. Park (Eds.), *Posttraumatic growth: Positive changes in the aftermath of crisis.* Mahwah, N. J.: Erlbaum.

Ardelt, M. (2004). Wisdom as expert knowledge system: A critical review of a contemporary operationalization of an ancient concept. *Human Development, 47,* 257–285.

Assmann, A. (1994). Wholesome knowledge: Concepts of wisdom in a historical and cross-cultural perspective. In D. L. Featherman, R. M. Lerner, & M. Perlmutter (Eds.), *Life-span development and behavior* (Vol. 12, pp. 187–224). Hillsdale, NJ: Erlbaum.

Azmitia, M. (1996). Peer interactive minds: Development, theoretical, and methodological issues. In P. B. Baltes & U. M. Staudinger (Eds.), *Interactive minds: Life-span perspectives on the social foundation of cognition* (pp. 133–162). New York: Cambridge University Press.

Bales, R. F., & Strodtbeck, F. L. (1951). Phases in group problem solving. *Journal of Abnormal and Social Psychology, 46,* 485–495.

Baltes, P. B. (1993). The aging mind: Potentials and limits. *The Gerontologist, 33,* 458–467.

Baltes, P. B. (1995). *Wisdom.* Unpublished Manuscript. Berlin: Max-Planck-Institut für Bildungsforschung.

Baltes, P. B., & Kunzmann, U. (2004). The two faces of wisdom: Wisdom as a general theory of knowledge and judgment about excellence in mind and virtue vs. wisdom as everyday realization in people and products. *Human Development, 47,* 290–299.

Baltes, P. B., Lindenberger, U., & Staudinger, U. M. (2006). Life-span theory in developmental psychology. In R. M. Lerner (Ed.), *Handbook of child psychology: Volume 1* (6th ed., pp. 569–664). New York: Wiley.

Baltes, P. B., & Smith, J. (1990). The psychology of wisdom and its ontogenesis. In R. J. Sternberg (Ed.), *Wisdom: Its nature, origins, and development* (pp. 87–120). New York: Cambridge University Press.

Baltes, P. B., Smith, J., & Staudinger, U. M. (1992). Wisdom and successful aging. In T. B. Sonderegger (Ed.), *Nebraska symposium on motivation* (Vol. 39, pp. 123–167). Lincoln, NE: University of Nebraska Press.

Baltes, P. B., & Staudinger, U. M. (1993). The search for a psychology of wisdom. *Current Directions in Psychological Science, 2,* 75–80.

Baltes, P. B., & Staudinger, U. M. (2000). Wisdom: A metaheuristic to orchestrate mind and virtue toward excellence. *American Psychologist, 55,* 122–136.

Baltes, P. B., Staudinger, U. M., Maercker, A., & Smith, J. (1995). People nominated as wise: A comparative study of wisdom-related knowledge. *Psychology and Aging, 10,* 155–166.

Berg, C. A., Strough, J., Calderone, K. S., Sansone, C., & Weir, C. (1998). The role of problem definitions in understanding age and context effects on strategies for solving everyday problems. *Psychology and Aging, 13,* 29–44.

Bloom, B. (1985). *Developing talent in young people.* New York: Ballantine.

Bluck, S., & Glück, J. (2004). Making things better and learning a lesson: Experiencing wisdom across the lifespan. *Journal of Personality, 72,* 543–572.

Brandtstädter, J. (1984). Personal and social control over development: Some implications of an action perspective in life-span developmental psychology. In P. B. Baltes & O. G. Brim, Jr. (Eds.), *Life-span development and behavior* (Vol. 6, pp. 1–32). New York: Academic Press.

Bronfenbrenner, U. (1979). *The ecology of human development: Experiments by nature and design.* Cambridge, MA: Harvard University Press.

Butler, R. N. (2006). Combating ageism: A matter of human and civil rights. In *Ageism in America.* International Longevity Center: New York.

Clayton, V. P., & Birren, J. E. (1980). The development of wisdom across the life span: A reexamination of an ancient topic. In P. B. Baltes & J.O.G. Brim (Eds.), *Life-span development and behavior* (Vol. 3, pp. 103–135). New York: Academic Press.

Clipp, E., & Elder, G. H., Jr. (1996) The Aging Veteran of World War II: Psychiatric and Life Course Perspectives. In P. E. Ruskin and J. A. Talbott, *Aging and posttraumatic stress disorder.* Arlington, VA: American Psychiatric Press.

Cohen, G. (2000). If you were an old woman who lived in a shoe, what would you do? *Geriatric Psychiatry, 8,* 93–95.

Cole, M. (1990). Cultural psychology: A once and future discipline? *Nebraska Symposium on Motivation, 38,* 279–335.

Cole, M. (1996). Interacting minds in a life-span perspective: A cultural/ historical approach to culture and cognitive development. In P. B. Baltes & U. M. Staudinger (Eds.), *Interactive minds: Life-span perspectives on the social foundation of cognition* (pp. 59–87). Cambridge University Press: New York.

Csikszentmihalyi, M., & Rathunde, K. (1990). The psychology of wisdom: An evolutionary interpretation. In R. J. Sternberg (Ed.), *Wisdom: Its nature, origins, and development* (pp. 25–51). New York: Cambridge University Press.

D'Andrade, R. (1995). *The development of cognitive anthropology.* Cambridge, UK: Cambridge University Press.

Donlon, M, Ashman, O., & Levy, B. (2005). Creating a defense against television's ageism. *Journal of Social Issues, 61,* 307–319.

Erikson, E. H. (1959). Identity and the life cycle: Selected issues. *Psychological Issues, 1,* 1–171.

Freund, A. M., & Baltes, P. B. (2002).The adaptiveness of selection, optimization, and compensation as strategies of life management: Evidence from a preference study on proverbs. *Journals of Gerontology: Psychological Sciences*, P426–P434.

Goodwin, P. D., & Wenzel, J. W. (1981). Proverbs and practical reasoning: A study in socio-logic. In W. Mieder & A. Dundes (Eds.), *The wisdom of many: Essays on the proverb* (pp. 140–159). New York: Garland.

Greenwald, A. G., Banaji, M. R., Rudman L. A., Farnham, S. D., Nosek, B. A., & Mellott, D. S. (2002). A unified theory of implicit attitudes, stereotypes, self-esteem, and self-concept. *Psychology Review, 109,* 3–25.

Heckhausen, J., Dixon, R. A., & Baltes, P. B. (1989). Gains and losses in development throughout adulthood as perceived by different adult age groups. *Developmental Psychology, 25,* 109–121.

Helson, R., & Srivastava, S. (2001). Three paths of adult development: Conservers, seekers, and achievers. *Journal of Personality and Social Psychology, 80,* 995–1010.

Helson, R., & Srivastava, S. (2002). Creative and wise people: Similarities, differences, and how they develop. *Personality and Social Psychology Bulletin, 28,* 1430–1440.

Helson, R., & Wink, P. (1987). Two conceptions of maturity examined in the findings of a longitudinal study. *Journal of Personality and Social Psychology, 53,* 531–541.

Holliday, S. G., & Chandler, M. J. (1986). *Wisdom: Explorations in adult competence* (Vol. 17). Basel, Switzerland: Karger.

Kessler, E.-M., & Staudinger, U. M. (2006). Plasticity in old age: Micro and macro perspectives on social contexts. In H. W. Wahl, C. Tesch-Römer & A. Hoff (Eds.), *Emergence of new person-environment dynamics in old age: A multidisciplinary exploration* (pp. 263–283). Amityville, NY: Baywood.

Kunzmann, U., & Baltes, P. B. (2003). Wisdom-related knowledge: Affective, motivational, and interpersonal correlates. *Personality and Social Psychology Bulletin, 29,* 1104–1119.

Lerner, R. M. (1984). *On the nature of human plasticity.* New York: Cambridge University Press.

Levy, B. (1996). Improving memory in old age by implicit self-stereotyping. *Journal of Personality and Social Psychology, 71,* 1092–1107.

Levy, B. (2003). Mind matters: Cognitive and physical effects of aging self-stereotypes. (New Directions in Aging Research.) *Journal of Gerontology: Psychological Sciences, 58,* 203–211.

Levy, B. & Banaji, M. (2002). Implicit ageism. In T. Nelson (Ed.), *Ageism: Stereotyping and prejudice against older persons.* Cambridge, MA: MIT Press.

Levy, B., Hausdorff, J., Hencke, R., & Wei, J. (2000). Reducing cardiovascular stress with positive self-stereotypes of aging. *Journal of Gerontology: Psychological Sciences, 55,* 1–9.

Levy, B., & Langer, E. (1999). Aging. In M. Runco & S. Pritzer (Eds.), *Encyclopedia of Creativity* (pp. 45–52). New York: Academic Press.

Levy, B., & Schlesinger, M. (2005). When self-interest and age stereotypes collide: Elders' preferring reduced funds for programs benefiting themselves. *Journal of Aging and Social Policy, 17,* 25–39.

Levy, B., Slade, M., & Kasl, S. (2002). Longitudinal benefit of positive self-perceptions of aging on functioning health. *Journal of Gerontology: Psychological Science, 57,* 409–417.

Levy, B., Slade, M., Kunkel, S., & Kasl, S. (2003). Longevity increased by positive self-perceptions of aging. *Journal of Personality and Social Psychology, 83,* 261–270.

Meacham, J. A. (1983). Wisdom and the context of knowledge: Knowing that one doesn't know. In D. Kuhn & A. Meacham (Eds.), *On the development of developmental psychology* (pp. 111–134). Basel, Switzerland: Karger.

Mead, G. H. (1982). *Mind, Self and Society.* Chicago: The University of Chicago Press.

Meegan, S. P., & Berg, C. A. (2002). Contexts, functions, forms, and processes of collaborative everyday problem solving in older adulthood. *International Journal of Behavioral Development, 26,* 6–15.

Mickler, C., & Staudinger, U. M (2006). How can we define measure insight into one's own life: Reliablity and validity of a new instrument to measure personal wisdom. Manuscript in preparation Bremen, Germany: International University Bremen.

Orwoll, L., & Perlmutter, M. (1990). The study of wise persons: Integrating a personality perspective. In R. J. Sternberg (Ed.), *Wisdom: Its nature, origins, and development* (pp. 160–177). New York: Cambridge University Press.

Oser, F. K., Schenker, C., & Spychiger, M. (1999). Wisdom: An action-oriented approach. In K. H. Reich, F. K. Oser, & W. G. Scarlett (Eds.), *Psychological studies on spiritual and religious development.* Lengerich, Germany: Pabst.

Oxford Dictionary of the English Language. (Vol. 12). (1933). Oxford, UK: The Clarendon Press.

Pasupathi, M., Staudinger, U. M., & Baltes, P. B. (2001). Seeds of wisdom: Adolescents' knowledge and judgment about difficult matters of life. *Developmental Psychology, 37,* 351–361.

Rudolph, K. (1987). Wisdom. In M. Eliade (Ed.), *Encyclopedia of religion: Wisdom* (Vol. 15, pp. 393–401). New York: Macmillan.

Sameroff, A. J. (1975). Transactional models in early social relations. *Human Development, 18,* 65–79.

Schaie, K. W. (1996). *Adult intellectual development: The Seattle Longitudinal Study.* New York: Cambridge University Press.

Searle, J. R. (1992). *The rediscovery of the mind.* Cambridge, MA: MIT Press.

Simonton, D. K. (1998). Career paths and creative lives: A theoretical perspective on later life potential. In C. Adams-Price (Ed.), *Creativity and successful aging: Theoretical and empirical approaches* (pp. 3–18). New York: Springer.

Smith, J., & Baltes, P. B. (1990). Wisdom-related knowledge: Age/cohort differences in responses to life planning problems. *Developmental Psychology, 26,* 494–505.

Smith, J., Staudinger, U. M., & Baltes, P. B. (1994). Occupational settings facilitative of wisdom-related knowledge: The sample case of clinical psychologists. *Journal of Consulting and Clinical Psychology, 62,* 989–1000.

Sowarka, D. (1989). Weisheit und weise Personen: Common-Sense-Konzepte älterer Menschen [Wisdom and wise individuals: Common-sense-concepts of older adults]. *Zeitschrift für Entwicklungspsychologie und Pädagogische Psychologie, 21,* 87–109.

Staudinger, U. M. (1989). *The study of life review: An approach to the investigation of intellectual development across the life span.* Berlin: Edition Sigma.

Staudinger, U. M. (1996). Wisdom and the social-interactive foundation of the mind. In P. B. Baltes & U. M. Staudinger (Eds.), *Interactive minds: Life-span perspectives on the social foundation of cognition* (pp. 276–315). New York: Cambridge University Press.

Staudinger, U. M. (1999a). Older and wiser? Integrating results on the relationship between age and wisdom-related performance. *International Journal of Behavioral Development, 23,* 641–664.

Staudinger, U. M. (1999b). Social cognition and a psychological approach to the art of life. In T. M. Hess & F. Blanchard-Fields

(Eds.), *Social cognition and aging* (pp. 343–375). San Diego, CA: Academic Press, Inc.

Staudinger, U. M. (2001). Life reflection: A social-cognitive analysis of life review. *Review of General Psychology Special Issue: Autobiographical Memory, 5,* 148–160.

Staudinger, U. M. (2005). Personality and aging. In M. Johnson, V. L. Bengtson, P. G. Coleman, & T. Kirkwood (Eds.), *Handbook of age and aging* (pp. 237-244). Cambridge, UK: Cambridge University Press.

Staudinger, U. M., & Baltes, P. B. (1996). Interactive minds: A facilitative setting for wisdom-related performance? *Journal of Personality and Social Psychology, 71,* 746–762.

Staudinger, U. M., Dörner, J., & Mickler, C. (2005a). *Ways to enhance and measure self-insight:* Unpublished manuscript. Bremen, Germany: International University Bremen.

Staudinger, U. M., Dörner, J., & Mickler, C. (2005b). Wisdom and personality. In R. J. Sternberg & J. Jordan (Eds.), *Handbook of wisdom* (pp. 191–219). New York: Cambridge University Press.

Staudinger, U. M., & Lindenberger, U. (Eds.). (2003). *Understanding human development: Dialogues with lifespan psychology.* Dordrecht, Netherlands: Kluwer Academic Publishers.

Staudinger, U. M., Lopez, D., & Baltes, P. B. (1997). The psychometric location of wisdom-related performance: Intelligence, personality and more? *Personality and Social Psychology Bulletin, 23,* 1200–1214.

Staudinger, U. M., Maciel, A., smith, J., & Baltes, P. B. (1998). What predicts wisdom-related knowledge? A first look at personality, intelligence, and facilitative experiential contexts. *European Journal of Personality, 12,* 1–17.

Staudinger, U. M., Pasupathi, M. (2003). Correlates of wisdome-related performance in adolescence and adulthood: Age-graded differences in "paths" toward desirable development. *Journal of Research on Adolescence, 13.*

Staudinger, U. M., Smith, J., & Baltes, P. B. (1992). Wisdom-related knowledge in a life review task: Age differences and the role of professional specialization. *Psychology and Aging, 7,* 271–281.

Staudinger, U. M., Smith, J., & Baltes, P. B. (1994). *Manual for the assessment of wisdom-related knowledge.* Berlin: Max-Planck-Institut für Bildungsforschung.

Sternberg, R. J. (1985). Implicit theories of intelligence, creativity, and wisdom. *Journal of Personality and Social Psychology, 49,* 607–627.

Sternberg, R. J. (1998). A balance theory of wisdom. *Review of General Psychology, 2,* 347–365.

Strough, J., Berg, C. A., & Sansone, C. (1996). Goals for solving everyday problems across the life span: Age and gender differences in the salience of interpersonal concerns. *Developmental Psychology, 32,* 1106–1115.

Vaillant, G. (1993). *The wisdom of the ego.* Cambridge, MA: Harvard University Press.

3

Social Influences on Adult Personality, Self-Regulation, and Health

Daniel K. Mroczek, Avron Spiro III, Paul W. Griffin, and
Shevaun D. Neupert

There are many definitions of self-regulation, especially conceptualized as a developmental phenomenon (Brandtstadter & Renner, 1990; Heckhausen & Schulz, 1995; Lachman & Burack, 1993), but most theories mention three basic components: mood regulation (with a particular emphasis on the regulation of negative affect), planfulness or impulse control, and control beliefs (as well as actual control; Heckhausen & Schulz, 1995). Although comprehensive theories of self-regulation (e.g., Carver & Scheier, 1982, 1998, 1999) suggest that there may be more to self-regulation than this group of concepts, much of what is meant by the term self-regulation is captured by this trio of individual difference concepts. In many senses, self-regulation is a broad type of personality characteristic, as Bandura (1999) has argued for many years. Moreover, like personality dimensions, people display individual differences in self-regulation in the ways it is manifested and how it functions within their lives. In this chapter, we will first define self-regulation via the three basic personality components we have mentioned. Second, we will discuss how changes in these constituents can influence changes in self-regulatory behavior with an important impact on physical health. Third and last, we will tie these themes to social structure and aging, describing how social or societal factors may impact self-regulation change, which in turn could potentially change self-regulation and even physical health and mortality further down the line.

A previous version of this paper was presented at the Penn State Gerontology Center Conference on Social Structures, Aging, and Self-Regulation in the Elderly, October 4–5, 2004, Penn State University, State College, PA.

SELF-REGULATION AS AN EMERGENT CONSTRUCT FORMED BY PERSONALITY

As mentioned above, we believe three broadly-construed personality dimensions are particularly salient for self-regulation: mood regulation, impulse control, and control beliefs. We contend that these three combine to form self-regulation as an emergent construct (also known as a "formative" construct; Bollen & Lennox, 1991; Edwards & Bagozzi, 2000). In an emergent construct, the defining constructs are distinct, but together they have emergent properties. This definition contrasts with the better-known concept of the latent construct (e.g., the common factor model), which assumes the latent variable causes the observed variables that are used to measure it. However, the personality variables that we believe play a major role in defining self-regulation are distinct constructs in and of themselves; they are not manifestations of an underlying causal, latent variable. Nevertheless, they may be brought together into a common composite or "formative" construct that is integrative in nature (Bollen & Lennox, 1991; Edwards & Bagozzi, 2000).

Mood regulation, the first of these three constructs, refers to a person's ability to govern mood over a period of time (Gross, 1999; Larsen, 2000). Recent theory has suggested that moods fluctuate around a set point (Headey & Wearing, 1989), and that people vary in their capacity to bring their moods back to this set point (Eid & Diener, 1999). Some people are highly variable around their set point, while others exert a greater degree of control over their moods. While not synonymous with mood regulation, individual differences in the personality trait neuroticism vary with individual differences in within-person mood variability (Eid & Diener, 1999; Larsen, 2000). People high in trait neuroticism tend to show greater fluctuations around their set point over short periods of time (Bolger & Schilling, 1991). They are more variable in their moods, leading some to label this trait "emotional stability" (Goldberg, 1992) or "emotionality" (Eysenck & Eysenck, 1968). We believe these forms of mood regulation should be a major constituent of any self-regulation construct.

The second aspect of self-regulation is planfulness. Better regulation implies an ability to control one's impulses and live life in a more organized and planful manner (Roberts & Bogg, 2004). Less planfulness is likely to result in worse health because precautions or preventive steps to maintain or improve health were not taken, or due to blind impulse-gratification resulting in exposure to grave health risks (e.g., sexually-transmitted diseases or fatal accidents). In fact, the personality trait conscientiousness encompasses many of the planfulness elements of self-regulation. Indeed, prior research has indicated that people low in personality trait conscientiousness and other forms of unplanfulness engage in more risky health behaviors such as drug and alcohol abuse (Caspi et al., 1997) and have higher rates of mortality (Friedman et al., 1993) than those higher in the trait. Planfulness and more effective and organized life management are all key aspects of self-regulation, which in turn lead to less risk-taking and better health behaviors, creating better physical and mental health and lower mortality over the lifespan.

The third and last set of defining variables for our emergent self-regulation construct is control beliefs. Some people believe they can influence events in their lives, giving rise to a sense of mastery and efficacy and the belief that one can achieve goals, including health goals. Others feel less control over their lives and events in their lives, producing the belief that they cannot do much to change the course of their lives or their health (Lachman, Ziff, & Spiro, 1994; Perrig-Chiello, Perrig, & Stahelin, 1999). Control and the sense of mastery it confers is an integral part of developmental regulation (Brandtstadter & Renner, 1990; Heckhausen & Schulz, 1995; Lachman & Burack, 1993). It indexes one of the cognitive elements of self-regulation in that it taps into people's belief systems and provides a window into an important aspect of how people think about and manage (and consciously regulate) their lives.

Each of these three constructs (mood regulation, planfulness, and control beliefs) are well understood, and there is a large nomological net connecting them with other variables (Contrada, Cather, & O'Leary, 1999). Despite this, researchers do not think of the three as connected to one other within a common conceptual structure. The overarching concept of self-regulation, however, provides a broad conceptual structure that allows this trio of empirically and theoretically distinct constructs to be understood together within a framework that has important consequences for behavior. That said, for most of the remainder of this chapter we will focus mainly on only one of the three, mood regulation (often operationalized as neuroticism). We will describe how it influences self-regulation as well as downstream outcomes such as health and mortality.

MOOD REGULATION AND STRESS REACTIVITY: AN ISSUE OF SELF-REGULATION

It is well known that high neuroticism is associated with higher levels of negative affect in general. However, neuroticism is also associated with greatly elevated negative affect during specific types of situations, such as stressful conditions (e.g., during a fight with one's spouse or boss). The tendency of people who are high in neuroticism to react to stressful situations with high negative affect is called the *stress reactivity effect* (Bolger & Schilling, 1991; Suls, 2001), and is perhaps the central concept in understanding individual differences in mood regulation. When people high in neuroticism encounter stressful events, they tend to experience them as more aversive and react with much higher levels of negative affect than those low in this trait (Bolger & Schilling, 1991; Bolger & Zuckerman, 1995; David & Suls, 1999; Gunthert, Cohen, & Armeli, 1999). Suls (2001) calls this process "hyperreactivity," or a large change in negative affect in response to a stressor (Suls, Green, & Hillis, 1998).

The theoretical underpinnings of this hyperreactivity are fourfold (Mroczek & Almeida, 2004), and each one of the four sheds light on why the effect is fundamentally an issue of self-regulation. First, persons high in neuroticism report larger numbers of stressful events in their lives, implying greater exposure to stress or to the creation of stressful situations (Bolger & Zuckerman, 1995; Ormel & Wohlfarth, 1991). Optimal self-regulation requires an ability to identify and avoid situations that may elevate negative affect, and persons high in neuroticism may lack this particular regulatory ability.

Second, persons high in neuroticism are more likely to appraise stressors as threats instead of as challenges, increasing the probability of experiencing negative affect as a response to stressful life events (Lazarus & Folkman, 1984; Suls, 2001). During the appraisal process, persons high in neuroticism also tend to focus more on the negative features of stressful events than people low in neuroticism (Hemenover, 2001). Optimal self-regulation demands healthy appraisal of the events that occur in our lives. If we see everything as a threat, we run the risk of activating threat-response systems, such as Gray's (1991) fight-or-flight response, when they are not necessary. Such over-activation of threat response systems not only results in elevated negative affect or distress when there is no need, but also prolongs their physiological consequences, such as elevated levels of stress hormones (e.g., cortisol) and immune system parameters (e.g., interleukin-6). Chronic levels of these hormones indicate dysregulation, and can ultimately cause both cardiovascular and neurological damage (Kendler, Thornton, & Gardner, 2001; Wilson, Bienas, Mendes de Leon, Evans, & Bennett, 2003; Wilson, Mendes de Leon, Bienas, Evans, & Bennett, 2004). This physical dysregulation is a consequence of psychological dysregulation.

Third, after a stressful event has occurred, persons high in neuroticism are more likely to remember events as more stressful or traumatic than people low in neuroticism. In essence, they encode life events differently (Larsen, 1990). Again, we believe this a type of regulatory failure. Healthy, optimal self-regulation demands that individuals have a realistic view of events that is not overly negative. If I looked back on any event in my life and focused on only the bad things that happened, discarding the good, then my memories would likely provoke unnecessary feelings of negative affect. Again, this represents an inability (or compromised ability) to maintain a healthy balance of negative to positive or neutral affect. Such imbalance implies dysregulation.

Fourth and last, persons high in neuroticism may employ less productive coping strategies, especially emotion-focused coping (Bolger, 1990; David & Suls, 1999), or utilize strategies that are unproductive (Bolger & Zuckerman, 1995). Suboptimal coping is again a problem of self-regulation, and results in prolonged experiences of negative affect, as opposed to re-regulation back to a state of lessened negative affect.

In each of these four underpinnings of the stress reactivity effect, the end result is elevated negative affect or prolonged periods of heightened negative affect, as well as potential elevations of dangerous stress hormones. Stress reactivity is in many ways an inability (or lessened ability) to re-regulate back to a more optimal emotional state. This is bad enough if it occurs frequently. However, what are the consequences if negative affect is repeatedly activated over long periods of time? What are the potential effects of an inability to self-regulate with respect to negative affect? Kendler et al. (2001) and Wilson et al. (2003, 2004) have hypothesized that neuroticism, and the constant elevated levels of negative affect that accompany that trait over periods of many years or decades, leads to a negative emotion "hair trigger" in older adulthood. They suggest that as people high in neuroticism grow older, they become more susceptible to elevated negative affect. Indeed, neuroticism and prolonged negative affect have been linked to dysregulation of the hypothalamic-pituitary-adrenal stress axis (HPA) (Kendler et al., 2001).

KINDLING EFFECTS: A SELF-REGULATORY FAILURE

Many studies, including some of our own, have shown that negative affect is lower in older than younger adults (Carstensen, Pasupathi, Mayr, & Nesselroade, 2000; Mroczek, 2001; Mroczek & Almeida, 2004; Mroczek & Kolarz, 1998). More importantly, longitudinal studies using growth-curve models have documented that negative affect declines as we age (Charles, Reynolds, & Gatz, 2001; Griffin, Mroczek, & Spiro, in press). Yet, little is known about older adults who are high in neuroticism. What do their levels of negative affect look like? We mentioned earlier that adults who are high in neuroticism might grow more susceptible to elevated negative affect as they grow older (Kendler et al., 2001; Wilson et al., 2003, 2004). The repeated activation of negative affect over a lifetime may increase reactivity by older adulthood. Repetition of negative affect activation, rather than causing habituation, may lead to its opposite, sensitization. Heightened sensitivity in turn may lead to easier activation of negative affect when a person encounters stressful stimuli. In other words, super-heightened stress reactivity (and concomitant elevated negative affect) may come to characterize people with high neuroticism as they age as a consequence of frequent activation. A lifetime of repeated activations, perhaps of the neural systems that mediate negative affect, may lead to a "hair trigger" in which states of elevated negative affect are prompted by relatively weak stimuli.

These heightened sensitivities are called kindling effects. Kindling occurs when repeated exposure to some stimulus causes sensitization (Gilbert, 1994; Kendler et al., 2001; van der Kolk, 1996, 1997; Woolf & Costigan, 1999). Kindling effects have been observed with respect to chronic pain, drug abuse, epilepsy, traumatic stress, anxiety, and depressive episodes. For example, major depressive episodes are frequently triggered by stressful life events (among those who are predisposed to major depression, of course). However, after repeated depressive episodes, the likelihood increases that these people will spontaneously slip into a depressive episode without the trigger of a stressful life event (Kendler et al., 2001). An individual in a kindled state is also more sensitive to triggering stimuli; depression is more likely to be triggered when a stressful life event takes place. In other words, the stimulus threshold becomes lower. Similarly, kindling effects occur in chronic pain. Many people become more sensitive to pain rather than developing tolerance over the long term (Woolf & Costigan, 1999). Kindling is a relatively permanent state of heightened susceptibility (Gilbert, 1994), brought on by past experience.

Some contend that kindling effects are a result of neuroplasticity, the ability of groupings of neurons to change and realign themselves in response to repeated exposure to stimuli (Gilbert, 1994; van der Kolk, 1997; Wilson et al., 2003; Woolf & Costigan, 1999). Neural networks that govern some processes (the sensation of pain, an epileptic seizure, feelings of depression, or negative affect) can themselves become molded by stimuli, causing these networks to become even more sensitive to stimuli and to sometimes even react spontaneously (van der Kolk, 1996, 1997; Woolf & Costigan, 1999). We suggest that persons high in neuroticism may become similarly molded over time, resulting in hypersensitivity to stress. Thus, older adults who have been high in neuroticism over their life course should display greater reactivity to stress in older adulthood when the opposite would be more beneficial to their health.

We do have some evidence consistent with this perspective. The 3-way moderator effect shown in Figure 3.1 lends support to the aforementioned perspective. These data are from 1,012 adults (54.5% women, 45.5% men) who are participants in the National Study of Daily Experiences (NSDE; Almeida, 2005; Almeida, Wethington, & Kessler, 2002; Mroczek & Almeida, 2004), one of the few daily experience studies that is national in scope. NSDE respondents completed a questionnaire about daily events, stressors, and affect for eight consecutive days, and these data were analyzed using multilevel models. Figure 3.1 illustrates that older adults high in neuroticism are more reactive to stress than any other group. On stressor days (days when any of seven broad stressful events may have occurred), daily negative affect is extremely elevated among older adults with high neuroticism. Interestingly, older adults with low neuroticism display levels of negative affect much lower than their younger or midlife counterparts low in neuroticism. This may indicate that older adults who are low in neuroticism may do a better job of regulating their moods, or at least their negative affect, than any other age group. Better emotion regulation may be a benefit of older adults who are lucky to have low neuroticism. Yet, older adults who are high in neuroticism have the bad fortune of poorer control or regulation of their negative affect, at least when stress occurs.

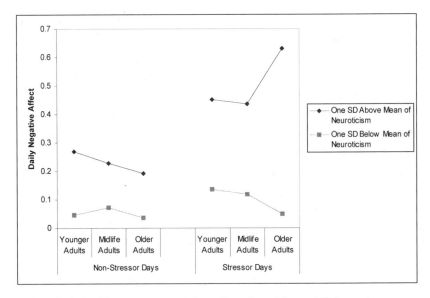

FIGURE 3.1 The stress reactivity effect for older, midlife, and younger adults: Neuroticism and age group moderate the association between daily stress and daily negative affect.

The heightened reactivity among older adults with high neuroticism is consistent with the kindling hypothesis (van der Kolk, 1996, 1997; Woolf & Costigan, 1999). A lifetime of frequent activation of the neural pathways associated with negative affect may bring about such sensitization, causing increased susceptibility to stimuli, including daily stress, that produce negative affect. In essence, the excessive activation of negative affect systems that plagues people high in neuroticism may, over years and decades, make the regulation of negative affect even more problematic. The difficulties in controlling negative affect are one of the key self-regulation problems for people high in neuroticism that may become worse over time. We do not know that this is exactly what underlies the effect in Figure 3.1, but it is one plausible explanation, backed up by recent work in several disciplines on kindling effects.

Tying the kindling hypothesis to the theme of social structure, we can easily imagine people who are high in neuroticism and are exposed to excessive amounts of stress due to social circumstances. For example, there are surely people who were born both high in dispositional neuroticism and to low socioeconomic status. The stressors of poverty combined with a proclivity toward stress reactivity would presumably put such individuals at a much higher risk for the development of kindling effects and hyperreactivity.

THE HEALTH CONSEQUENCES OF POOR REGULATION OF NEGATIVE AFFECT

It is clear that hypersensitivity to stressful stimuli takes away from the quality of one's life and very likely has implications for mental health. However, there is emerging evidence that such deficits in mood regulation have consequences for physical health as well. Many studies have documented that acute and chronic stressors can elicit cortisol elevation (Dickerson & Kemeny, 2004). Experiencing stress increases corticotrophin-release hormone, activates the HPA-axis, and promotes secretion of glucocorticoids (e.g., cortisol) into blood circulation. Persistent elevated levels of cortisol or non-response of cortisol levels to challenge (blunted sensitivity) are symptomatic of general poor physical health, especially wear and tear on the HPA-axis (Kiecolt-Glaser & Glaser, 1986). Such blunted sensitivity is, in essence, a failure of physical self-regulation brought on by a failure of psychological self-regulation.

Moreover, an elevated level of glucocorticoids in general blood circulation is associated with heart disease and hippocampal cell death, including hippocampal atrophy (Seeman, Singer, McEwen, Horwitz, & Rowe, 1997). Thus, persons who are more effective at managing stress may show less heart disease and hippocampal atrophy than those who have self-regulatory difficulties with respect to stress management (e.g, those high in neuroticism). Self-regulation should moderate the effect of stress on the development of such physical problems as heart disease and hippocampal atrophy, ultimately influencing downstream variables such as mortality. Indeed, recent studies have provided evidence that is consistent with this view. Wilson et al. (2004) documented that high neuroticism in a sample of older adults was associated with a higher risk of mortality, and even earlier mortality, which had been previously linked to other personality traits such as low conscientiousness. These findings highlight the potential damage to physical health that self-regulatory problems can bring about, especially those that are due to personality traits such as high neuroticism and its associated difficulties in managing stress.

CHANGE IN HEALTH RISKS AS A FUNCTION OF CHANGE IN PERSONALITY

Thus far, we have painted a pessimistic picture of problematic self-regulation. We have conjured up images of persons high in neuroticism experiencing difficulty in regulating their moods in response to stress, maximizing negative affect, in turn leading to widespread physical damage in their brains and arteries, culminating in an earlier death. This is perhaps too bleak a picture, considering the evidence that neuroticism can change as we age. If neuroticism changes over time for a given person, it is possible that the health risks associated with high levels of this trait (and perhaps other traits) also change across that person's lifespan.

The debate over change in personality and psychological well-being has quietly evolved over the past several years (Caspi & Roberts, 1999; Roberts & DelVecchio, 2000; Roberts & Wood, in press). The old question of whether or not personality traits are stable has given way to the more subtle perspective that change is an individual difference variable in and of itself (Mroczek & Spiro, 2003a, 2003b). Some people are stable, whereas others change in varying degrees. Recent studies have documented individual differences in rate of change for numerous personality traits (Helson, Jones, & Kwan, 2002; Jones & Meredith, 1996; Jones, Livson, & Peskin, 2003; Mroczek & Spiro, 2003a, 2003b; Mroczek, Spiro, & Almeida, 2003; Small, Hertzog, Hultsch, & Dixon, 2003). These are illustrations of the lifespan developmental tenet of plasticity (Baltes, 1987; Roberts, 1997; Roberts & Wood, in press), which states that developmental constructs remain somewhat malleable throughout the lifespan. Roberts (1997) has argued that personality is an "open system" that remains sensitive to contextual life experiences and socialization processes through the lifespan.

With respect to neuroticism, these studies have generally found that this trait declines in general (across people) as we age, but that there are considerable individual differences around the overall trajectory. Thus, some people go down faster than others, some track the sample trajectory, some remain stable, and still others may see a rise in neuroticism over time. There is a range of change, and it likely has implications for health risk. For example, a person at age 40 who is one standard deviation above the mean on neuroticism has some quantifiable risk for dying younger than someone at the mean of neuroticism, based on the Wilson et al. (2004) study. However, as in most epidemiological studies of risk factors, Wilson's study used neuroticism as assessed at one point in time. If high neuroticism is associated with higher risk of mortality several years down the road, then what happens to the risk when someone increases or decreases on this trait? Does risk of dying at a given age rise or fall as level of neuroticism changes? We can ask the same question of other findings in the area of personality and mortality. For instance, Friedman et al. (1993) found that lower conscientiousness measured early in life predicted later mortality. Surely, some individuals will remain stable and low in conscientiousness over periods of many years, and these people will remain at high risk for early mortality, but does that risk fall if a person increases on conscientiousness? There is a general (mean-level) decline in neuroticism and a general increase in conscientiousness as people age (Roberts & Walton, 2004). However, imagine the aforementioned person who was a standard deviation above the mean at age 40 experiences a decrease in neuroticism greater than the norm (via psychotherapy or some other intervention) and by age 50 is at the mean level. We may infer that with such a considerable drop in neuroticism, this person's risk of early mortality would drop as well.

This may not be the case if the physical damage (e.g., hippocampal atrophy) done prior to age 40 is extensive enough to keep the risk of an earlier death high even after a substantial drop in neuroticism. However, there is reason to believe that such changes can have a significant impact on health risk. As an analogy, consider high LDL cholesterol and the increased risk of suffering from some event, such as having a heart attack or dying from cardiac failure. LDL cholesterol can drop, like neuroticism, especially with intervention. One's risk of a heart attack declines as the risk factor declines. Getting your LDL back into a specified safe range brings the risk of the adverse health event back to the norm. Just as changes in cholesterol, blood pressure, or body mass index can change the risk of a cardiac event or early mortality, it may be that change in certain personality traits such as neuroticism or conscientiousness may also change the risk of similar undesirable health events.

Speculatively, people who are high in neuroticism may (through intervention) learn to regulate their moods better relatively early in life, perhaps in their 20s or 30s, before the potential damage of kindling effects sets in. Those who changed would presumably be better able to regulate negative affect and its ill effects, and may short-circuit some of the physical damage brought on by chronically high levels of negative emotion. Similarly, people who are low in planfulness (or high in impulsivity) may improve their ability to plan and control their impulses relatively early in their adult lives (again, through intervention), leading to fewer of the risky health behaviors that are hypothesized to account for the conscientiousness-mortality associations (Friedman et al., 1993). These are interesting possibilities involving the way change in personality leads to change in self-regulatory behaviors (especially health-relevant self-regulation), which leads to change in the risks of health events or mortality.

A similar causal chain may exist among control beliefs, self-regulatory behaviors, and health. A strong feeling of control leads to greater flexibility in the management of one's life goals and choices. It is known that people who feel a greater sense of control over their life, especially their work, tend to be in better health and live longer (Marmot, 2004). However, social factors, such as socioeconomic status, also influence sense of control. Indeed, social influences exert at least some influence over all three of the personality dimensions that impact self-regulation. This finally brings us back to the title of this chapter.

SOCIAL INFLUENCES ON PERSONALITY DIMENSIONS

Families, societies, and cultures each have an impact on the development of neuroticism, conscientiousness, and control beliefs. Earlier, we hinted at proactive methods, such as interventions, that may alter personality trajectories and subsequent health risks. However, larger social forces also shape the level and direction of certain personality trajectories. We acknowledge that genetic factors place limits on the influence of social factors; there is no doubt that biological factors play a strong role in the development of personality characteristics. Yet, recent theory (Caspi & Roberts, 1999; Roberts & Wood, in press) and empirical research (Mroczek & Spiro, 2003a) support the view that personality traits are at least somewhat responsive to environmental forces.

For example, families differ in the extent to which they socialize children and adolescents to deal with stress in an effective and healthy manner. These differences among families likely alter mood regulation trajectories (although within families, shared influences have little impact, as behavior genetics studies have shown). Certainly, genetically-based temperament dimensions create a starting point for where mood regulation trajectories begin, but environmental presses mold them throughout childhood and adolescence. A person may be predisposed to poor mood regulation, especially a proneness to chronically high negative affect. However, if that person learns ways to minimize negative affect—through family, peer or spouse influence—the potential negative health effects would be blunted. There is other evidence as well that sociocultural factors influence mood regulation. Two recent studies have noted cohort effects in mood regulation (operationalized by neuroticism), indicating that time and place may have some effect on development of this regulatory ability (Mroczek & Spiro, 2003a; Twenge, 2000).

With respect to planfulness and conscientiousness, people are exposed to different social forces that either promote or restrain impulsive behavior. An individual may possess a genetically-based proclivity toward impulsive behaviors, including those that may harm his or her health, but through familial, educational, or cultural forces learns to restrain those impulses. This would alter the course of that person's planfulness and conscientiousness trajectories, having long-term effects on health and health behaviors. Similarly, the influence of getting married or having children may alter conscientiousness trajectories, causing previously low-conscientiousness individuals to check their impulses more than they had before. In other words, they gain a greater degree of self-regulation. Thus, it is not difficult to imagine how family influences impact health via the shifting of planfulness or conscientiousness trajectories and its effect on self-regulation. School and other educational influences may also mitigate the negative impact of impulsivity and low planfulness. Henry, Caspi, Moffitt, Harrington, and Silva (1999) found that impulsive (undercontrolled) boys were less likely to engage in crime the longer they stayed in school.

Finally, families and cultures exert influence over control beliefs as well. The extent to which a person believes he or she is in control of his or her life (external versus internal sense of control) differs across cultures and across families within particular cultures. Yet, peer and spouse influence, as well as the influence of education and work, can potentially alter one's trajectory of control, with downstream effects on self-regulation and health. For example, a person may have come from a family that fostered fatalistic attitudes, creating an initial sense of low control within that person. However, through peer and spouse influence, this person eventually gains a greater sense of control over his or her life, including control over health. Believing that one's actions actually have an effect (internal sense of control) leads that person to take better care of his or her health. Thus, the environmental influences of peer and spouse shifted this hypothetical person's control trajectories, leading to changes in self-regulatory health behaviors and in turn better health.

THE STRUGGLE AGAINST ONE'S OWN PERSONALITY

In the above examples, we have made the argument that a combination of biological and environmental factors impact personality trajectories, leading to changes in self-regulatory behaviors, in turn influencing health. However, we entertain the possibility that some personality dimensions do not change, but the behaviors associated with them do. That is, someone who is very impulsive (low in planfulness and conscientiousness) learns to restrain impulsive behaviors, but nonetheless still feels the urge to fulfill the impulse. In this case, the underlying, genetically-influenced personality disposition of high impulsivity has not changed, but one's control over the manifest behaviors that flow from the disposition does change. In this case, the person has gained self-regulation abilities. The person gains the ability to *go against his or her own nature,* but the underlying trait may still be there in relatively unaltered form. The person struggles against his or her own personality dispositions, yet in doing so, gains the ability to self-regulate. Again, while this comes naturally to some, others need to actively work for it.

Consequently, it is not clear whether the changes observed in long-term studies of personality, such as our own (Mroczek & Spiro, 2003a), reflect underlying or manifest personality change. This of course goes against the emergent variable model we presented at the beginning of this paper in which mood regulation, planfulness, and control beliefs defined self-regulation. These dimensions change, and by necessity, self-regulation abilities change. Yet, in the underlying versus manifest model, this may not be the case. Only empirical research can verify which model is better.

CONCLUSION

With respect to the health outcomes we have discussed, it almost does not matter whether the underlying self-regulation dimensions change or if only the manifest behaviors change. If people who find it difficult to regulate negative affect gain the ability to regulate it more effectively early in life, they will likely obtain the health benefits. There may be many paths to improved regulation of negative affect. People may restructure their lives to avoid negative-affect producing situations, or they make seek out cognitive-behavioral therapy, or they may begin meditating regularly. Ultimately, perhaps the underlying disposition does decline for these people who have taken such proactive action. Or it may be that the latent proclivity still lurks, but the manifest behaviors (in this case, feelings of negative affect) are better controlled. Yet, with respect to the health outcomes, it may not matter. A person who possesses a genetic predisposition to produce excess LDL cholesterol never loses that genotypic trait; however, through treatment, the manifest effect (actual excess LDL) is controlled, although the underlying predisposition remains. In this sense, the underlying dispositions may remain stable at a latent level, but if the behaviors that flow from them become better regulated, people will gain health benefits. This is the hopeful message that we wish to convey.

We have focused on health outcomes in this chapter. However, improvements in some of the self-regulatory processes we have described, such as stress reactivity or impulse control, have benefits that go beyond physical health. They can lead to better mental health, enhanced functioning of social relationships, and improved productivity in work. Handling stress without experiencing negative affect or containing impulsive desires comes naturally for some people, who need not change because they already possess functioning self-regulation abilities. Any attempts at intervention need to be targeted at those most at risk. This is where the area of lifespan personality development can be of great use to those who study the development of self-regulation across the life course.

Commentary: From Kindling to Conflagration: Self-Regulation and Personality Change

Brent W. Roberts

On the whole, I agree with much of what Mroczek, Spiro, Griffin, and Neupert (this volume) have to say. Specifically, I concur with three global ideas contained in their essay: (a) that self-regulation should be conceptualized as part of personality trait psychology, (b) that individual differences in personality change are the most important developmental phenomena to study and explain, and (c) that social structures are partly responsible for the changes in personality that we see.

On the first point, the authors have stepped into the breach that often befuddles personality psychology. How should structural aspect of personality, which is often seen as some variant of personality traits such as the Big Five, be integrated with the process aspect of personality—the ways in which individual differences work in day-to-day activities? More often than not, it seems as if researchers interested in self-regulation and researchers interested in personality traits lead parallel lives in which they investigate strikingly similar concepts without acknowledging or thinking about the links between their programs and the implications of those links. For example, self-regulatory self-efficacy has often been conceptualized as a key personality variable that affects functioning in many social domains (Bandura, Caprara, Barbaranelli, Gerbino, & Pastorelli, 2003). Yet, constructs such as self-regulatory self-efficacy have been offered as alternatives to personality traits rather than integrated with them (Bandura, 1999). It is refreshing to find the willingness to seek a

A previous version of this commentary was presented at the Penn State Gerontology Center Conference on Social Structures, Aging, and Self-Regulation in the Elderly, October 4–5, 2004, Pennsylvania State University, State College, PA.

minor concilience between these domains that are clearly linked within Mroczek et al.'s chapter.

Once linked, of course, the key questions become in what direction does causality flow. Mroczek et al. implicitly prioritize the causal role of personality traits in determining patterns of self-regulation, which is a legitimate point. The portrait of those high in neuroticism being more susceptible to stress reactivity, appraisal deficits, encoding burdens, maladaptive coping mechanisms, and kindling effects is indisputably one way in which neurotic people remain more neurotic by using less than effective self-regulatory strategies.

The second point, that individual differences in personality change are important developmental phenomena, is apparently a difficult point to consume in personality psychology. This is somewhat ironic, as in the study of cognitive development it has long been known that the general trend for decrease in cognitive abilities is a misrepresentation of the data. That is, most people decrease on one or two skills rather than on all skills across the board (for a review, see Schaie, Willis, & Caskie, 2004). One person may lose fluid abilities faster than a second person because the latter has a job in which fluid ability is reinforced (e.g., Kohn & Schooler, 1978). Although the aggregate trend that results looks as if we decrease on all of our facilities, each person is in actuality changing in his or her own unique fashion, albeit typically losing cognitive abilities rather than gaining them.

Of course, this same phenomenon exists with personality trait development. Despite robust rank-order stability and meaningful mean-level changes, people demonstrate individual differences in personality trait change throughout the life course (Mroczek & Spiro, 2003a; Roberts, 1997; Roberts, Helson, & Klohnen, 2002; Small et al., 2003). That is the transition from kindling to conflagration. We move from the potential to change to actual change just as the kindling catches fire. Nonetheless, the obsession in personality psychology has been with demonstrating the rank-order stability of traits and the lack of mean-level change (e.g., McCrae & Costa, 1999). This has to be attributable, in part, to the unfortunate legacy of the person-situation debate, which erroneously challenged the existence of personality traits altogether, leaving many personality psychologists focused on demonstrating the impressive continuity of personality traits rather then investigating the full developmental repertoire of change (Caspi & Roberts, 1999; Roberts &

Pomerantz, 2004). This has left the field of personality development catching up with perspectives well accepted among those studying cognitive development. Mroczek et al., not are captured the significance of this domain and exemplify the next generation of research in the field of personality trait development.

Of course, the second and third points are intrinsically linked. If people do change in their own unique way, then we would want to know why they change in this fashion. That is, what is the match that causes the kindling to catch fire? One of the most reasonable hypotheses is that experiences within social structures facilitate changes in personality traits. Again, this perspective is non-controversial within cognitive aging, as studies have demonstrated that experiences at work may facilitate gains, or more realistically, lack of declines, in cognitive functioning over time (Kohn & Schooler, 1978; Schooler, Mulatu & Oates, 1999), and that cognitive ability can be increased through interventions (Schaie & Willis, 1986). Likewise, if personality develops through socialization experiences structured in social institutions in childhood and adolescence, why would this pathway suddenly turn off in adulthood? Once again, I see much to like in the position that the authors' espouse concerning the ways in which social structures may contribute to changes in personality traits that will in turn affect patterns of self-regulation.

In order to expand on these points and to highlight some areas where I would chose a different interpretation, I now turn to some empirical examples from our ongoing study of the development of conscientiousness.

THE DEVELOPMENT OF CONSCIENTIOUSNESS IN ADULTHOOD

Conscientiousness is defined as individual differences in the propensity to follow socially prescribed norms for impulse control, to be goal-directed, planful, able to delay gratification, and to follow norms and rules (John & Srivastava, 1999). Like neuroticism, conscientiousness has clear links to self-regulation. It takes a modicum of self-control in order to avoid the compelling rewards that tend to inhibit long-term goals and plans. Recently, we have concentrated our research on the link between conscientiousness and health behaviors. The latter tend to be concrete examples of self-regulation, such as not overeating, exercising regularly, not smoking or drinking to excess, and avoiding risky sexual encounters. Interestingly, health-related behaviors are the primary factors contributing to poor health outcomes such as cardiovascular disease and cancer (McGinnis & Foege, 1993). In the United States, the leading behavioral contributors to mortality are tobacco use, diet and level of physical activity, excessive alcohol use, shootings, sexual behavior, risky driving/accidents, and drug use (McGinnis & Foege, 1993). These behaviors are relevant to health and longevity through their relations to cardiovascular disease, cancer, AIDS, and accidental deaths.

In several studies, we have tested the relationship between conscientiousness, broadly conceived, and the health behaviors that contribute to poor health outcomes. We have found that most aspects of conscientiousness are negatively related to both alcohol and drug abuse (Walton & Roberts, 2004). These patterns replicate using observer ratings of personality, demonstrating that the correlations are not the result of response biases or social desirability. In turn, we have found that conscientiousness is positively related to preventative and accident control behaviors such as seeing a doctor regularly and checking smoke alarms around the house (Chuah, Drasgow, & Roberts, in press). From these preliminary studies, it is clear that conscientiousness is linked to several domains of risky health behaviors and several domains of preventative health behaviors, both of which epitomize self-regulation.

Our most recent research shows that the influence of conscientiousness is more pervasive than these initial studies indicate. We have conducted one of the most comprehensive meta-analyses of the relationship between conscientiousness-related traits and health behaviors to date (Bogg & Roberts, 2004). In this study, data was compiled on the relationships between conscientiousness-related traits and the nine different health behaviors that are among the leading correlates of mortality, including alcohol use, disordered eating (including obesity), drug use, physical activity, risky sexual practices, risky driving practices, tobacco use, suicide, and violence (McGinnis & Foege, 1993). Conscientiousness predicted each and every outcome. The scope of the effects is rather significant. People who are not conscientious have quite a number of ways to experience premature mortality. They can die through car accidents, the acquisition of AIDS through risky sexual practices, through violent activities such as fights and suicides, and through drug overdoses. People low in conscientiousness can still suffer from an attenuated life span through not eating well, not exercising, and smoking tobacco, which all lead to heart disease and cancer. Clearly, conscientiousness plays a significant role in facilitating self-regulatory behaviors that promote positive health benefits.

What makes the relationship of conscientiousness to health behaviors and longevity so compelling is that, like neuroticism, conscientiousness changes in adulthood. For example, cross-sectional studies show that conscientiousness increases even in middle and old age (Srivastava, John, Gosling, & Potter, 2003). In addition to the cross-sectional studies, two reviews of the longitudinal data concluded that people continued to increase in conscientiousness well into adulthood. Helson and Kwan (2000) reviewed data from three cross-sectional studies and three longitudinal studies that covered the majority of the life course from 20–80 years of age and concluded that there was significant mean-level change in norm-adherence, which is most similar to the reliability facet of conscientiousness. Roberts, Robins, Caspi, and Trzesniewski (2003) reviewed a more comprehensive list of cross-sectional and longitudinal studies than previously captured in narrative reviews. According to their interpretation of the data, measures of conscientiousness increased across the life course from age 18–60+, a finding subsequently confirmed in a meta-analytic review of longitudinal studies (Roberts, Walton, & Viechtbauer, 2006).

From a self-regulatory perspective, the news appears to be mostly good. People tend to get better at regulating their impulses and planning for their future as they age. These findings beg two additional questions: Do these increases net people better health practices and increased longevity? Why do people increase in conscientiousness? We have yet to address the first question. As for the second question, we see two reasons for the increase in conscientiousness from young adulthood to middle age. First, people change their levels of conscientiousness by changing the way they behave with age (Caspi & Roberts, 1999; Roberts & Caspi, 2003). In the case of conscientiousness and health, the behaviors most relevant to change in conscientiousness are, of course, health behaviors. So the question is whether participating in certain health behaviors or changing one's health behavior is associated with changes in conscientiousness. Consistent with the idea that change in one's behaviors can lead to change in personality, women who decreased their tobacco and marijuana consumption increased in conscientiousness more than their peers who did not change their behavior (Roberts & Bogg, 2004). These findings provide initial support for the idea that enacting or changing behaviors can then translate into more global changes in one's personality.

The second reason for the increase in conscientiousness has to do with experiences people have within different social structures. There is now consistent evidence derived from longitudinal studies that social investment in work and marriage is associated with increases in conscientiousness. For example, women who achieved higher levels of occupational attainment at work tended to increase on achievement, responsibility, and self-control, demonstrating that more continuous investment in work is related to increases in facets from the domain of conscientiousness (Roberts, 1997). Results from an ongoing longitudinal study of both men and women replicated and extended these findings. Success and involvement in work were associated with increases in achievement and control, two facets of conscientiousness, from 18–26 years of age (Roberts, Caspi, & Moffitt, 2003).

In the domain of relationships, remaining in a close intimate relationship in young adulthood is related to increases in constraint, a facet of conscientiousness related to impulse control (Robins, Caspi, & Moffitt, 2002). Similarly, engaging in a serious partnership for the first time in young adulthood is associated with decreases in neuroticism and increases in conscientiousness (Neyer & Asendorpf, 2001). Avoiding divorce and maintaining a marriage-like relationship for a longer period of time in young adulthood is also associated with increases in responsibility, prospectively in midlife (Roberts & Bogg, 2004). These longitudinal studies show that investment in the conventional roles of work and intimate relationships can explain, in part, the increases in conscientiousness found in young and middle adulthood.

In sum, people who are more conscientious, and by definition are more successful at self-regulation, tend to live longer and do so most likely because of their health practices. Moreover, people increase in conscientiousness in young adulthood, midlife, and old age. People increase in conscientiousness because they see themselves behaving differently over time and because they respond to contingencies in social roles. The latter comes about through investing in conventional social institutions, such as marriage and work. Overall, our program of research on the consequences and development of conscientiousness reaffirms many of the points made by Mrozcek et al. Personality traits and self-regulation are intrinsically linked. People continue to change in terms of personality in adulthood, and experience of changes in self-regulatory behaviors and experience of demands in social structures are linked to these changes in conscientiousness.

A POINT OF DEPARTURE

I do have one perspective on the linkages of personality and self-regulation that departs from the treatment of the topic given by Mroczek et al. Specifically, I have found it useful to make a hierarchy of breadth clear when considering the way seemingly disparate or related constructs are linked (Roberts & Pomerantz, 2004). Specifically, personality constructs and situational constructs can be ordered from broad to narrow (see Figure 3.2).

For example, on the person side of the equation, traits are often considered broad constructs because they entail aggregation of thoughts, feelings, and behaviors across many situations. They also conform nicely to the broad level of the bandwidth-fidelity trade-off, in that like other broad bandwidth constructs, they predict more outcomes at more modest levels, than constructs more narrowly conceived (Roberts & Donahue, 1994). At the mid-level of breadth, we prefer the concept of the role identity, which is the perspective people have about how they behave in a subset of the role-based situations of their lives (Wood & Roberts, in press). Research

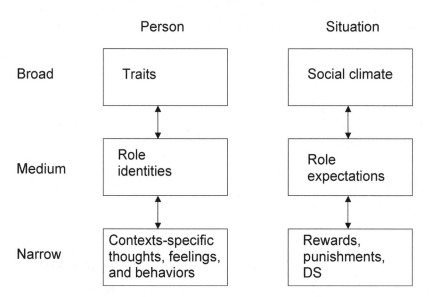

FIGURE 3.2 Hierarchical model of the person and the situation.

has shown repeatedly that we see systematic differences in ourselves across various roles (Donahue & Harrary, 1998; Roberts & Donahue, 1994; Wood & Roberts, in press). At the most narrow level, we find the constituent elements of personality traits, thoughts, feelings, and behaviors. Similarly, situations can be arranged hierarchically, as we have seen in Figure 3.2.

Why is this important and how does it inform the relationship between personality traits and self-regulation? Moreover, how does this relate to personality development? In most research, self-regulatory actions are conceptualized at the lower level of abstraction as specific types of thoughts, feelings, or behaviors. This is one reason why trait psychologists and those who study self-regulatory behaviors often talk past one another. They study similar phenomena at different levels of abstraction. Locating self-regulation at the lower level of the model provides an interesting permutation on the implicit model set forth by Mroczek et al. Specifically, rather than seeing self-regulation only as an outcome of traits, we can also see that self-regulatory behaviors may feed back onto traits and potentially mediate the relationship between environmental experiences and personality trait change.

For example, Figure 3.3 shows a hypothetical scenario detailing the relationship between work experiences and the trait of conscientiousness. In this example, the person has taken their first job right out of high school or college. The model details how self-regulatory thoughts would hypothetically mediate the changes in behaviors called upon by new role demands that might in turn affect changes in the higher-order trait of

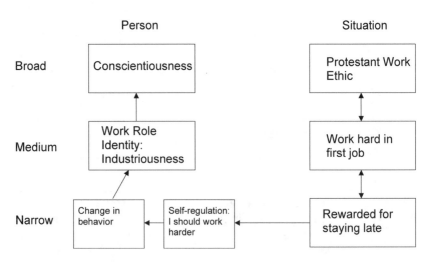

FIGURE 3.3 Hierarchical relationship between expectations for change, self-regulatory thoughts, and personality change.

conscientiousness. In this example, we see that the new work role brings with it a press to work harder than the person had previously done in school. Moreover, responding to the press is rewarded with social regard or more tangible rewards such as raises and promotions. In a simple socialization scenario, the effect of the environmental press would be direct and this person would then change his or her behavior and, through these behavioral changes, grow to become more conscientious.

Alternatively, self-regulatory thoughts could serve as a mediator of personality change. In one situation, a person would clearly see the new demands, and by becoming cognizant of them, facilitate changes in his or her behavior to fit the expectations—in essence, receiving the message that they should work harder. In a second situation, a person may miss the demand or choose to ignore it and then not regulate the change in his or her behavior successfully. He or she would then not enact the behavioral change and would therefore not come to be more conscientious over time.

Through this example, one can see how separating traits and self-regulatory behaviors across levels of abstraction can shed light on some of the processes that play out in the relationship between social structures and changes in personality that happen in adulthood. Rather than conceptualizing self-regulation as a simple manifestation of a personality trait, self-regulatory acts may work in a reciprocal fashion. Thus, self-regulatory thoughts may mediate the relationship between the press to change, behavioral change, and ultimately change in personality.

SUMMARY

In summary, I have made four points about the Mroczek et al. chapter (this volume). I agree that self-regulation should be conceptualized as part of personality psychology, that individual differences in personality change are the most important developmental phenomena to study and explain, and that social structures are partly responsible for the changes in personality that we see. Moreover, our program of research on the development and consequences of the self-regulatory trait of conscientiousness dovetails perfectly with the perspective outlined by Mroczek et al. Where I deviate slightly is on how self-regulation can be conceptualized and utilized as a lower-order phenomena that serves as a catalyst or mediator of change in personality traits caused by experiences in social structures. That being said, the integration of traditional personality traits with self-regulatory concepts in a developmental context appears to be a perfect marriage.

Can Self-Regulation Explain Age Differences in Daily, Weekly, and Monthly Reports of Psychological Distress?

David M. Almeida, Daniel K. Mroczek, and Michelle Neiss

There is growing evidence that psychological distress rarely increases over the course of the adult life span (Malatesta & Kalnok, 1984; Smith & Baltes, 1993). In fact, a number of studies have reported a general decrease in distress across the adult years (Carstensen, Pasupathi, Mayr, & Nesselroade, 2000; Charles, Reynolds, & Gatz, 2001; Costa, McCae, & Zonderman, 1987; Diener, Sandvik, & Larsen, 1985; Rossi & Rossi, 1990; Vaux & Meddin, 1987). Such results seem surprising in the face of the stressful experiences that often accompany advancing age, such as declining physical health and deaths of peers and spouse (Baltes & Baltes, 1990).

This commentary reviews previous research that uses concepts of self-regulation to explain such age differences. In addition we extend this line of inquiry by presenting a series of analyses that assess self-reports of negative affect across monthly, weekly, and daily time frames. Because the daily and weekly reports of psychological distress occurred over the same period of time, these analyses offer a unique opportunity to assess the extent to which frequency of psychological distress reported on a daily basis is recalled at the end of the week. Finally, the analyses explored the differences in how people of various ages recall emotions. We examined the extent to which the most distressing day in a given week predicted the recall of distress over the same week. Final analyses tested whether this relationship was greater for younger adults than for older adults.

DEVELOPMENTAL CHANGES IN SELF-REGULATION

Explanations for lower levels of psychological distress among older adults often focus on age differences in the ability to control or regulate emotions. In a study of emotion-specific autonomic nervous system activity, older adults exhibited lower levels of somatic activity when reliving a remembered emotion than did younger adults (Levenson, Carstensen, Friesen, & Ekman, 1991). Furthermore, skills in emotional regulation, or attempts to control emotions, do seem to increase over the life span. Labouvie-Vief (1997) proposes that emotion becomes better integrated with cognitive processes as people age. One dimension of this integration is affective complexity, evidenced by the ability to integrate both positive and negative emotions. A benefit of increased integration is greater understanding of one's own emotions, a possible mechanism for greater effectiveness in regulating affect (Labouvie-Vief, DeVoe, & Bulka, 1989).

Socioemotional selectivity theory also provides insight into change in emotional experiences over the life span by focusing on how the primacy of emotional goals changes as we age (Carstensen, 1991; Carstensen, Isaacowitz, & Turk-Charles, 1999). Socioemotional selectivity theory suggests that as people approach the end of the life span, they view time as limited. Awareness of time constraints alters emotional experience by leading people to give greater weight to emotional goals rather than to knowledge-related goals. In addition to increased salience of emotion, awareness of endings may also bring about more mixed reactions. To the extent that older adults face endings, they may experience both positive and negative feelings, or a sense of poignancy (Carstensen et al., 2000). Self-reports of emotional regulation support the proposition that regulatory skills increase with age. Across culturally and ethnically diverse samples, older adults report greater emotional control than do younger adults (Gross et al., 1997). Greater skills in regulating emotion suggest that quality of life for older adults may be more positive even in the face of losses.

Much of the empirical evidence supporting decreases in psychological distress across adulthood comes from studies that rely on longer-term retrospective accounts of affect recalled over one month or more (Costa et al., 1987; Charles et al., 2001; Rossi & Rossi, 1990; Vaux & Meddin, 1987). For example, Mroczek and Kolarz's (1998) analysis of the National Survey of Midlife in the Unites States (MIDUS) showed that older adults experienced more frequent positive affect and less frequent psychological distress than their younger counterparts. These findings were based on respondents' recall of positive and negative affect over the previous 30 days. In a more recent study of daily emotional experiences, Carstensen, Pasupathi, Mayr, and Nesselroade (2000) found age-related declines in frequency of negative affect. The present paper extends this work by examining age differences in distress using daily, weekly, and monthly reports of psychological distress from a subsample of MIDUS respondents. A focus on differing time intervals of recalled emotions allows for the comparison of age differences in psychological distress using molar time referents (i.e., monthly) and more micro time referents (i.e., daily and weekly).

AGE DIFFERENCES IN CONCURRENT VERSUS RETROSPECTIVE REPORTS OF EMOTIONS

The length of the recall period may play an important role in people's reports of their emotional experiences. Winkielman, Knauper, and Schwarz (1998) found that questions with a shorter recall period (1 day) were interpreted by respondents as referring to less extreme and therefore less memorable events, whereas questions with a longer recall period (1 year) were interpreted as referring to rare and more memorable events. These interpretations are reflected in empirical findings of actual reported emotions across differing recall periods. Weekly retrospective accounts of positive and negative affect tend to be higher than daily reports (Thomas & Diener, 1990) and daily reports tend to be higher than momentary ratings (Parkinson, Briner, Reynolds, & Totterdell, 1995). A general pattern seems to indicate that longer reference periods are prone to a systematic bias for recall of more intense emotional experiences. We will extend this research by examining whether similar bias occurs when recalling frequency of negative emotions across a wide age span.

Another potential problem with longer-term retrospective reports of emotions is the assumption of temporal integration where individuals average their affective experiences equally over a given interval. Kahneman (1999) proposes an alternative process of recollection, the peak-end hypothesis. Based on this hypothesis, retrospective evaluations will be best predicted by the average of the peak affective experience during a given episode and the affective experience at the end of the episode. In a series of studies, Kahneman and colleagues found support for this hypothesis by comparing individuals' ongoing reports of emotions during actual events with recollections of emotions at the end of the experience (Fredrickson & Kahneman, 1993; Redelmeier & Kahnamen, 1996; Varey & Kahneman, 1992). For example, in a study of patients' discomfort during a colonoscopy, retrospective evaluations were best predicted by the average of the highest discomfort during the procedure with the level of discomfort at the end of the procedure (Redelmeier & Kahnamen, 1996). Although most evidence for peak-end recollection processes come from studies of intensity of emotion over specific episodes (e.g., colonoscopy), the present study will assess peak-end recollection of frequency of emotion across a specific interval (i.e., week). Accordingly, the peak experience (most frequent distress day of the study week) and the end experience (frequency of distress on the last day of the week) should be more memorable and therefore have a greater effect on retrospective reports.

There may be age differences in temporal integration and peak-end-recollection processes. Differences in emotional regulation may play a role in how younger and older adults recall emotions. Investigating the salience of affect in potential social interactions, Carstensen and Fredrickson (1998) found that older adults placed more importance on the affective dimension of possible social partners than younger adults. This increased salience of affect has been found to impact older adults' recall of material. Furthermore, Carstensen and Turk-Charles (1994) found that older adults recalled proportionately more emotional material than neutral material. The proportion of emotional material recalled increased linearly with age, suggesting emotional material was more salient for older adults. Greater attention to affect may enable older adults to better recall all of their emotional experiences than younger adults. If this is the case, age-related declines in psychological distress may not be reflecting actual differences in experienced emotions. Rather, age declines in distress may be due to age differences in how younger and older adults recall emotional experiences. During recall, older adults may temporally integrate their emotional experiences while younger adults use peak-end processing.

RESEARCH QUESTIONS FROM A DAILY DIARY STUDY

The remainder of this commentary will focus on a series of analyses that show how age differences in self-regulation processes are manifested in how individuals recall naturally occurring emotions. By comparing daily, weekly, and monthly reports on psychological distress, we have the ability to test several research questions. First, do age differences in psychological distress generalize across different recall periods? The second question centers on age differences in discrepancy of daily and weekly recall. Because emotions are more pertinent to older adults, do they recall affective experiences more consistently? The third set of questions pertains to age differences in the peak-end hypothesis of retrospective evaluations. Greater affective complexity may allow older adults to better process their emotional experience, perhaps by being able to temporally integrate both mundane and more salient emotions. When younger adults recall their emotions, they may be more likely to rely on extreme negative emotional experiences than on more mundane emotional experiences. Thus, we predicted that the relationship between weekly recall of distress and the most distressful day (i.e., peak day) would be higher for young adults. A competing hypothesis was that older adults would show less accuracy in their recall of emotions. Due to age-related declines in memory, older adults may rely on more recent emotions (end day) than do younger adults. When recalling psychological distress across a week, for example, older adults may be more likely to base their report on the current day's experience.

THE NATIONAL STUDY OF DAILY EXPERIENCES

We attempt to answer these questions by analyzing data from the National Study of Daily Experiences (NSDE). Respondents were 1,031 adults (562 women, 469 men), all of whom had previously participated in the Midlife in the United States Survey (MIDUS), a nationally representative telephone-mail survey of 3,032 people 25–74 years of age, carried out in 1995–1996 under the auspices of the John D. and Catherine T. MacArthur Foundation Network on Successful Midlife (for descriptions of the MIDUS project, see Keyes & Ryff, 1998; Lachman & Weaver, 1998; Mroczek & Kolarz, 1998). Respondents in the NSDE were randomly selected from the MIDUS sample and received $20 for their participation in the project. Of the 1,242 MIDUS respondents who we attempted to contact, 1,031 agreed to participate, yielding a response rate of 83%. Over the course of eight consecutive evenings, respondents completed short telephone interviews about their daily experiences. On the final evening of interviewing, respondents also answered several questions about their previous week. Data collection spanned an entire year (March 1996–March 1997) and consisted of 40 separate "flights" of interviews, with each flight representing the 8-day sequence of interviews from approximately 38 respondents. The initiation of interview flights was staggered across the days of the week to control for the possible confounding between day of study and day of week. Respondents completed an average of seven of the eight interviews, resulting in a total of 7,221 daily interviews. The present analyses used the 571 respondents (244 men, 327 women) who completed all eight interviews. To assess distress across one week, we dropped the first interview day. Thus our analyses involved 3,997 days (571 respondents over seven days). For many of the analyses that follow, we used the *week* as the unit of aggregation by calculating the mean of the distress score across the seven days.

The MIDUS and NSDE samples had very similar distributions for age, marital status, and parenting status. The NSDE had slightly more females, fewer minority respondents, and better-educated respondents than the MIDUS sample. Respondents for the present study were 47 years old on average. Seventy-seven percent of the women and 85% of the men were married at the time of the study. Forty-seven percent of the households reported having at least one child in the household. The average family income was between $50,000–$55,000. Younger adults (25–39 years of age) had less household income, while older adults (56–74 years of age) were less likely to have children in the household.

Our analyses used five measures of psychological distress that differed in interval of recall and level of aggregation. Each distress measure used the same inventory of six emotions from the Non-Specific Psychological Distress Scale (Mroczek & Kolarz, 1998). This scale was developed from several well-known instruments: The Affect Balance Scale (Bradburn, 1969), the University of Michigan's Composite International Diagnostic Interview (Kessler et al., 1994), the Manifest Anxiety Scale (Taylor, 1953), and the Center for Epidemiological Studies Depression Scale (Radloff, 1977). The scale consists of six emotions across a range of intensity, including sad, hopeless, anxious, restless, depressed, and worthless. Respondents indicated how much of the time they experienced each emotion on a 4-point scale from *none of the time* to *all of the time*. For each of the following measures of distress across these items, sum scores were calculated.

Daily distress was assessed during the daily telephone interviews in which respondents indicated how often they felt each of the emotions "during the past 24 hours." On each day, sum scores across the six items were computed (Cronbach's alpha = .89). A *Weekly Aggregate Distress* measure was created by computing the mean frequency of distress across the seven diary days. *Peak Day Distress* was measured by selecting the highest of the seven daily distress scores (Cronbach's alpha = .91). *End Day Distress* was daily distress score on the last day of the interview (Cronbach's alpha = .84). *Weekly Distress Recall* was assessed at the conclusion of the final day of interviewing when respondents were asked how often they felt each of the six emotions "during the past week" (Cronbach's alpha = .85). *Monthly Distress Recall* was measured approximately eight months prior to the daily interviews during the initial baseline MIDUS data collection via questionnaire items asking respondents to indicate how often they felt each of the six emotions "during the past thirty days" (Cronbach's alpha = .87).

RESULTS

Descriptive Results

The first set of analyses provides some descriptive information on the psychological distress measures. Table 3.1 shows the average level of distress for each of the measures for the total sample and separately by gender. Although gender is not a main focus of the present investigation, we describe gender differences in this first set of analyses and use gender as a covariate in subsequent analyses. Several studies have shown that women report higher levels of psychological distress than men (for review, see Nolen-Hoeksema, 1987) including daily distress (Almeida & Kessler, 1998). Mean differences in the measures of psychological distress and gender were examined through a 2 × 4 (Gender × Type of Measure) mixed model MANOVA with type of measure as the within-person factor and gender as a between-person factor. This analysis revealed a main effect for gender and type of measure. Women reported significantly higher levels of distress across all four measures. Only the weekly aggregate of distress yielded similar levels of distress across both men and women. A significant Gender × Type of Measure interaction indicated that the gender difference was greatest for the monthly recall measure.

These analyses also showed significant mean differences in psychological distress by recall period (F (3, 568) = 11.0, $p < .01$). A series of subsequent paired t-tests revealed that measures with longer recall intervals yielded higher mean levels of psychological distress. Respondents' monthly recall distress scores were higher than their weekly recall scores (t (570) = 14.2, $p < .01$) and their weekly aggregated scores (t (570) = 21.1,

TABLE 3.1 Description of Psychological Distress Variables by Gender and Reference Period

Psychological Distress	Total Sample	Men	Women	Gender
Variable	Mean (SD)	Mean (SD)	Mean (SD)	F
Weekly Aggregate	1.17$_a$ (.26)	1.15$_a$ (.22)	1.19$_a$ (.29)	4.05*
Weekly Recall	1.28$_b$ (.37)	1.25$_b$ (.32)	1.31$_b$ (.40)	6.27**
Monthly Recall	1.55$_c$ (.62)	1.47$_c$ (.52)	1.62$_c$ (.68)	13.05**
Peak Day	1.47$_d$ (.53)	1.42$_d$ (.48)	1.51$_d$ (.51)	6.25**

Notes: N = 571. Means with different subscripts in the same column differ at $p < .01$. Responses range from 1 "none of the time" to 4 "all of the time." * $p < .05$. ** $p < .01$.

$p < .01$). In fact, the monthly estimate of distress was greater than the peak daily distress score ($t(570) = 4.1, p < .01$). There was also a significant difference between the weekly recall and weekly aggregate of distress scores ($t(570) = 17.2, p < .01$). Respondents, on average, reported greater levels of distress when asked to recall over the entire week as compared to the aggregate of daily reports of distress across that same week. The discrepancy between the aggregate and the recall measures suggested that respondents tended to report more frequent distress when they recalled their emotions over longer time intervals.[1]

1. It is important to mention the particularly low mean for weekly aggregate, suggesting that individuals reported very little psychological distress across the study days. There are several possible reasons for these low scores including: (a) few respondents actually reported any distress across the study week; (b) few days which were days of reported distress; (c) only a few items endorsed on the distress scale; or (d) some combination of these factors. A detailed evaluation of the distribution of distress scores across respondents, study days, and distress items revealed that 82% of participants experienced at least some distress (i.e., a distress score above 1 on the aggregate measure) across the study week. Across the study days, respondents reported some distress on 48% of the study days. Furthermore, respondents endorsed one distress item (i.e., experienced this emotion more than never) on 18% of the days, two distress items on 14% of the days, and three or more distress items on 16% of the days. The most frequently endorsed item was anxious (21% of study days) and least endorsed item was worthless (4% of study days) Thus it appears that the low weekly aggregate reflects a combination of the number of days of distress reported and the number of distress items endorsed.

Age Differences in Recalling Distress

The next series of analyses assessed the first research question, whether age differences existed in this pattern of recall of distress. Hierarchical multiple regressions were computed using each of the distress measures as criterion variables. On the first step, Gender as well as linear and quadratic functions of Age were entered. On the second step, interactions of Gender and the Age functions were entered. Figure 3.4 plots mean age differences for each of the distress measures. Standardized regression coefficients for the linear Age term are shown in parentheses.

The quadratic functions of Age and the Age × Gender interactions were not significantly associated with any of the psychological distress measures. For the monthly and weekly recall measures, age was negatively related to level of distress. Older respondents reported less frequent distress than their younger counterparts. However, age was not related to level of psychological distress for the weekly aggregate, peak day, or end day distress scores. Furthermore, age slopes for weekly aggregate distress and peak day distress were significantly less than the age slopes for weekly recall distress ($t = 2.8$ (568), $p < .05$; $t = 2.2$ (568), $p < .05$) and monthly recall distress ($t = 4.5$ (568), $p < .05$; $t = 3.8$ (568), $p < .05$). This pattern of results, with age differences present only in weekly and monthly recall, suggested that length of recall interval played a role in age differences in psychological distress. A subsequent analysis assessed age differences in day-to-day variation in psychological distress. Using each of the seven daily psychological distress scores, a within-person standard deviation

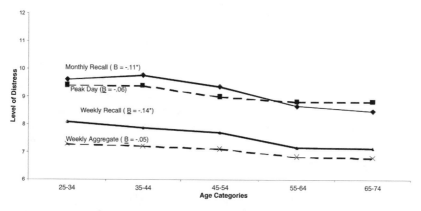

FIGURE 3.4   Age differences in psychological distress.

was calculated for each respondent. The mean within-person standard deviation was 1.11. Age, Gender, and the Age × Gender interaction were not associated with within-person variation.

We further explored the pattern of age differences by examining the discrepancy between the weekly aggregate and weekly recall distress scores. As noted earlier, weekly recall scores were, on average, greater than the weekly aggregate scores collected during the same week. In the next set of analyses we wanted to see if this discrepancy was associated with age. To this end, difference scores were calculated between the weekly aggregate and recall scores. Positive difference scores were interpreted as an overestimate in the recall of distress and negative difference scores were interpreted as an underestimate. These difference scores were then used as the criterion variable in a multiple regression with linear and quadratic functions of age and gender as predictors. Age, gender, and their interaction were significant. Figure 3.5 illustrates the results of this analysis. Men's and women's standardized regression coefficients for the linear age term are shown in parentheses. Older individuals' weekly recall of psychological distress was closer to their aggregated daily scores of distress. The Age × Gender interaction indicated that this was especially the case for men in the sample. The discrepancy between the weekly aggregate score and the weekly recall of distress for older men was close to zero.[2]

The next set of analyses tested the final research question, whether there were age differences in the peak-end hypothesis for recalling emotions. One explanation for age differences in recall discrepancy is that older adults may be more likely to average their emotions equally across the days of the week (temporal integration), while younger adults may be more likely to give more weight to those days when they experience more frequent

---

2. Findings for the age differences could be biased due to floor effects in the weekly aggregate variable especially if older adults are more likely to have no days of distress. This does not appear to be the case. First, we recomputed the regressions for the weekly aggregate and peak day measures using only those respondents who reported having some distress across the study week (i.e., a weekly aggregate score above 1). The age slopes for weekly aggregate ($\beta = -.08, p > .05$) and peak day ($\beta = -.05, p > .05$) were almost identical to the slopes estimated on the entire sample. Second, we recomputed the regression testing age difference in the discrepancy between weekly aggregate and weekly recall again using only those respondents whom reported having some distress across the study week. The pattern of results did not differ from the results for the entire sample. The age slope for men was ($\beta = -.27, p < .01$) and the age slope for women was ($\beta = -.13, p < .05$).

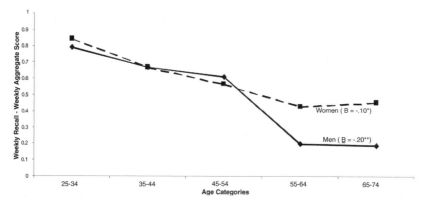

FIGURE 3.5   Age differences in the discrepancy between weekly aggregate of psychological distress and weekly recall of psychological distress.

distress (peak day). For example, an older and a younger respondent may both report particularly distressing Mondays, but report emotionally calm days for the remainder of the week. Because the older adult is more sensitized to, and a better regulator of, his or her emotions, he or she is likely to average the distressing Monday and the calm days equally. The younger adult, not yet having acquired these skills, might be more attuned to the distressing Monday and therefore give this day more weight when he or she recalls his or her emotions over the entire week. To address this hypothesis, we tested whether age moderated the associations of the peak day distress (i.e., the most distressing day in the week) with the weekly recall of distress. In addition, older adults might be more likely than their younger counterparts to rely on the most current assessment of distress (end day) because of declines in memory functioning. Thus we assessed whether peak day distress was more predictive of weekly recall of distress for younger adults, and whether end day distress was more predictive of weekly recall for older adults. Table 3.2 shows the results of a hierarchical multiple regression using linear function of age, gender, peak day distress, end day distress, and interactions between age and the two daily distress scores as predictors.

On the first step of the analysis, Gender and Age significantly predicted weekly recall of distress. On the second step, both Peak Day Distress and End Day Distress predicted weekly recall of distress, accounting for an additional 58% of the variance beyond the effects of gender and age. On the third step, the Age $\times$ Peak Day Distress interaction significantly predicted weekly recall of distress. On this step, the age effect decreased to

TABLE 3.2 Hierarchical Multiple Regression of Age, Peak Day Distress, Final Day Distress Predicting Weekly Recall of Psychological Distress

Predictors	Step 1 B (SE) β	Step 2 b (SE) β	Step 3 b (SE) β
Age	−.024 (.006) −.15*	−.015 (.004) −.07*	.020 (.012) .09
Gender	.300 (.155) .06*	.047 (.106) .01	0.50 (.098) .01
Peak Day Distress	.365	(.017) .59*	.487 (.069) .73*
End Day Distress	.339	(.027) .27*	.423 (.100) .39*
Age × Peak Day Distress			−.004 (.001) −.25*
Age × End Day Distress			.002 (.002) .09
R^2	.03*	.61*	.65*
Change in R2		.58*	.04*

*Notes: N = 571. * p < .01.*

non-significance, suggesting that age differences in weekly recall of distress are mediated by the interaction between age and peak distress day. Figure 3.6 shows the nature of this interaction. We plotted regression lines representing the prediction of weekly recall of distress from peak daily distress for younger (25–39 years of age), middle aged (40–55 years of age), and older adults (56–74 years of age). Standardized regression coefficients for the peak daily distress terms are shown in parentheses. As hypothesized, peak daily distress was a stronger predictor of weekly recall of distress for younger adults than for older adults.

One explanation for these findings is that younger adults place more weight on peak days because they are more likely to experience particularly distressing days. The logic is that more days with more severe distress are more memorable. Recalculating the peak-end analysis two ways tested this possibility. First, we omitted respondents who did not report any weekly aggregate distress. Second, we omitted respondents who scored lower than the mean on the Peak Day Distress variable. The pattern of results for both of these subsamples was identical to the original sample. In both of these supplementary analyses, the significant Age × Peak Day Distress interactions (β = −.25, p < .01 and β = −.24, p < .01) indicated

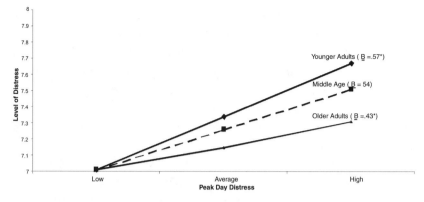

FIGURE 3.6   Weekly recall of psychological distress as a function of peak day distress for younger, middle aged, and older adults.

that peak daily distress was a stronger predictor of weekly recall of distress for younger adults than for older adults.

Another possible explanation for these findings is that older adults may have more difficulty recalling the most distressing day in their week because of declines in memory processing (Smith, 1996). In other words, younger adults place more weight on particularly distressing experiences when recalling emotions because they remember them better than older adults do. Our final analysis tested potential age differences in the ability to recall psychological distress over our 7-day study period. In a multiple regression, daily distress scores from the first study day and the final study day were used to predict the weekly recall of distress. If age-related decline in memory was a factor in the weekly recall of distress, we would expect a negative age by first-day distress score interaction and a positive age by last-day distress score interaction. For example, the relationship between first day distress and weekly recall of distress should be less for older adults. Although the main effects for the first and last day distress scores were significant ($\beta = .41, p < .01; \beta = .47, p < .01$, respectively), the interactions of age by daily distress scores were not significant. Thus it appears older adults did not differ from their younger counterparts in their ability to recall earlier distressing experiences.

DISCUSSION

Using daily, weekly, and monthly reports of psychological distress from a national sample of adults, these analyses examined several issues related to age differences in how adults recall negative emotions. Respondents tended to recall more frequent distress when reporting over longer time frames compared to shorter time frames. When asked to report their level of distress over the entire week, respondents recalled greater frequency compared to the aggregate of their daily reports of distress across that same week. Thomas and Diener (1990) found a similar pattern of results, and attributed such discrepancy to recall bias that occurs in measures that use longer time intervals. Such bias may be due to differences in peak-end recollection processes. Extreme emotional experiences (i.e., peak experience) are more likely to occur over longer intervals. For example, the feeling of distress is more likely to occur over a given week than on a given day. To the extent that individuals place more weight on peak emotions during recollection, we would expect to find higher scores for longer intervals.

An alternative explanation is that lower scores are due to respondents finding it more plausible to give a "none of the time" response for shorter recall periods than for longer recall periods. The percentage of respondents who reported experiencing no monthly, weekly, and daily distress was 22%, 26%, and 18% respectively. Chi square tests revealed no significant differences across these three measures. However, the distribution of the daily scores across the study days revealed that respondents reported never experiencing distress on 52% of the study days. Although we did show evidence for peak-end processes, we cannot rule out the possibility that recall differences may be partially due to respondent interpretations of questions across differing recall periods.

Age Differences in Monthly, Weekly, and Daily Psychological Distress

Compared to older adults, younger adults recalled experiencing greater levels of distress over monthly and weekly time frames. These findings are consistent with previous work on age differences in affect (e.g., Mroczek & Kolarz, 1998). However, we found no age differences in distress for shorter time frames. Younger and older adults did not differ in their daily reports of psychological distress aggregated across the week or in their peak distress score during that week. These results differ from Carstensen et al. (2000) findings on momentary assessments of affect. At least three reasons can account for this discrepancy. First, this study used a more restricted age range than the Carstensen sample. If we had a younger sample, our pattern might be more similar. Second, our method of assessment relied on self reports at the end of a day, not momentary assessments across the day. Third, there may have been floor effects present in our study. Although the majority of our respondents reported at least some distress across the study week, the mean of the weekly aggregate variable suggests that the level of distress experienced was very low. It is important to mention, however, that subsequent analyses attempting to control for low level did not alter the pattern of results.

Our pattern of results suggests that frequency of emotional experience does not differ at the daily level; rather, age differences are apparent in recall of emotional experience over weekly and monthly intervals. Previously reported age differences in reports of distress may be partially due to differences in how younger and older adults recall emotions. Older adults may be better able to recall their emotion because they pay more attention to their emotional experiences (Carstensen et al., 1999). Alternatively, older adults may be less able than their younger counterparts to recall their emotional experiences because of declines in memory processing (West & Craik, 1999). The subsequent analysis more fully examined age-related differences in recall.

Age Differences in Recalling Psychological Distress

Our findings indicate that older adults' weekly recall is more consistent with their daily reports of distress. Although respondents overall showed a general tendency to recall more frequent psychological distress over the week compared to the aggregate of daily distress reports, this discrepancy decreased with age. This pattern supported the hypothesis that older adults would more accurately recall their emotions. Interestingly, more consistent recall by older adults does not follow the general pattern of age-related declines in memory usually found in cognitive studies (e.g., West & Craik, 1999). However, older adults' greater consistency in recalling emotion does add to a base of literature suggesting that emotions become better integrated with cognitive processes throughout adulthood (Labouvie-Vief & DeVoe, 1991; Labouvie-Vief et al., 1989). Consistent with laboratory studies investigating recollection of emotions (Carstensen & Turk-Charles, 1994), our study suggests that older adults may be better than younger adults at recalling their own emotions in real-life settings as well.

We also found that men reported lower levels of psychological distress on each of the measures than did women. This gender difference in psychological distress is similar to other studies of negative mood (Almeida & Kessler, 1998; Nolen-Hoeksema, Larson, & Grayson, 1999). However, it is important to point out that a negative age effect was present for women as well. This suggests that, regardless of gender, older and younger adults recall their emotions in a different manner.

Younger Adults are More Likely to Recall Particularly Distressing Days

For both older and younger adults, the peak day distress is a significant predictor of weekly reports of psychological distress. However, younger adults' weekly recall of psychological distress is more influenced by the peak day distress than older adults' recall of distress. This is consistent with our hypothesis that younger adults would rely more on salient negative experiences when evaluating their overall distress over the past week.

Why might peak day distress more substantially affect recall of psychological distress among younger adults as compared to older adults? Labouvie-Vief and DeVoe (1991) suggest that older adults perhaps have a clearer understanding of their own affective experience and are better able to integrate both positive and negative aspects of their emotional experiences. In a recent study of momentary assessments of emotions, Carstensen et al. (2000) found age to be positively associated with more differentiated emotional experiences. In their study, differentiation was exhibited through endorsement of more specific emotions and the co-occurrence of positive and negative emotions at a given time frame. If older adults are in fact more likely to experience positive emotions even when experiencing feelings of psychological distress, they may have a more balanced perspective, so that a particularly distressful day does not exert such a strong influence on their assessment of affect over longer time frames. This greater cognitive complexity might facilitate greater temporal integration across all emotional experiences within a given interval. An alternative explanation could be age differences in the quality of distress on a peak day. Our analysis found no age difference in within-person variation of distress scores across the study days or in the mean level of peak day distress. However, there may be other age-related differences such as activity, volatility, and lifestyle that make peak day distress more memorable or distinctive for younger adults. Unfortunately we were unable to consider these possible explanations.

Conclusions

Findings from these analyses should be interpreted in light of this study's limitations. First, it is constrained by the fact that it is cross-sectional. As with all studies examining *age differences,* we are unable to rule out cohort effects. For example, older individuals in this sample may have under-reported distress in the weekly and monthly recall measures because they have been exposed to more severe life events such as challenges of economic survival and war (Kling, Seltzer, & Ryff, 1997). This may have altered their assessment of what they considered distressing. Further, because of the cross-sectional design, we cannot make any interpretations regarding age changes. Future research should attempt to track the trajectories of various measures of psychological distress across the adult life course.

It is important to note the age restriction in our sample. Some recent evidence suggests that an increase in psychological distress can be found among the oldest old (Carstensen et al., 2000). Adults of very old age might report higher levels of psychological distress, a pattern different than that seen among our respondents. Nevertheless, a unique aspect of this study is our ability to demonstrate how age differences in psychological distress display different patterns over various time frames.

Finally, another limitation of these analyses revolves around our assessment of negative emotions. The response format across the three time intervals used the same vague quantifiers (e.g., "some of the time"), thus mean differences across the measures should not be directly interpreted as differences in objective frequency of psychological distress. In addition, we did not obtain accompanying measures of positive emotions. The role of positive emotions may be key to understanding the greater weight younger adults seem to place on distressing days. We can speculate that for younger adults, a particularly distressing day may subjectively seem more important as it is less likely to also involve positive emotions. Our understanding of how age moderates discrepancies in recall of distress could be informed by research examining the role of both positive and negative emotions. In addition, younger adults may give more weight to distressful days because they are less able to regulate or control their negative emotions. Perhaps older adults, with greater skills in emotional regulation, feel more control over their negative emotions and are therefore not as adversely affected by distressful experiences.

These limitations not withstanding, this commentary offers unique insight into our understanding of age differences in emotional self-regulation. Previous research on adult age differences in psychological distress has largely relied on either single reports of affect recalled over long periods (e.g., Mroczek & Kolarz, 1998), or several reports of affect over only shorter time frames (e.g., Carstensen et al., 2000). The study of how people recall emotions has benefited from daily studies that compare reports of affect collected over differing time frames (Thomas & Diener, 1990; Winkielman, Knauper, & Schwarz, 1998). The present study expands on previous research by using daily telephone interviews from an U.S. national sample of adults across a broad age range. Such a design allowed for a comparison of distress, as it is recalled day to day across a week, with recollection of distress across that same week. Although younger adults reported higher levels of distress over longer time frames, younger and older respondents did not differ in their levels of distress as reported in daily interviews. Interestingly, when we compared weekly aggregate to weekly recall measures of distress, older adults were more consistent in their recall of psychological distress. Subsequent analyses showed that this finding was not due to adults merely forgetting their distressing experiences. Thus it appears that older adults are actually better at remembering their emotions than younger adults. Due to experience in adapting to daily stress, older adults may have greater self-awareness and self-knowledge which lessens bias when remembering distress. Future research should investigate the processes that shape the ways people remember their emotional experience.

REFERENCES

Almeida, D. M. (2005). Resilience and vulnerability to daily stressors assessed via diary methods. *Current Directions in Psychological Science, 14,* 64–68

Almeida, D. M., & Kessler, R. C. (1998). Everyday stressors and gender differences in daily distress. *Journal of Personality and Social Psychology, 75,* 670–680.

Almeida, D. M., Wethington, E., & Kessler, R. C. (2002). The daily inventory of stressful events (DISE): An interview-based approach for measuring daily stressors. *Assessment, 9,* 41–55.

Baltes, P. B. (1987). Theoretical propositions of life-span developmental psychology: On the dynamics between growth and decline. *Developmental Psychology, 23,* 611–626.

Baltes, P. B., & Baltes, M. M. (1990). Psychological perspectives on successful aging: The model of selective optimization with compensation. In P. B. Baltes & M. M. Baltes (Eds.), *Successful aging: Perspectives from the behavior sciences* (pp. 1–34). Cambridge, MA: Cambridge University Press.

Bandura, A. (1999). Social cognitive theory of personality. In L. Pervin & O. P. John (Eds.), *Handbook of personality: Theory and research* (2nd ed., pp. 154–196). New York: Guilford.

Bandura, A., Caprara, G. V., Barbaranelli, C., Gerbino, M., & Pastorelli, C. (2003). Role of affective self-regulatory efficacy in diverse spheres of psychosocial functioning. *Child Development, 74,* 769–782.

Bogg, T., & Roberts, B. W. (2004). Conscientiousness and health behaviors: A meta-analysis of the leading behavioral contributors to mortality. *Psychological Bulletin, 130,* 887–919.

Bolger, N. (1990). Personality as a personality process: A prospective study. *Journal of Personality and Social Psychology, 59,* 525–537.

Bolger, N., & Schilling, E. A. (1991). Personality and problems of everyday life: The role of neuroticism in exposure and reactivity to daily stressors. *Journal of Personality, 59,* 356–386.

Bolger, N., & Zuckerman, A. (1995). A framework for studying personality in the stress process. *Journal of Personality and Social Psychology, 69,* 890–902.

Bollen, K. A., & Lennox, R. (1991). Conventional wisdom on measurement: A structural equation perspective. *Psychological Bulletin, 110,* 305–314.

Bradburn, N. M. (1969). *The structure of psychological well-being.* Chicago, IL: Aldine.

Brandstadter, J., & Renner, G. (1990). Tenacious goal pursuit and flexible goal adjustment: Explication and age-related analysis of assimilative and accommodative strategies of coping. *Psychology and Aging, 5,* 58–67.

Carstensen, L. L. (1991). Selectivity theory: Social activity in life-span context. In K. W. Schaie (Ed.), *Annual Review of Gerontology and Geriatrics* (Vol. 11, pp. 195–217). New York: Springer.

Carstensen, L. L., & Fredrickson, B. L. (1998). Influence of HIV status and age on cognitive representations of others. *Health Psychology, 17,* 494–503.

Carstensen, L. L., Isaacowitz, D. M., & Turk-Charles, S. (1999). Taking time seriously: A theory of socioemotional selectivity. *American Psychologist, 54,* 165–181.

Carstensen, L. L., Pasupathi, P., Mayr, U., & Nesselroade, J. R. (2000). Emotional experience in everyday life across the adult life span. *Journal of Personality and Social Psychology, 79,* 644–655.

Carstensen, L. L., & Turk-Charles, S. (1994). The salience of emotion across the adult life span. *Psychology and Aging, 9,* 259–264.

Carver, C. S., & Scheier, M. F. (1982). Control theory: A useful conceptual framework for personality-social, clinical and health psychology. *Psychological Bulletin, 92,* 111–135.

Carver, C. S., & Scheier, M. F. (1998). *On the self-regulation of behavior.* New York: Cambridge University Press.

Carver, C. S., & Scheier, M. F. (1999). Stress, coping and self-regulatory processes. In L. A. Pervin & O. P. John (Eds.), *Handbook of personality: Theory and research* (pp. 553–575). New York: The Guilford Press.

Caspi, A., Begg, D., Dickson, N., Harrington, H., Langley, J., Moffit, T. E., & Silva, P. A. (1997). Personality differences predict health-risk behaviors in young adulthood: Evidence from a longitudinal study. *Journal of Personality and Social Psychology, 73,* 1052–1063.

Caspi, A. & Roberts, B. W. (1999). Personality change and continuity across the life course. In L.A. Pervin & O.P. John (Eds.), *Handbook of personality: Theory and research* (pp. 300–326). New York: The Guilford Press.

Charles, S. T., Reynolds, C. A., & Gatz, M. (2001). Age-related differences and change in positive and negative affect over 23 years. *Journal of Personality and Social Psychology, 80,* 136–151.

Chuah, S. C., Drasgow, F., & Roberts, B. W. (in press). Personality Assessment: Does The Medium Matter? No. *Journal of Research in Personality.*

Contrada, R. J., Cather, C., & O'Leary, A. (1999). Personality and health: Dispositions and processes in disease susceptibility and adaptation to illness. In L. A. Pervin & O. P. John (Eds.), *Handbook of personality: Theory and research* (pp. 576 604). New York: Guilford.

Costa, P. T., McCrae, R. R., & Zonderman, A. B. (1987). Environmental and dispositional influences on well-being: Longitudinal follow-up of an American national sample. *British Journal of Psychology, 78,* 299–306.

David, J. P., & Suls, J. (1999). Coping efforts in daily life: Role of big five traits and problem appraisals. *Journal of Personality, 67,* 265–294.

Dickerson, S. S. & Kemeny, M. E. (2004). Acute stressors and cortisol responses: A theoretical integration and synthesis of laboratory research. *Psychological Bulletin, 130,* 355–391.

Diener, E., Sandvik, E., & Larsen, R. J. (1985). Age and sex effects for emotional intensity. *Developmental Psychology, 21,* 542–546.

Donahue, E. M., & Harary, K. (1998). The patterned inconsistency of traits: Mapping the differential effects of social roles on self-perceptions of the Big Five. *Personality and Social Psychology Bulletin, 24,* 610–619.

Edwards, J. r., & Bagozzi, R. P. (2000). On the nature and direction of relationships between constructs and measures. *Psychological Methods, 5(2),* 155–174.

Eid, M., & Diener, E. (1999). Intraindividual variability in affect: Reliability, validity, and personality correlates. *Journal of Personality and Social Psychology, 76,* 662–676.

Eysenck, H. J., & Eysenck, S.B.G. (1968). *Manual for the Eysenck Personality Inventory.* San Diego, CA: Educational and Industrial Testing Service.

Fredrickson, B. L., & Kahneman, D. (1993). Duration neglect in retrospective evaluations of affective episodes. *Journal of Personality and Social Psychology, 65,* 45–55.

Friedman, H. S., Tucker, J. S., Tomlinson-Keasey, C., Schwartz, J. E., Wingard, D. L., & Criqui, M. H. (1993). Does childhood personality predict longevity? *Journal of Personality and Social Psychology, 65,* 176–185.

Gilbert, M. E. (1994). The phenomenology of limbic kindling. *Toxicology and Industrial Health, 10,* 343–358.

Goldberg, L. R. (1992). The development of markers for the Big-Five factor structure. *Psychological Assessment, 4,* 26–42.

Gray, J. A. (1991). Neural systems, emotion, and personality. In J. Madden IV (Ed.), *Neurobiology of learning, emotion, and affect* (pp. 273–306). New York: Raven Press.

Griffin, P., Mroczek, D. K., & Spiro, A. (in press). Trajectories of positive and negative affect over 10 years. *Journal of Research in Personality.*

Gross, J. J. (1999). Emotion and emotion regulation. In L. A. Pervin & O. P. John (Eds.), *Handbook of personality: Theory and research* (pp. 525–552). New York: The Guilford Press.

Gross, J. J., Carstensen, L. L., Pasupathi, M., Tsai, J., Skorpen, C. G., & Hsu, A.Y.C. (1997). Emotion and aging: Experience, expression, and control. *Psychology and Aging, 12,* 590–599.

Gunthert, K. C., Cohen L. H., & Armeli, S. (1999). The role of neuroticism in daily stress and coping. *Journal of Personality and Social Psychology, 77,* 1087–1100.

Headey, B., & Wearing, A. (1989). Personality, life events, and subjective well-being: Toward a dynamic equilibrium model. *Journal of Personality and Social Psychology, 57,* 731–739.

Heckhausen, J., & Schulz, R. (1995). A life-span theory of control. *Psychological Review, 102,* 284–304.

Helson, R., Jones, C., & Kwan, S. Y. (2002). Personality change over 40 years of adulthood: Hierarchical linear modeling analyses of two longitudinal samples. *Journal of Personality and Social Psychology, 83,* 752–766.

Helson, R., & Kwan, V.S.Y. (2000). Personality development in adulthood: The broad picture and processes in one longitudinal sample. In S. Hampson (Ed.), *Advances in personality psychology* (Vol. 1, pp. 77–106). London: Routledge.

Henry, B., Caspi, A., Moffitt, T. E., Harrington, H. L., & Silva, P. A. (1999). Staying in school protects boys with poor self-regulation in childhood from later crime: A longitudinal study. *International Journal of Behavioral Development, 23,* 1049–1073.

Hemenover, S. M. (2001). Self reported processing bias and naturally occurring mood: Mediators between personality and stress appraisals. *Personality and Social Psychology Bulletin, 27,* 387–394.

John, O. P., & Srivastava, S. (1999). The Big Five trait taxonomy; History, measurement, and theoretical perspectives. In L. A. Pervin & O. P. John, (Eds.), *Handbook of Personality Theory and Research* (Vol. 2, pp. 102–138). New York: The Guilford Press.

Jones, C. J., & Meredith, W. (1996). Patterns of personality change across the life-span. *Psychology and Aging, 11,* 57–65.

Jones, C. J., Livson, N., & Peskin, H. (2003). Longitudinal hierarchical linear modeling analyses of California Psychological Inventory data from age 33 to 75: An examination of stability and change in adult personality. *Journal of Personality Assessment, 80,* 294–308.

Kahneman, D. (1999). Objective happiness. In D. Kahneman, E. Diener, & N. Schwartz (Eds.), *Well-being: The foundations of hedonic psychology* (pp. 1–25). New York: Russell Sage Foundation.

Kendler, K. S., Thornton, L.M., & Gardner, C. O. (2001). Genetic risk, number of previous depressive episodes, and stressful life events in predicting onset of major depression. *American Journal of Psychiatry, 158,* 582–586.

Kessler, R. C., McGonagle, K. A., Zhao, S., Nelson, C. B., Hughes, M., Eshleman, S., et al. (1994). Lifetime and 12-month prevalence of DSM-II-R psychiatric disorders in the United States. *Archives of General Psychiatry, 51,* 8–19.

Keyes, C.L.M., & Ryff, C. D. (1998). Generativity in adult lives: Social structural contours and quality of life consequences. In D. P. McAdams & E. de St. Aubin (Eds.), *Generativity and adult development: How and why we care for the next generation* (pp. 227–263). Washington, D.C.: American Psychological Association.

Kiecolt-Glaser, J. K., & Glaser, R. (1986). Psychological influences on immunity. *Psychosomatics: Journal of Consultation Liaison Psychiatry, 27,* 621–624.

Kling, K. C., Seltzer, M. M., & Ryff, C., D., (1997). Distinctive late-life challenges: Implications coping and well-being. *Psychology and Aging, 12,* 288–295.

Kohn, M. L., & Schooler, C. (1978). The reciprocal effects of the substantive complexity of work and intellectual flexibility: A longitudinal assessment. *American Journal of Sociology, 84,* 24–52.

Labouvie-Vief, G. (1997). Cognitive-emotional integration in adulthood. In K. W. Schaie (Ed.), *Annual review of gerontology and geriatrics* (Vol. 17, pp. 207–237). New York: Springer.

Labouvie-Vief, G., & DeVoe, M. R. (1991). Emotional regulation in adulthood and later life: A developmental view. In K. W. Schaie (Ed.), *Annual review of gerontology and geriatrics* (Vol. 11, pp. 172–194). New York: Springer.

Labouvie-Vief, G., DeVoe, M., & Bulka, D. (1989). Speaking about feelings: Conceptions of emotion across the life span. *Psychology and Aging, 4,* 425–437.

Lachman, M. E., & Burack, O. R. (1993). Planning and control processes across the life course: An overview. *International Journal of Behavioral Development, 16,* 131–145.

Lachman, M. E., & Weaver, S. L. (1998) The sense of control as a moderator of social class differences in health and well-being. *Journal of Personality and Social Psychology, 74*, 763–773.

Lachman, M. E., Ziff, M., & Spiro, A., III. (1994). Maintaining a sense of control in later life. In R. P. Abeles, H. C. Gift, & M. G. Ory (Eds.), *Aging and quality of life* (pp. 216–232). New York: Springer.

Larsen, R. J. (2000). Toward a science of mood regulation. *Psychological Inquiry, 11*, 129–141.

Lazarus, R. S., & Folkman, S. (1984). *Stress, appraisal, and coping.* New York: Springer.

Levenson, R. W., Carstensen, L. L., Friesen, W. V., & Ekman, P. (1991). Emotion, physiology, and expression in old age. *Psychology and Aging, 6*, 28–35.

Malatesta, C. Z., & Kalnok, M. (1984). Emotional experience in younger and older adults. *Journal of Gerontology, 39*, 301–308.

Marmot, M. (2004). *Status syndrome: How your social standing directly affects your health and life expectancy.* London: Bloomsbury.

McCrae, R. R., & Costa, P. T. Jr. (1999). A Five-Factor theory of personality. In L. A. Pervin & O. P. John (Eds.), *Handbook of personality: Theory and research* (2nd ed., pp. 139–153). New York: Guilford.

McGinnis, M., & Foege, W. (1993). Actual causes of death in the United States. *Journal of the American Medical Association, 270*, 2207–2212.

Mroczek, D. K. (2001). Age and emotion in adulthood. *Current Directions in Psychological Science, 10*, 87–90.

Mroczek, D. K., & Almeida, D. M. (2004). The effects of daily stress, age, and personality on daily negative affect. *Journal of Personality, 72*, 354–378.

Mroczek, D. K., & Kolarz, C. M. (1998). The effect of age on positive and negative affect: A developmental perspective on happiness. *Journal of Personality and Social Psychology, 75*, 1333–1349.

Mroczek, D. K., & Spiro, A., III. (2003a). Modeling intraindividual change in personality traits: Findings from the Normative Aging Study. *Journals of Gerontology. Series B, Psychological Sciences and Social Sciences, 58B*, 153–165.

Mroczek, D. K., & Spiro, A., III. (2003b). Personality structure and process, variance between and within: Integration by means of a developmental framework. *Journals of Gerontology. Series B, Psychological Sciences and Social Sciences, 58B,* 305–306.

Mroczek, D. K., Spiro, A., & Almeida, D. M. (2003). Between- and within-person variation in affect and personality over days and years: How basic and applied approaches can inform one another. *Aging International, 28,* 260–278.

Neyer, F. J., & Asendorpf, J. B. (2001). Personality-relationship transaction in young adulthood. *Journal of Personality and Social Psychology, 81,* 1190–1204.

Nolen-Hoekema, S. (1987). Sex differences in unipolar depression: Evidence and theory. *Psychological Bulletin, 101,* 259–282.

Parkinson, B., Briner, R. B., Reynolds, S., & Totterdell, P. (1995). Time frames for mood: Relations between momentary and generalized ratings of affect. *Personality and Social Psychology Bulletin, 21,* 331–339.

Perrig-Chiello, P., Perrig, W., & Stahelin, H. B. (1999). Health control beliefs in old age: Relationship with subjective and objective health and health behavior. *Journal of Psychology: Health and Medicine, 4,* 84–94.

Ormel, J., & Wohlfarth, T. (1991). How neuroticism, long-term difficulties, and life situation change influence psychological distress. *Journal of Personality and Social Psychology, 60,* 744–755.

Radloff, L. S. (1977). The CES-D scale: A self-report depression scale for research in the general population. *Applied Psychological Measurement, 1,* 385–401.

Redelmeier, D., & Kahneman, D. (1996). Patients' memories of painful medical treatments: Real-time and retrospective evaluations of two minimally invasive procedures. *Pain, 116,* 3–8.

Roberts, B. W. (1997). Plaster or plasticity: Are adult work experiences associated with personality change in women? *Journal of Personality, 65,* 205–232.

Roberts, B. W., & Bogg, T. (2004). A longitudinal study of the relationships between conscientiousness and the social-environmental factors and substance-use behaviors that influence health. *Journal of Personality, 72,* 325–353.

Roberts, B. W., & Caspi, A. (2003). The cumulative continuity model of personality development: Striking a balance between continuity and change in personality traits across the life course. In R. M. Staudinger & U. Lindenberger (Eds.), *Understanding human development: Lifespan psychology in exchange with other disciplines* (pp. 183–214). Dordrecht, NL: Kluwer Academic Publishers.

Roberts, B. W., Caspi, A., & Moffitt, T. (2003). Work experiences and personality development in young adulthood. *Journal of Personality and Social Psychology, 84,* 582–593.

Roberts, B. W., & DelVecchio, W. F. (2000). The rank order consistency of personality traits from childhood to old age: A quantitative review of longitudinal studies. *Psychological Bulletin, 126,* 3–25.

Roberts, B. W., & Donahue, E. M. (1994). One personality, multiple selves: Integrating personality and social roles. *Journal of Personality, 62,* 201–218.

Roberts, B. W., Helson, R., & Klohnen, E. C. (2002). Personality development and growth in women across 30 years: Three perspectives. *Journal of Personality, 70,* 79–102.

Roberts, B. W., & Pomerantz, E. M. (2004). On traits, situations, and their integration: A developmental perspective. *Personality and Social Psychology Review, 8,* 402–416.

Roberts, B. W., Robins, R. W., Caspi, A., & Trzesniewski. K. (2003). Personality trait development in adulthood. In J. Mortimer & M. Shanahan (Eds.), *Handbook of the life course* (pp. 579–598). New York: Kluwer Academic Publishers.

Roberts, B. W., & Walton, K. (2004). *Patterns of mean-level change in personality traits across the life-course: A meta-analysis of longitudinal studies.* Unpublished manuscript, University of Illinois, Champaign-Urbana.

Roberts, B. W., Walton, K., & Viechtbauer, W. (2006). Patterns of mean-level change in personality traits across the life course: A meta-analysis of longitudinal studies. *Psychological Bulletin, 132,* 1–25.

Roberts, B. W., & Wood, D. (in press). *Personality development in the context of the neo socioanalytic model of personality.* In D. K. Mroczek & T. D. Little (Eds.), *Handbook of Personality Development.* Mahwah, NJ: Erlbaum.

Robins, R. W., Caspi, A., & Moffitt, T. E. (2002). It's not just who you're with, it's who you are: Personality and relationship experiences across multiple relationships. *Journal of Personality, 70,* 925–964.

Rossi, A. S., & Rossi, P. H. (1990). *Of human bonding: Parent-child relations across the life course.* Hawthorne, NY: Aldine De Gruyter.

Schaie, K. W., & Willis, S. L. (1986). Can intellectual decline in the elderly be reversed? *Developmental Psychology, 22,* 223–232.

Schaie, K. W., Willis, S. L., & Caskie, G.I.L. (2004). The Seattle Longitudinal Study: Relationship between personality and cognition. *Aging, Neuropsychology and Cognition, 11,* 304–324.

Schooler, C., Mulatu, M. S., & Oates, G. (1999). The continuing effects of substantively complex work on the intellectual functioning of older workers. *Psychology and Aging, 14,* 483–506.

Seeman, T. E., Singer, B., McEwen, B. S., Horwitz, R., & Rowe, J. W. (1997). The price of adaptation—allostatic load and its health consequences: MacArthur Studies of successful aging. *Archives of Internal Medicine, 157,* 2259–2268.

Small, B. J., Hertzog, C., Hultsch, D. F., & Dixon, R. A. (2003). Stability and change in adult personality over 6 years: Findings from the Victoria Longitudinal Study. J*ournals of Gerontology. Series B, Psychological Sciences and Social Sciences, 58B,* 166–176.

Smith, D. D. (1996). Memory. In J. E. Birren & K. W. Schaie (Eds.), *Handbook of the psychology of aging* (4th ed., pp. 236–250). San Diego: Academic Press.

Smith, J., & Baltes, P. B. (1993). Differential psychological aging: Profiles of the old and very old. *Aging and Society, 13,* 551–587.

Srivastava, S., John, O. P., Gosling, S. D., & Potter, J. (2003). Development of personality in early and middle adulthood: Set like plaster or persistent change? *Journal of Personality and Social Psychology, 84,* 1041–1053.

Suls, J. (2001). Affect, stress and personality. In J. P. Forgas (Ed.), *Handbook of affect and social cognition* (pp. 392–409). Mahwah, NJ: Erlbaum.

Suls, J., Green, P., & Hillis, S. (1998). Emotional reactivity to everyday problems, affective inertia, and neuroticism. *Personality and Social Psychology Bulletin, 24,* 127–136.

Taylor, J. A. (1953). A personality scale of manifest anxiety. *Journal of Abnormal and Social Psychology, 48,* 285–290.

Thomas, D. L., & Diener, E. (1990). Memory accuracy in the recall of emotions. *Journal of Personality and Social Psychology, 59,* 291–297.

Twenge, J. M. (2000). The age of anxiety? The birth cohort change in anxiety and neuroticism, 1952–1993. *Journal of Personality and Social Psychology, 79,* 1007–1021.

van der Kolk, B. S. (1996). The body keeps score: Approaches to the psychobiology of posttraumatic stress disorder. In B. A. van der Kolk & A. C. McFarlane (Eds.), *Traumatic stress: The effects of overwhelming experience on mind, body and society* (pp. 214–241). New York: Guilford.

van der Kolk, B. S. (1997). The psychobiology of posttraumatic stress disorder. *Journal of Clinical Psychiatry, 58,* 16–24.

Varey, C., & Kahneman, D. (1992). Experiences extended across time: Evaluations of moments and episodes. *Journal of Behavioral Decision Making, 5,* 169–186.

Vaux, A., & Meddin, J. (1987). Positive and negative life change and positive and negative affect among the rural elderly. *Journal of Community Psychology, 15,* 447–458.

Walton, K., & Roberts, B. W. (2004). On the relationship between substance use and personality traits: Abstainers are not maladjusted. *Journal of Research in Personality, 38,* 515–535.

West, R., & Craik, F.I.M. (1999). Age-related decline in prospective memory: The roles of cue accessibility and cue sensitivity. *Psychology and Aging, 14,* 264–272.

Wilson, R. S., Bienas, J. L., Mendes de Leon, C. F., Evans, D. A., & Bennett, D. A. (2003). Negative affect and mortality in older persons. *American Journal of Epidemiology, 158,* 827–835.

Wilson, R. S., Mendes de Leon, C. F., Bienas, J. L., Evans, D. A., & Bennett, D. A. (2004). Personality and mortality in old age. *Journal of Gerontology. Series B, Psychological Sciences and Social Sciences, 59B,* 110–116.

Winkielman, P., Knauper, B., & Schwarz, N. (1998). Looking back at anger: Reference periods change the interpretation of emotion frequency questions. *Journal of Personality and Social Psychology, 75,* 719–728.

Wood, D., & Roberts, B. W. (in press). Cross-sectional and longitudinal tests of the personality and role identity structural model (PRISM). *Journal of Personality.*

Woolf, C. J., & Costigan, M. (1999). Transcriptional and posttranslational plasticity in the generation of inflammatory pain. *Proceedings of the National Academy of Sciences, 96,* 7723–7730.

4

Social Norms, Rules of Thumb, and Retirement: Evidence for Rationality in Retirement Planning

Gary Burtless

This chapter was prepared for a conference on "Social Structures, Aging, and Self Regulation in the Elderly," at the Penn State Gerontology Center, University Park, Pennsylvania, October 4–5, 2004. I am grateful to Lisa Bell for excellent research assistance and to Ellen Peters of Decision Research, Joseph Quinn of Boston College, and the editors of this volume for providing unusually helpful comments on an earlier draft of the chapter. The views are solely those of the author and should not be attributed to the Gerontology Center or the Brookings Institution.

Workers who anticipate reaching old age must make three choices about their retirement. They must decide at what age they will retire, the percentage of their wages to set aside so they can live comfortably when earnings cease, and the allocation of their retirement savings across different kinds of investments, such as stocks, bonds, bank and insurance accounts, and real estate. The three decisions are interrelated. Workers who do not expect to retire until shortly before they die do not need to save much for retirement. Those who anticipate retiring in their early 50s should plan to save a sizeable fraction of their pay. People who invest in risky assets, like biotechnology stocks and swamp real estate, may obtain terrific rewards for accepting great risk. If they are lucky they can use some of the rewards to retire young and live sumptuously. Less fortunate investors may be left with too little savings to retire.

Over the past couple of decades economists have devoted increasing efforts to understand retirement decisions. Labor economists focus on the timing of retirement and on retirees' work patterns after they leave career jobs. Microeconomists have examined workers' preretirement saving and postretirement consumption behavior. Finance economists have theorized about workers' choices regarding the allocation of retirement saving across risky and less risky investments.

In thinking about decision-making, economists usually assume agents are well informed, farsighted, and rational (i.e., that agents use sound logic when deciding on a course of action). They combine all the information at their disposal, including knowledge of their own preferences and long-term interests, to make logical choices that maximize their well-being given the constraints they face. This does not mean people never make choices they later regret. Stock prices might fall 50% and house prices rise 50% after a worker has placed all his or her retirement savings in the stock market. When these outcomes become known, most people would regret investing in stocks rather than real estate. At the time the worker decides to invest in stocks, however, the choice is assumed to be based on good information and a prudent evaluation of the potential risks and rewards of alternative investments. Economists' presumption that agents are rational simply means they think people make decisions calculated to produce the greatest long-term satisfaction given the trade-offs and uncertainties that a person faces when the decision is made.

Many observers, including some economists, are skeptical that workers make retirement decisions in the farsighted and logical manner just described. Unlike other economic choices, which are repeated many times over the course of adulthood, retirement only occurs once in a lifetime for most workers. People are not given the opportunity to improve on their decision making through constant repetition, as is the case when consumers learn how to budget and shop for groceries, clothing, apartments, and even marriage partners. It is therefore hard to argue that workers can eventually learn from experience about choosing an advantageous retirement age or an optimal rate of saving. When people decide when to retire or how much to save for retirement, their choices may be poorly informed, short sighted, and less than rational.

What alternative decision-making rules might workers follow when making these choices? One possibility is that workers economize on independent decision making by imitating the decisions of other workers. If a worker's colleagues or friends retire around age 60, age 60 may seem like a desirable age to leave a job. Another possibility is that workers use simple rules of thumb, which may not be farsighted or fully rational. Instead of considering the financial implications of retiring at every future age, some workers may retire as soon as available pension income replaces a target percentage of earnings, say, 75% of preretirement pay. Simple rules of thumb may produce decisions that are correlated with optimal decisions, but rules of thumb can also produce a retirement that occurs much too early or much too late compared with the age selected under a farsighted plan. For example, a 75% income replacement rate may support a comfortable retirement for someone who is in excellent health, which is likely to be the case in the first years after a worker retires. However, the same replacement rate may be grossly inadequate to pay for necessities and medical bills if the retiree's health deteriorates. A farsighted planner would take account of this risk by delaying retirement or building up a bigger nest egg before leaving a career job.

Does it matter which of these decision-making models is more accurate in describing workers' retirement choices? It matters if we are concerned about the well-being of the aged. This is particularly true if we are considering policies that place greater responsibility on individual workers to save and invest for their own retirement. At the moment, all industrial countries have state-sponsored pension and health insurance programs to support consumption in old age. Workers are automatically enrolled in these programs when they take a job. Industrial countries also face the prospect of rapidly aging populations, a development that is likely to lead to the insolvency of state pension schemes unless pension contributions are raised and benefits cut. One way to reduce the long-term burden of state pensions is to gradually replace them with individual investment accounts. Under this kind of system, workers might have to decide how much savings to place in their accounts, how to allocate their savings across different investment options, and when and how fast to make withdrawals from their accounts. After they retire, workers would depend on withdrawals from their accounts to pay for consumption in old age. Some countries including Japan and Great Britain have moved in this direction, and policymakers in other countries including the United States urge reforms along the same lines.

Policies that rely on workers to make their own decisions about retirement saving and investment seem reasonable if most workers make these choices rationally and competently. The same policies are less appealing when a large fraction of workers base their retirement and saving choices on herd behavior, faulty logic, or defective information. If workers are forced to assume more responsibility to save for their own retirement, allocate their pension contributions, and withdraw funds in retirement, policymakers should be confident that few workers will make big planning mistakes. A big mistake can lead to serious hardship if state pensions are small. By the time aged workers discover they have retired too early or saved too little, they may have no opportunity to undo this mistake by saving more or returning to work.

In the remainder of this chapter I will consider what economists have learned about the rationality and farsightedness of workers' retirement decisions. Do workers retire at a reasonable age? Do they save enough to afford the retirement ages they choose? Do they invest their retirement savings in a rational and prudent way?

The literature on these topics is lengthy and growing, and is unsurprisingly open to competing interpretations. When polled about their preparations for retirement, large minorities of Americans acknowledge they have given no thought to the subject, have saved little or nothing in pension and other retirement accounts, and lack confidence they will be able to afford retirement. A number of economists (Bernheim, 1992; Moore & Mitchell, 2000) and financial planners have published alarming studies suggesting that middle-aged and older workers face large saving shortfalls compared with the nest eggs needed to retire at the typical retirement age. On the other hand, careful analysis of the best survey evidence on workers' earnings, pension accumulations, Social Security entitlements, and non-pension saving reveals that very few workers have nest eggs that obviously and substantially fall short of what is optimal under some conceivably rational plan. To be sure, many workers have little or no retirement saving, as already noted. However, most low-saving workers can fall back on Social Security or public assistance to support minimal consumption in old age. While the annual consumption reported by newly retired workers is lower than workers' consumption before they retired, the decline is relatively small, is anticipated by many people approaching retirement, and is not clearly associated with a drop in retirees' well-being.

Recent research findings on worker savings and retiree consumption do not *prove* that retirement and saving decisions are made in a fully rational and farsighted way (Engen, Gale, & Ucello, 1999; Scholz, Seshadri, & Khitatrakum, 2004). The evidence only shows it is hard to rule out rationality and farsightedness using available information on households' consumption and savings. One problem is that we do not directly observe the underlying preferences of individual workers. This makes it nearly impossible to rule out rational decision making, even when we observe very odd patterns of work, saving, and consumption. When a worker suffers a 50% drop in consumption upon retirement, we might interpret this as evidence of poor (irrational) planning. Alternatively, it may reflect the unfortunate effect of an unexpected early exit from the labor force, possibly because of a factory shutdown or onset of serious disease. Even if the possibility of a plant closing or poor health were fully reflected in the worker's saving plan, he or she may have rationally intended to accept a big cut in consumption if his or her career came to a premature end. This means that we cannot rule out rational foresight when workers enter retirement with little savings or when they experience big drops in consumption over the course of their retirement. Bad outcomes may have been fully anticipated, and accepted, in a farsighted and plausible retirement plan.

In the next section of this chapter, I will examine what is known about the determinants of retirement and the role of farsighted planning in the choice of retirement age. What evidence have economists found that the age of retirement is the result of a deliberate and rational plan involving lifetime optimization? The following section contains a review of saving behavior. Do workers save enough to retire comfortably? Or is there substantial under-saving compared with what is needed in light of the distribution of retirement ages? I will not treat the rationality of workers' observed investment choices. Since there is deep division among economists and financial planners on what constitutes a sensible investment strategy, the soundness of most workers' portfolios is not easy to evaluate. The chapter will conclude with a brief summary of implications.

EVIDENCE ON AGE AT RETIREMENT

When workers retire, they withdraw from their normal occupation and reduce their work effort or stop work altogether. At the beginning of the last century, retirement was relatively rare but not unknown. Two out of three American men past age 65 were employed, but one-third were not (U.S. Department of Commerce, Bureau of the Census, 1975). By the middle of the century, retirement was much more common. Fewer than half of men 65 and older held a job in 1950. In 2000, the proportion at work had fallen still further. Just 18% of men over 65 were employed or actively seeking a job. Eighty-two percent were outside the active labor force. The proportion of women past 65 who were employed also fell during the 20th century, but the reduction was far smaller than among men because the percentage of older women in paid work has always been low.

The decline in labor force participation among older men has not been confined to the United States. It is characteristic of all rich, industrialized countries. In most European countries, employment rates among the aged are now significantly below those in the United States (Burtless, 2004; Quinn & Burkhauser, 1994). Along with a shrinking work week and rising labor force participation among women, earlier retirement has been a distinctive feature of economic development in all the rich countries.

Theory

When economists think about retirement, they naturally focus on the financial aspects of the decision. In this section, I will reflect on the basic theory economists have used to explain retirement choice and the evidence they have analyzed to test the theory. Although the economic literature on retirement age choice did not begin in earnest until the mid-1970s, it has grown rapidly since that time (Burtless, 1999; Hurd, 1990; Lumsdaine & Mitchell, 1999; Quinn & Burkhauser, 1994; Quinn, Burkhauser, & Myers, 1990). The first aspect of retirement to attract economists' interest was the effect, or hypothesized effect, of retirement on individual and national saving. The classic statement of this relationship is contained in a series of articles written or co-authored by Nobel prize-winning economist Franco Modigliani (Ando & Modigliani, 1963; Modigliani & Brumberg, 1954). His theory has had a wide influence on economists' thinking about the timing of retirement as well as the determination of saving.

Modigliani's basic hypothesis was that farsighted workers will rationally plan their consumption over a full lifetime. In devising their lifetime consumption plans, they take account of the likely path of their labor earnings as they age and then prudently accumulate savings in anticipation of their retirement. The goal of a good consumption plan is to maximize the worker's lifetime well-being, subject to the constraint that lifetime consumption cannot exceed the worker's lifetime wealth. Lifetime wealth consists of the worker's initial assets and the present discounted value of anticipated labor earnings and other kinds of income that are not derived from initial assets or labor earnings. Rational and farsighted workers will plan to avoid situations in which all of their lifetime wealth has been consumed long before they expect to die. In the absence of public aid or private charity, the effects of such a planning error are not appealing.

When workers first enter the labor force their earnings are low, but wages typically rise as workers gain extra skill and experience. In the United States, earnings often reach a peak around age 50 and then begin to gradually decline. Since 1985, the average age at retirement for U.S. men and women has been about 62 years of age. One-half of the people who work in their early 50s have withdrawn from the labor force by the time they reach age 63. When most workers retire, their earnings cease altogether, although about one-fifth of male retirees continue to earn reduced wages, at least temporarily. In simple versions of the life-cycle consumption model, workers are well informed about the path of their future earnings, their age at death, and the interest rate they are able to earn on their savings. If workers have stable preferences throughout their lives, their planning problem is formidable but tractable.

A worker who successfully solves the consumption planning problem will plot out a desired path of consumption for each future year of life, and will stick with the plan unless there is an unanticipated change in his or her financial outlook. The most advantageous plan will depend on the relationship between the worker's subjective rate of time preference and the interest rate that can be obtained on savings. The rate of time preference is a measure of the worker's impatience in consumption. Persons who immediately consume nine-tenths of a box of cookies, leaving only one-tenth of it for consumption tomorrow, are said to have a high rate of time preference; they are very impatient in their consumption. If the worker's rate of time preference is equal to the market interest rate, the consumption path will be level throughout the worker's life (the situation assumed in the top panel of Figure 4.1). If instead the rate of time preference is higher than the interest rate, the worker will attempt to shift consumption toward the early part of life, and consumption will fall as the worker grows older. People with a very low rate of time preference—who are very patient in their consumption—will shift consumption to later stages of their life, and will plan to increase their consumption as they age. Workers may wish to leave bequests to survivors, in which case they will consume all their lifetime wealth except the amount they plan to leave to heirs.

Figure 4.1 shows one solution to the life-cycle consumption problem for a worker who expects to live to age 85, faces a 5% interest rate, chooses to retire at age 65, and has no intention of leaving anything to an heir. The worker's potential wage is $10,000 a year when entering the workforce at age 20, gradually rises to a little more than $22,000 a year when reaching age 50, and then declines at later ages. The value of expected lifetime earnings is a little more than $850,000, but the total lifetime consumption can be greater than this if part of earnings are saved and invested in an account that bears 5% per year. If the worker consumes the entire sum of lifetime

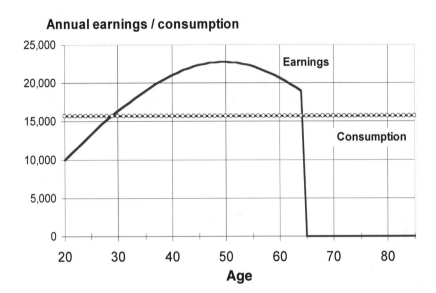

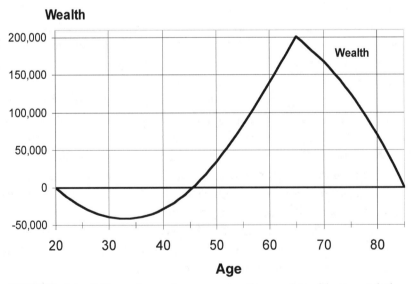

FIGURE 4.1 Life-cycle earnings, consumption, and wealth accumulation of a farsighted saver.

income (including anticipated interest earnings) steadily throughout life, the annual consumption will be greater than the annual earnings in the worker's early career. Consumption will be less than earnings in the middle of the worker's career when wages reach their peak. After retirement, earnings will fall to zero, and the worker will live off accumulated wealth. The lower panel in Figure 4.1 shows the worker's wealth holdings at successive stages of a career. Note that the nest egg is negative when the worker is young, because money must be borrowed in order to consume more than is earned. (Young workers who cannot borrow are limited to consuming what they earn, but most consumption surveys suggest that Americans in their 20s and early 30s consume more than they earn and accumulate substantial debt.) By age 30, the worker's wages exceed annual consumption, and the worker can begin to repay some debts. At age 45, debts have been paid off and the worker begins to accumulate wealth. Wealth holding reaches a lifetime peak at retirement, and then declines as the nest egg is depleted to pay for old-age consumption.

Modigliani's life-cycle consumption model emphasizes the single most important financial aspect of retirement, namely, the sharp drop or complete cessation of labor earnings when work hours decline. Most worker households rely heavily on labor earnings to pay for consumption. When earnings cease at retirement, workers must find another way to pay for their consumption. Modigliani stressed personal saving as an alternative source of support in old age. Even though other income sources are quite important nowadays, it is useful to think about the choice of retirement age in a world in which retired workers rely solely on their own savings to finance consumption. A crucial implication of the life-cycle theory is that farsighted workers will simultaneously select both a retirement age and a pattern of lifetime consumption. Their choice will be decisively affected by the expected pattern of their wage income, the interest rate they pay on money they borrow, and the interest earnings they obtain on money they save. Another implication of the theory is that year-to-year changes in consumption should be much smaller than year-to-year changes in earnings, especially around the planned age of retirement. Workers with farsighted plans will smooth consumption using saving and spending out of their savings over the course of their careers.

The characteristic pattern of increasing and then declining asset holdings over the life cycle, displayed in the bottom panel of Figure 4.1, is a central empirical prediction of life-cycle consumption theory. The asset buildup would not be needed if workers did not expect to retire. In the absence of retirement, saving would be needed mainly to finance bequests and to smooth out consumption in comparison with earnings. Several of the assumptions I have mentioned are highly stylized and are not likely to be true in real life. For example, workers cannot borrow money at the same interest rate they obtain on their investments. Usually they must pay a higher interest rate for loans than the one they can safely earn on their investments. More importantly, few workers can borrow huge sums of money to finance current consumption. They are constrained in the amount they can borrow. These are comparatively minor issues for many workers, however, and addressing them does not really change most of the implications of the theory.

A more serious problem arises when we introduce a realistic picture of the worker's uncertainty about the future. In formulating an ideal retirement and consumption plan, it obviously helps if workers are completely confident about their future earnings, their age at death, and the future interest rate. Unfortunately, few people can predict these things very accurately. In formulating their consumption plans, workers must take account of the possibility that the future may turn out to be more or less congenial than they anticipate. When they experience an unexpected change in earnings, workers face the problem of deciding whether the change will be long lasting or only temporary. These considerations are crucial in determining how much workers should adjust their flow of consumption once they have obtained new information about future income flows. In theory, alert consumers will formulate a new lifetime consumption plan every time they receive new information about the future. If an employer's quarterly earnings report shows an unexpected drop in profits, employees in the company should scale back their consumption in anticipation of layoffs or slower future wage growth. If interest rates rise, workers should postpone consumption until later in life to take greater advantage of higher earnings on their investments. If a worker suffers an unexpected heart attack, the worker may boost saving in anticipation of an earlier retirement and lower lifetime earnings.

New information about the future state of the world is seldom clear cut. Does a heart attack mean that retirement will last longer because the victim may be forced to leave a job earlier? Or will it shorten retirement because the worker can expect an earlier reunion with his deceased relatives? The two outcomes, if fully anticipated, would have opposite effects on the rate of consumption over the remainder of life, but a farsighted worker will take account of both possibilities in formulating a consumption plan. Will an interest rate hike be temporary or permanent? Even financial market specialists do not have enough information to answer this question with much confidence.

Setting aside the effects of uncertainty for a moment, the life-cycle model can be used to analyze workers' choice of a retirement age. To simplify the analysis, assume that workers will stop working completely when they retire. If a worker's potential wages at each future age are known with reasonable certainty, the planning problem is to select the most satisfying combination of years at work and lifetime consumption that is available to him or her. Economists usually assume that, other things equal, workers would prefer to work fewer years (holding constant their lifetime consumption) and to consume more goods and services (holding constant their years at work). In other words, additional consumption of goods and services is a *good* and an additional year at work is a *bad*. If workers postpone their retirement (accepting more of a *bad*), they can also consume more over their lifetime (a *good*). Of course, this characterization of employment is not really accurate for many people who enjoy work and derive great satisfaction from their accomplishments and social interactions on the job. The theory is not very helpful in explaining retirement among this kind of worker, but it is useful for explaining retirement among the much larger number of people who dislike or eventually grow tired of their jobs.

Retirement Incentives

One reason workers retire is that their potential earnings decline in old age, so the payoff from accepting a longer work life grows smaller with advancing age. When the payoff falls below the perceived value of the extra goods and services a worker can consume as a result of working longer, they will retire. Employer and government pension plans can reduce the financial payoff from extra work, which may be another reason work may appear less attractive at older ages. Social Security and company pensions affect the lifetime trade-off between consumption and retirement in a complicated way. Consider the effects of Social Security. Its impact on retirement depends on the contributions workers must make for the pensions they will receive and on the benefit formula that links monthly pensions to a worker's past covered earnings. U.S. employers and workers currently pay a combined tax equal to 12.4% of wages into the system. The tax thus reduces workers' wages by about 12% in comparison with the wages they would receive if the program were abolished. On the other hand, contributions allow a worker to earn credits toward a bigger Social Security pension. The monthly pension goes up as the worker's covered lifetime wages increase. Whether the increase in the pension entitlement is large enough to compensate workers for their extra contributions is an empirical question. Low-wage workers receive favorable treatment under Social Security, so they usually receive a generous return on their contributions. High-wage and long-service workers typically receive much lower returns.

Because the Social Security system has historically been quite generous, all generations retiring up to the present have received larger pensions than their contributions could have paid for if the contributions had been invested in safe assets. In effect, this generosity raised the lifetime wealth of older workers who became entitled to pensions under the system. If they consumed all of the Social Security benefits paid to them, they enjoyed higher lifetime consumption than their labor income alone could have financed. The fortunate generations that received this windfall may have retired earlier than they would have if Social Security had not been introduced or if the program had offered less generous pensions.

On the margin, Social Security can have another effect on the payoff from extra work. Workers who delay their retirement until after age 62 are at least temporarily passing up the opportunity to receive a Social Security check, which can begin when the worker turns 62. If a worker is entitled to $800 per month in pension, for example, the worker gives up $800 in retirement income every month he or she delays retirement past age 62. If the worker's regular monthly pay is $10,000, this represents a comparatively small sacrifice. But if her usual pay is $1,000 a month, the sacrifice amounts to 80% of wages. If the worker can only earn $800 a month, the sacrifice is equal to the *entire* monthly pay. The sacrifice is so large the worker would be an idiot to continue working past age 62, unless some adjustment is made in future pension to compensate for the sacrifice. This presumes, of course, that the person is only working for financial gain. Many people, including volunteers, are happy to work for no pay at all, which is precisely the situation of a worker who gives up $800 every month in pensions in exchange for a monthly pay envelope that contains just $800.

Between the ages of 62–64, the Social Security formula offers workers a fair compensation for giving up a year's pension. Monthly benefits are adjusted upwards about 8% for each year's delay in claiming a pension. For workers who have average life expectancy and a moderate rate of time preference, this adjustment is large enough so that the sacrifice of a year's benefits is compensated by eligibility for a bigger pension in the future. After age 65, however, the benefit formula was historically much less generous toward delayed retirement. Postponement of retirement after that age was not fairly compensated by increases in the monthly pension. (Because of changes in the benefit formula, that is no longer true. Regardless of when workers retire between age 62–69, these days most will receive fair compensation in the form of higher monthly pensions if they delay their retirement by one extra year.) In effect, the historical benefit formula required workers to give up part of the accumulated value of their lifetime pensions if they delayed retirement after age 65. It should not be surprising under these circumstances if a sizeable fraction of workers stopped working at age 65 and began collecting Social Security pensions.

It is worth noting that very few workers are exactly "average." A benefit calculation rule that is age-neutral (or "actuarially fair") on average can still provide a worker who has below-average life expectancy with a strong financial incentive to retire. The worker may not expect to live long enough for the future benefit increase to make up for the benefits he or she gives up by delaying retirement for one more year. Similarly, a worker who applies a high discount factor when evaluating future benefits may not be impressed with the "fair" pension adjustment for an average worker. For workers who are impatient to consume, an 8% hike in benefits starting one year from the present day may not be enough to compensate for the loss of 12 monthly pension checks over the next year. Even an actuarially fair pension adjustment might be too small to persuade workers who are tired of their jobs to delay retirement.

The Social Security program imposes an earnings test in calculating the annual pension, which is why many people must retire in order to begin collecting their benefits. Workers who are between 62–64 and who earn more than $11,640 a year lose a dollar in annual benefits for every two dollars in earnings they receive in excess of $11,640. At one time the earnings limitation was much lower, the tax on excess earnings was much higher, and the age range in which the earnings test applied was much wider. Social Security pensioners were discouraged from working, and some workers may have been induced to postpone claiming a pension until they were confident their earnings would remain low.

Many company pension plans are structured similarly to Social Security pensions. Workers who are covered under an old-fashioned defined-benefit plan earn pension credits for as long as they work for the employer that sponsors the plan (sometimes up to a maximum number of years). The longer they work, the higher their monthly pension. Most defined-benefit plans are structured to encourage workers to remain with the employer for a minimal period—say, 10 years—or until a critical age—say, age 55. Workers who stay for shorter periods may receive very little under the plan. On the other hand, workers who stay in the job too long may see the value of their pension accumulation shrink. This would happen if the plan offered benefits to workers starting at age 55 but then failed to significantly increase the monthly benefit for workers who delayed retirement after age 55. If a 55 year old worker can collect a monthly pension of $2,000 when retiring immediately and a monthly check of $2,001 if retirement is delayed for one year, the worker will clearly lose a substantial amount of lifetime benefits—nearly $24,000—for each year that retirement is postponed. The worker essentially suffers a pay cut when reaching age 55, and the cut is equal to the loss in lifetime benefits suffered by postponing retirement. Many employers find this kind of pension formula to be an effective inducement to push workers into early retirement.

Evidence

Some rough indication of the possible influence of Social Security on retirement is provided by examining the relationship between Social Security incentives and the observed distribution of retirement ages. Social Security is now the principal source of cash income of American households headed by someone 65 years of age or older. Tabulations of the Current Population Survey show that Social Security accounts for slightly more than 40% of the total cash income of the aged. For almost three-fifths of aged families, Social Security represents half or more of the family's total cash income (Employee Benefit Research Institute, 2002, Figure 9.1; Grad, 2002, Table 9.6.A2). Until 1941, Social Security provided no income at all to the elderly. Today the program replaces about 40% of the final wage earned by a full career single worker who earns the average wage and claims a pension at age 65. If the worker has a non-working dependent spouse, the benefit replaces approximately 60% of the worker's final wage. Benefits are clearly high enough so they can be economically significant in influencing the choice of retirement age.

As noted above, labor force participation rates at older ages fell substantially over the 20th century. What role did Social Security incentives play in this trend? The distributions of male retirement ages in selected years between 1940–2000 are plotted in Figure 4.2. The figure shows the percentage of men leaving the labor force at each age from 55–72, computed as a fraction of men in the labor force at age 54. The calculations are based on male labor force participation rates for successive years of age in each of the indicated years. Not surprisingly, the retirement distributions for more recent years are skewed toward the left, reflecting the fact that men have withdrawn from the workforce at younger and younger ages. The tabulations in all of the years show evidence of clustering in retirement at particular ages. There are peaks in the 1940 distribution at ages 60, 65, and 70, indicating that retirement at those ages was more common than at other ages. By 1960, however, there is only one main peak in the retirement distribution, at age 65. In 1970 there is evidence of a secondary peak in the distribution at age 62. By 1980, the percentage of retirements that occurred at age 62 was almost as high as the percentage at age 65. In 1990 and 2000, retirement at age 62 was much more common than retirement at 65.

The earlier discussion of Social Security incentives suggests an explanation for the clustering of retirements at ages 62 and 65. Between 1941–2000, workers eligible for Social Security who continued to work beyond age 65 gave up pensions for which they were not fairly compensated. The earnings penalty in the benefit formula encouraged workers to retire at age 65. The clustering of retirements at age 62, which began after 1960, is also easy to explain. Starting in 1961, age 62 became the earliest age at which men could claim a reduced Social Security pension. Before 1961 men could not claim a pension until 65, and there was no evidence of clustering in retirements at age 62. By 1970, retirement was more common at 62 than at any other age except 65. By 1990, age 62 was the most popular age of retirement by a wide margin. In principle, the Social Security formula fairly compensates workers if they delay claiming a pension past age 62. As we have seen, however, a worker with a high rate of time preference or short life expectancy might not regard the compensation as fair. In that case, some workers will prefer retiring at age 62 rather than at a later age.

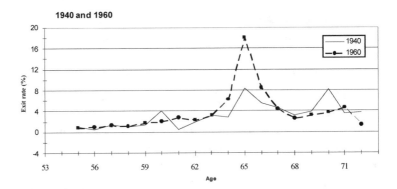

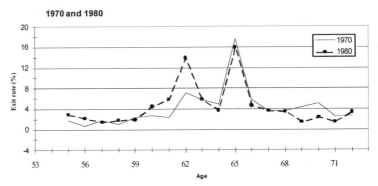

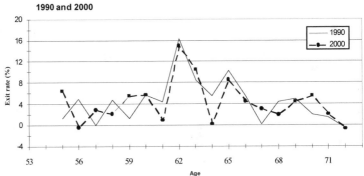

FIGURE 4.2   Male retirement rate by age, 1940–2000.

Notes: Percent retiring each year is a constructed number reflecting the fraction of men leaving the workforce at the designated age, measured as a percent of men in the labor force at age 54.

Source: Author's tabulations of participation rates reported by U.S. Census Bureau for 1940, 1960, and 1970 decennial censuses and tabulations of 12 monthly public-use Current Population Survey files for 1980, 1990, and 2000 calendar years.

The retirement age distributions displayed in Figure 4.2 are based on a crude approximation of workers' behavior in each of the indicated years. If the labor force participation rate of 60-year-old men is five percentage points lower than the participation rate at age 59, and if 90% of 54-year-old men are in the labor force in the same year, the calculation assumes that the retirement rate at age 60 is 5.5% [(5 ÷ 90) × 100]. A more refined estimate of workers' retirement ages can be obtained by interviewing the same people several times as they approach the end of their careers. The U.S. government has mounted two such panel surveys, the Longitudinal Retirement History Survey (LRHS) (Irelan, 1976), conducted between 1969–1979, and the Health and Retirement Survey (HRS), which began in 1992 (Gustman, Mitchell, & Steinmeier, 1995).

The LRHS was a 10-year panel survey covering about 11,000 families headed by people who were between 58–63 years old when the survey began in 1969. Retirement behavior in these 11,000 families has been ana-lyzed by a number of researchers who applied the life-cycle framework in their studies. Figure 4.3 displays information on the retirement behav-ior of men in the LRHS sample who had no disabilities. The top panel shows the distribution of retirement ages among men who were observed to retire by the end of the survey in 1979, when respondents were between 68–73 years old (Burtless & Moffitt, 1985). To determine the exact retire-ment age, I examined the lifetime pattern of respondents' work effort and selected the point in each worker's life when he or she made a discontinu-ous and apparently permanent reduction in labor supply. This definition excludes spells of unemployment that end with the worker's return to a full-time job. However, the definition includes movements from steady full-time work into part-time jobs. The picture misses the retirements of some men who did not retire before their last completed interviews, and this omission will lead to some under-representation of retirements that occur after age 67. Taking account of the different populations included in the tabulations and the differing definitions of retirement, the pattern of retirement in the top panel of Figure 4.3 is broadly similar to that shown in Figure 4.2 for 1970. As in Figure 4.2, there is a clustering of retirements at ages 62 and 65 with a much higher peak at the latter age.

The lower panel displays the pattern of earnings among retired but work-ing men who are age 62 or older in the first LRHS interview after they retired. Approximately one-fifth of retiring men were still working within the first two years after their retirements, and on average they worked a

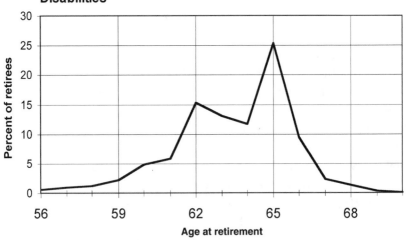

Distribution of Retirement Ages among Men without Disabilities

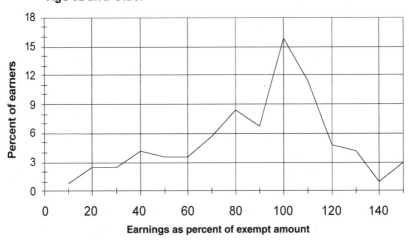

Distribution of Post-Retirement Earnings among Men Age 62 and Older

FIGURE 4.3   Retirement age and postretirement earnings distributions in the Longitudinal Retirement History Survey, 1969–1979.

Source: Burtless & Moffitt (1985), p. 225.

little more than 16 hours a week. The lower panel in Figure 4.3 shows the distribution of their earnings in relation to the earnings exempt amount in the Social Security benefit formula. Earnings below the exempt amount had no effect on a worker's pension; earnings above the exempt amount caused benefits to be reduced by 50% of the amount of excess wages over the exempt amount. (The tax rate on excess earnings was subsequently reduced for retirees age 65 and older. The retirement earnings test for workers older than the normal retirement age was eliminated altogether in 2000.)

Casual observation of the top and bottom panels of Figure 4.3 suggests Social Security had a powerful effect on both retirement ages and postretirement earnings. Note that the age distribution of retirements had two peaks, a lower one at age 62, when Social Security benefits could first be claimed, and a much higher one at age 65, when the Social Security formula stopped making generous adjustments for further delays in claiming a pension. The distribution of postretirement work effort shows an even larger effect of Social Security. Workers appear acutely sensitive to the high implicit tax on their earnings when annual wages exceed the exempt amount. Over a quarter of working retirees earn within 10% and over half earn within 30% of the exempt amount. While retirees may under-report their true earnings to Social Security to avoid paying the high implicit tax, the earnings estimates displayed in Figure 4.3 are based on workers' responses to a Census interviewer, not their earnings reports to the Social Security Administration. The evidence in Figures 4.2 and 4.3 strongly suggests that some fraction of men are quite sensitive to Social Security incentives when they retire. It is less obvious whether this shows most of them are choosing their retirement age on the basis of a farsighted and rational plan. As noted earlier, workers following a simple rule of thumb may retire as soon as available retirement income replaces a target percentage of their monthly pay. It does not require long-term planning to recognize this target is more likely to be met when the worker can first claim a Social Security pension. To be sure, the shifts in the peak of male retirement ages shown in Figure 4.2 conform broadly with the shifting incentives provided by Social Security. Still, it seems surprising that men were so slow to respond to the availability of early pensions, which began in 1961. The percentage of men retiring at age 62 approximately doubled between 1970 and 1980, yet it is hard to see how the incentives for retirement at that particular age changed appreciably over the decade. The innovation in pension rules occurred in 1961 when early retirement benefits were first made available.

Axtell and Epstein (1999) argue that the slow evolution of retirement ages after the 1961 rule change actually provides powerful evidence *against* the view that workers are fully rational in their choice of retirement age. They suggest instead that " . . . imitative behavior and social interactions—factors absent from traditional economic models—may be fundamental in explaining the sluggish response to policy" (p. 162). They argue that only a small percentage of workers may have the capacity or willingness to understand program rules and interpret their meaning for the choice of an optimal retirement age. Most workers imitate the behavior of their "neighbors," that is, older relatives, colleagues at work, or actual neighbors whose retirement behavior can be directly observed. If an imitator's neighborhood happens to include one or more farsighted planners, it is more likely the imitator will respond to new incentives in a farsighted way because the behavior imitated is more likely to be optimal. Axtell and Epstein show how rational behavior can cascade through a social network, even though very few members of the network may be farsighted or fully rational in their decision making. Eventually, retirement patterns attain a new equilibrium in which the rational behavior predominates. It is not obvious, however, whether the optimal, farsighted behavior of a neighbor offers a good guide to one's own behavior. A neighbor who has accumulated greater wealth or who expects a shorter life span can comfortably retire at a younger age. Axtell and Epstein's (1999) model works best in explaining imitative behavior when agents face a common change in incentives. The change in availability of Social Security pensions at age 62 is one example of such a change.

There is also some question whether the pattern of retirement ages and postretirement work effort reflects a sensible response to Social Security incentives. Many people retire shortly after their 62nd birthdays, apparently because they can immediately claim a Social Security pension. As noted earlier, however, the Social Security benefit formula compensates workers who delay claiming a pension after 62 by increasing their monthly pension in later years. For workers who have average or above-average life expectancy and who have a savings account that earns less than 5% a year, it should make sense to delay claiming Social Security for two or three years after age 62. The rate of return that these workers can obtain through delaying a benefit claim compares favorably to the return they obtain on their savings. For workers in these circumstances, there is no more reason to stop working at age 62 than there is at age 61. Only workers who have no liquid savings, who have a short life expectancy, or who apply a high rate of discount when evaluating future income gains have any special reason to retire at 62 years of age. Of course, men in those circumstances could account for all the extra retirements observed at age 62.

The postretirement work pattern shown in the lower panel of Figure 4.3 seems to reflect a powerful influence of the Social Security retirement earnings test on behavior. Pensioners avoid earning more than the Social Security exempt amount in order to avoid facing a 50% marginal tax rate on their earnings. On the other hand, the distribution of postretirement pay may also reflect a deep misunderstanding of the earnings test. Under the rules of Social Security, workers whose benefits are penalized because of application of the earnings test eventually have their monthly pensions recalculated to reflect this benefit reduction. Suppose a 64 year old worker earns enough wages above the earnings exempt amount to lose three months of benefit payments when age 64. According to the rules of the program, the basic monthly pension at age 65 and later is supposed to be increased to reflect the fact that no benefits were received for three months between ages 62–64. The adjustment is exactly the same as the one the worker would have received if claiming benefits had been postponed for three months. Since this delay in claiming pensions is compensated with an actuarially fair adjustment in monthly pensions, in effect the worker does not lose any lifetime benefits at all when benefits are reduced because of application of the retirement earnings test. For pensioners who are between 62 years of age and the normal retirement age, the earnings test results in the rearrangement of benefits over time. The worker receives smaller monthly benefits at the time he earns more than the annual exempt amount, but he receives permanently higher monthly benefits starting at a later age. In theory, the later benefit adjustment fairly compensates workers for the temporary reduction in benefits. If workers fully understood these rules, it is a little hard to understand why their postretirement earnings are so sensitive to the "tax" on earnings above the exempt amount and to changes in the annual exempt amount (Vroman, 1985).

One plausible theory is that workers misunderstand the program rules. Many interpret the rules to mean they face a simple benefit cut whenever their earnings exceed the exempt amount. The clustering of annual earnings around the exempt amount certainly seems consistent with this interpretation. It shows pensioners are responsive to Social Security incentives, but it does not show whether workers are knowledgeable about the true financial implications of the program rules. If they are knowledgeable about the program rules, the clustering of postretirement earnings at the exempt amount may ironically provide evidence that workers are short-sighted in their response to the earnings test.

Another way to analyze the impact of Social Security incentives is to examine the retirement age differences among people who face different incentives because the program has been altered in an unanticipated way. In 1969 and again in 1972, Social Security benefits were increased much faster relative to wages than at any time in the recent past. By 1973, benefits were 20% higher in inflation-adjusted terms than would have been the case if pensions had grown with wages as they did during the 1950s and 1960s. Congress passed amendments to the Social Security Act in 1977 that sharply reduced benefits to workers born in 1917 and later years (the "notch" babies) in comparison with benefits payable to workers born before 1917. Burtless (1986) examined the first episode, and Krueger and Pishke (1992) the second, using the life-cycle framework. In the period analyzed by Burtless, workers born in earlier years planned their retirements when Social Security was comparatively less generous; workers born in later years planned their retirement when Social Security was significantly more liberal. Krueger and Pischke analyzed a period in which younger workers received significantly less generous pensions than those available to older workers. Both studies reached an identical conclusion: Major changes in the generosity of Social Security produced small effects on the retirement behavior and labor force participation of older men, and the effects went in the direction predicted by the farsighted planning model. Burtless estimated, for example, that the 20% benefit hike between 1969–1993 caused a two month reduction in the work career of men who were fully covered by the more generous formula. This was equivalent to a reduction in the labor force participation rates of 62-year-old and 65-year-old men of about two percentage points.

The effects of the 1977 amendments found by Krueger and Pischke were smaller, but probably went in the direction predicted by theory. Of course, even if workers are using shortsighted rules of thumb rather than farsighted optimal planning to choose their retirement age, many will respond to the changed incentives in the same way these economists found. If monthly pensions are hiked 20%, as occurred between 1969–1972, even shortsighted workers may claim benefits a couple of months earlier. Moreover, the behavioral responses uncovered by Burtless and Krueger and Pischke may have been confined to a relatively small number of retirees. The great majority of workers may have failed to respond at all to the changed incentives.

Some economists have directly posed the question of whether the retirement behavior they observe is guided by simple-minded or farsighted planning. Lumsdaine, Stock, and Wise (1992) believe they found evidence suggesting that retirement age choice is often the result of a sophisticated decision-making rule. They examined the retirement choices of workers in a handful of company pension plans. They assessed these choices using three different decision-making rules, one an application of a simple rule, and the other two based on more sophisticated decision-making approaches. (One of the sophisticated approaches was based on an "option value" technique for evaluating the value of pension offers, and the other was based on a "dynamic reprogramming" rule.) The economists estimated their models using information from one period, and then they tried to predict retirement patterns in a later period under each of the three models. Perhaps surprisingly, they found that the models based on more complex and farsighted decision rules were more successful in predicting future retirement patterns. This evidence suggests at least some workers use information in a sophisticated way to decide when to retire. Of course, within a long-established company plan that covers many workers in the same workplace, information helpful in choosing an optimal retirement age that is discovered by one worker can easily be shared with coworkers. Where information sharing is more difficult, workers might rely on simpler decision-making rules, and some workers may end up retiring at an age that is less than optimal. Lumsdaine et al. (1992) analyzed the retirement decision in isolation. They did not assume workers were making farsighted and fully consistent plans for both work and consumption over a multi-year time horizon. Even the most sophisticated decision rule they consider is simpler than the planning methods needed to simultaneously select a retirement age and an optimal path for saving and consumption.

Other data are less supportive of the idea that workers use good information and farsighted plans to select their retirement age. The availability of longitudinal surveys of older workers allows researchers to ask people whether they have made retirement plans and selected an expected age of retirement. Information from later interviews can be used to determine whether respondents follow through on their plans. Abraham and Hausman (2004) analyzed information from the 1992–2000 HRS to determine how frequently older workers reported a retirement plan and how often they stuck to those plans. Workers in the HRS were in their 50s and early 60s when the question on retirement plans was first posed. This seems like a point in life when long-term planners would have formulated a retirement strategy. Abraham and Hausman report that " . . . the most common answer (38% of responses) was that the respondent had not given much thought to future work and retirement plans, or had no plans" (p. 9). Among workers who reported an expected retirement age or retirement strategy, a large percentage failed to follow through on their plans, even when the planned retirement was within two years of the time they described their plans. Among respondents reporting they would stop working altogether within two years of an interview, slightly more than one-third were still at work in the next biannual interview. Among workers who claimed they would *never* stop working, about one in seven had actually ceased working within two years. Of course, unexpected events may have intervened between the two surveys, disrupting the best laid plans of rational workers.

If workers wish to formulate a rational retirement strategy, a minimum requirement is to become familiar with the rules and benefit formulas governing the pension plans in which they are enrolled. The HRS provides a good source of information about older workers' knowledge of their pension plans. Workers were asked to describe some important features of their company plans, and their descriptions were compared to the descriptions of the same plan supplied by employers. Because of the method used to collect and verify the data, we should expect that employers provided more accurate plan descriptions than their employees. Gustman and Steinmeier (2004) offer a sobering comparison of the pension descriptions supplied by workers and employers in the HRS. Only about one-half of workers covered by a defined-contribution plan correctly identified the type of pension plan in which they were enrolled. Approximately the same percentage of workers enrolled in a defined-benefit plan correctly reported that their employer offered that form of pension.

A defined-benefit plan provides vested workers with a pension that is determined by the worker's years of service and final salary while enrolled in the plan. These plans ordinarily have an early entitlement age (when workers can first receive reduced benefits) and a full entitlement age (when workers can claim an unreduced benefit). In this kind of plan, the monthly pension is guaranteed by the employer. In contrast, a defined-contribution pension is essentially an individual investment account maintained on behalf of individual workers. The employer deposits annual contributions (usually a fixed percentage of a worker's pay), and the ultimate value of the investment account depends on the success of the worker's or employer's investment strategy. The worker bears the risk of poor investment outcomes, but the accumulation in the pension account is the property of the worker even if he leaves the employer long before the standard retirement age. If workers do not know whether they are enrolled in a defined-benefit or a defined-contribution pension plan, it is unlikely they are familiar with the retirement incentives in their plan. Indeed, Gustman and Steinmeier (2004) show startling discrepancies between workers' understanding and employers' descriptions of retirement incentives. Even among workers who correctly stated they were covered by a defined-benefit plan, only a minority accurately reported the youngest age at which they could claim pensions. For example, among workers in plans where the early eligibility age was 55, only 40% of workers correctly reported this age. Slightly more than 20% believed the early entitlement age was 62, and 7% reported it was 65 or higher. Gustman and Steinmeier show that workers are more accurate in describing their Social Security entitlements, although workers with very low entitlements often have an exaggerated estimate of their potential monthly benefits.

How does misinformation affect retirement decisions? Chan and Stevens (2003) offer some fascinating evidence. They focused their analysis on HRS respondents who worked in 1992 and were covered by a company pension plan according to the reports of their employers. Using the employer's description of the worker's pension entitlement, Chan and Stevens could reliably calculate the value of a pension if the worker retired immediately and compare that to the pension value if the worker retired at a future age. The average worker underestimated the value of the pension by about 55% of the amount reported by employers. Moreover, many workers offered wildly inaccurate estimates of the improvement in their pension if they delayed retirement to a later age. Using information from follow-up HRS interviews, Chan and Stevens found that workers' retirement choices were based on their (possibly inaccurate) interpretation of pension rules. For people with accurate information, retirement choices were closely aligned with the financial incentives in their plan. If a worker's understanding of the plan rules was in error, the retirement decision was often based on serious misunderstanding.

One of the most important financial determinants of an optimal retirement age is the increase or decline in the value of a pension if a worker postpones retirement for one or more years. Under some retirement plans, workers can actually lose lifetime pension wealth if they delay their retirement after attaining the plan's early or normal retirement age. Chan and Stevens (2003) found that workers who accurately reported the amount of pension gain from delaying retirement were several times more responsive than average workers to the true financial incentives in their pension plan. Most economists, including Gustman and Steinmeier (1986), Burtless and Moffitt (1985), and Burtless (1986), estimate life-cycle retirement models under the presumption that workers are responding to the true financial incentives in the pension plans in which they are enrolled. On the whole, they find aggregate responses to pension incentives that seem consistent with the basic life-cycle model. Chan and Stevens' findings suggest the pattern of aggregate response may reflect farsighted responses on the part of some well-informed workers and poorly informed or irrational choices for a sizeable minority or even a majority of workers.

LIFE-CYCLE SAVING

To help us understand whether saving decisions are guided by rational and farsighted planning, workers' saving behavior can also be compared with the predictions of the life-cycle model. It provides some clear predictions about how wealth is accumulated over a career and how workers should respond to unexpected events. The lower panel of Figure 4.1 implies that workers should build up significant savings in anticipation of retirement and then draw down their wealth during retirement. The model makes a clear and plausible distinction between (unanticipated) changes in flows of income that can be expected to last and changes that are only temporary. An unexpected income improvement that is permanent, such as an earnings gain that accompanies a promotion, will have a much bigger impact on a worker's consumption than an improvement that is only temporary, such as a one-time bonus for outstanding job performance. By the logic of the life-cycle model, a person who wins a lottery that pays $30,000 a year for 30 years will plan to make a much bigger change in consumption than the person who wins a one-time prize of $30,000. By the same reasoning, the lottery winner who obtains a prize paying a modest annual amount (say, $2,000 a year) that has a present discounted value of $30,000, will alter consumption by roughly the same amount as the winner of a one-time prize equal to $30,000. A fully anticipated drop in income, such as the one that accompanies a planned retirement, should have almost no effect on consumption.

Some evidence supports this theory (Lusardi & Browning, 1996). Most empirical research suggests that the life-cycle model is correct in emphasizing that households discount short-run fluctuations in their income when determining current consumption, and that retirement is one important motive for saving. There is competing evidence, however, that consumption is more volatile and closely related to current income changes than would be the case if there were complete smoothing of consumption over full lifetime resources. As the theory predicts, we observe a tendency among many workers to steadily, but gradually, build up their wealth, increasing their rates of saving in peak earning years and as they approach retirement. The life-cycle theory's implication that consumers have a target wealth-income ratio that increases with age up to retirement also seems to be valid for many households.

Nonetheless, some economists are skeptical of the theory because simple versions of it are not very successful in accounting for important aspects of personal saving. For example, many American workers enter retirement without any assets. A large percentage of workers who do have assets apparently continue to add to them after they retire. Neither fact is easy to reconcile with simple versions of the life-cycle model. Theorists have made modifications in the basic theory to account for obvious empirical contradictions. Different theorists have proposed different modifications to rescue the basic model. Whatever their criticisms of the model, however, few economists have strayed far from it in trying to explain the connection between saving and retirement behavior.

Preretirement Saving

Recent empirical research has focused on two questions about saving behavior in relation to retirement. First, do workers typically accumulate enough savings so that they can live comfortably during retirement? And second, is there evidence to support the prediction of the life-cycle model that consumption changes little when retirement occurs?

The first question has aroused considerable controversy because of disagreement over what constitutes adequate saving for retirement. Almost from the beginning of systematic analysis of the wealth distribution, economists have had to confront the fact that many workers reach old age with very little savings (Diamond & Hausman, 1984). This finding has been confirmed in many studies over the years. Lusardi (2001) recently tabulated the wealth holdings of HRS respondents who were not retired at the time of their first interview in 1992. Since these workers were between 50–61 years of age, it is reasonable to assume most of them were within a decade of retirement. Workers in the bottom one-tenth of the wealth distribution had no wealth at all except their Social Security wealth. Even workers at the 25th percentile had essentially no liquid wealth. That is, subtracting their short-term debt from the sum of their bank deposits, stocks, and bonds left these workers with no liquid savings. These workers' total wealth holdings, including equity in a home or business, IRAs and Keogh plan assets, and vehicles, amounted to less than $28,000 (at the value of a dollar in 1992). Lusardi points out that if all of this wealth were sold and converted into a lifetime annuity, it would provide workers with an income of less than $200 a month. One-quarter of 50–61-year-old workers in the HRS had even less wealth than this. One reason for low savings may be that workers have given little or no thought to retirement. Lusardi reports that the median wealth holdings of workers who have thought "hardly at all" about their retirement is less than one-half the median wealth of workers who have thought "some" or "a lot" about retirement.

Although the fraction of older workers who lack wealth may seem shockingly high, is it high enough to cause us to reject the hypothesis that workers save rationally for retirement? In some cases we can show that the optimal rate of preretirement saving is zero or very near zero. Many workers who earn low or erratic wages throughout their careers will qualify for a Social Security pension or an old age public assistance check. The amount of monthly benefits may equal or exceed the average net pay they received in their career. Since some of these workers may not be eligible for public assistance unless their liquid savings are very low, it may make no sense to accumulate preretirement wealth. The availability of Social Security, public assistance, and company provided pensions means that the optimal amount of savings depends critically on individual circumstances. Workers who can expect pensions or assistance payments that replace a large percentage of their net earnings have much less need for savings than workers who do not anticipate pensions or assistance payments.

Bernheim (1992, 1995) published two widely cited studies showing that many baby boomers, including high-wage workers, face large shortfalls in retirement saving. He calculated workers' optimal saving levels, taking into account the number of their current and anticipated dependents, earnings, expected Social Security and pension benefits, and other factors. He then compared workers' actual saving with the optimal saving amount and determined whether workers faced a surplus or deficit in their saving. His calculations implied that workers in the baby boom generation were saving at just one-third the rate needed to cover the costs of their retirement.

Other researchers have reached similar conclusions, often using much better survey data. Moore and Mitchell (2000) examined the 1992 wealth holdings of HRS respondents and calculated the additional saving they would need to retire without any loss of consumption at retirement. This calculation takes into account the Social Security and pension benefits that workers could obtain if they continued working. The calculations are repeated for two potential retirement ages, 62 and 65, the two ages that are most common (see Figure 4.2). Moore and Mitchell show that the median HRS household would have to increase its saving rate by 16% of earnings to maintain constant consumption after retirement at age 62. If retirement were delayed for three additional years to 65, the required extra savings for the median worker would represent 7% of earnings. When Moore and Mitchell compared required savings rates to actual savings rates among households approaching retirement, they found that actual savings rates typically fall far short of the required rate. A similar conclusion about the adequacy of household saving was reached by Warshawsky and Ameriks (2001).

Some recent analyses of wealth surveys have produced a very different picture of wealth adequacy. A number show that comparatively few workers have clearly under-saved, and the typical amount of under-saving is quite small. One reason for the difference is that the newer studies explicitly account for the income uncertainty workers face in the years before they retire. Earnings uncertainty is very important for an obvious reason. If workers cannot borrow much money, they must save a very large percentage of their earnings in high earnings years to ensure that their families do not have to reduce their consumption in low earnings years. This effect of earnings uncertainty is not reflected in Figure 4.1 because it is drawn under the assumption that annual earnings will rise and fall over a worker's career in a completely predictable way. In the real world, earnings are much less predictable than this. Every year many workers lose their jobs, and some must accept big pay cuts in order to get reemployed. Other workers receive unexpected promotions or take new jobs with higher salaries. If workers want to accumulate enough savings to fully smooth consumption, they must save a very large percentage of their pay to accumulate a buffer stock of savings. Rational planners will save less than the full amount needed to completely smooth consumption, and this will mean that large, unexpected wage reductions will sometimes cause workers to deplete their savings before they retire. As noted by Engen, Gale, and Uccello (1999), it is wrong to argue that there is a single optimal path of saving for all workers who expect to earn the same lifetime wages. Instead they find, even among workers who share the same preferences, that there is a range of optimal saving paths where each path depends on the exact sequence of earnings "surprises" received by the worker. Workers and retirees also face uncertainty about when they will die. If workers die at an unexpectedly early age, their savings will go unused and will not contribute much to their lifetime happiness. If they die in advanced old age, they may deplete all their savings and face many years of very low consumption. Rational workers will make a savings choice that balances these risks, but for many farsighted workers, the balance will mean their consumption falls as they live longer and longer beyond their retirement age.

In light of earnings and lifespan uncertainty, Engen et al. (1999) ask a somewhat different question about wealth holdings from the one posed by earlier analysts. They ask whether the observed distribution of wealth holdings seems consistent with the distribution that would be observed if each household responded to unexpected earnings changes and life-span uncertainty in an optimal way. Earlier analysts implicitly posed a different question: If the profile of lifetime earnings and date of death were known in advance, how much wealth would an optimizing worker have set aside by the time he reached the age when his wealth holdings were reported to the interviewer? If a worker's wealth falls short of this threshold, the worker is judged to have inadequate savings. Engen et al. do not actually observe the past sequence of earnings for any member of their sample, but they can use information from other sources to derive reasonable estimates of typical year-to-year variability in earnings. Combining this information with data about the worker's current earnings and survival probabilities in future years, they simulate the range of wealth holdings that would be observed if workers responded optimally to a simulated sequence earnings fluctuations and the known probabilities of future death. Their simulations unsurprisingly reveal that many prudent and rational savers will have little or no savings if they experience a big, unpleasant earnings surprise. Although Engen et al. conclude that there is probably some under-saving in a few population groups, the shortfall in saving seems quite modest compared with earlier estimates. This conclusion was confirmed in a recent study by Scholz, Seshadri, and Khitatrakun (2004), which used HRS data to calculate optimal saving accumulations based on workers' *actual* lifetime sequence of Social Security covered earnings. The optimal accumulations were then compared with wealth holdings reported by the same workers. Scholz et al. conclude that less than one-fifth of HRS households have lower saving than their optimal targets, and the saving shortfall of those households is typically quite small.

Postretirement Consumption

The findings by Engen et al. (1999) and Scholz et al. (2004) do not prove that the saving behavior of American workers is farsighted and rational. They demonstrate instead that it is difficult to rule out the hypothesis that saving choices are farsighted and rational for the overwhelming majority of workers. Some readers might find this conclusion more reassuring if analysts could offer clear evidence that retirees enjoy adequate income or consumption in old age. It is hard to define a reliable benchmark for assessing adequacy, however. One gauge is the official U.S. poverty line. Census Bureau statistics on income poverty suggest destitution is no more common these days among the aged than it is among non-aged adults (see Figure 4.4). This reassuring fact may suggest that poor planning and shortsightedness do not lead to any more hardship in old age than at younger ages. Of course, if the income needs of the aged are greater than those of the non-elderly, perhaps because of costly health problems, it still might be the case that retirees have inadequate resources to maintain postretirement consumption.

Economists have found reasonably reliable and consistent evidence suggesting that consumption falls after workers retire, although the implications of this decline are not always clear. Hamermesh (1985) found that couples' consumption early in retirement is 14% higher than their retirement income can support, forcing them to reduce their consumption in later old age. Hausman and Paquette (1987) uncovered more compelling evidence of a drop in consumption following retirement. Looking solely at food consumption among families represented in the LRHS, Hausman and Paquette found that retirement led to a decline in expenditures on food of about 14% of preretirement consumption. For the workers who were forced to leave their jobs because of a layoff or deterioration in health,

Percent in poverty

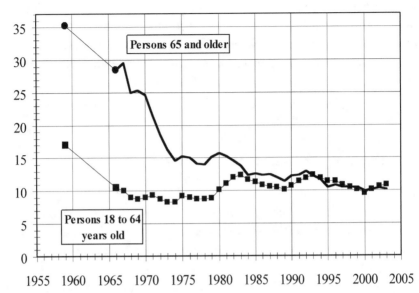

FIGURE 4.4   U.S. poverty rate among aged and non-aged adults, 1959–2003.

Source: U.S. Bureau of Census.

the drop in consumption was even bigger—an additional 9% of preretirement food consumption. For workers who had accumulated below average wealth, the drop in food expenditures was larger still. Banks, Blundell, and Tanner (1998) used many years of detailed household consumption data for British families to document the fall in consumption that occurs immediately after workers retire. Part of this decline can be explained by lower spending requirements for people who no longer need to go to work, but much of the falloff in consumption cannot be rationalized. Banks, Blundell, and Tanner conclude that for many households, retirement must have been accompanied by an unwelcome surprise that reduced the families' ability to consume.

Recent studies have shown that the drop in consumption following retirement is at least partly anticipated. Hurd and Rohwedder (2004) used interview responses in the HRS to compare respondents' preretirement expectations of consumption after retirement with the actual experiences of workers who had already retired. HRS respondents who were not yet retired were asked whether they expected consumption to fall after retirement and by how much. The responses of people who had not yet retired could be compared with the reported consumption changes of HRS respondents who had retired and already experienced the fall in income that accompanies retirement. Hurd and Rohwedder confirm that consumption falls at retirement, with an average decline of about 15–20% of preretirement consumption. They also show, however, that this fall in consumption is largely anticipated by workers. In fact, the reported decline in consumption among workers who had already retired is a bit smaller than the average decline predicted by workers who had not yet retired. These findings confirm earlier findings by Ameriks, Caplin, and Leahy (2002). Using survey responses obtained from participants enrolled in the TIAA-CREF pension program, Ameriks et al. discovered that a majority of active workers expect their consumption spending to fall after retirement. Among TIAA-CREF participants who had already retired, on the other hand, only about one-third report that their consumption has actually declined. Forty-four percent report their spending has remained unchanged, and 20% say consumption has risen. Thus, many older workers anticipate their spending will decline after retirement, but the actual experience of recent retirees suggests the drop in saving may be smaller than anticipated.

Even granting that consumption falls after retirement, the drop in spending may not reduce retirees' welfare. For example, retirees may spend less on food because they do not need to eat as many meals away from home or because they have more time to shop for bargains. Necessary spending on taxes, clothing, and transportation may also fall. Retirees have the time to produce some goods and services in the home that full-time workers typically purchase in the market. Thus, even if it is true that consumption expenditures fall in retirement, it is not clear that the decline is associated with a drop in well-being. The evidence on the reported happiness (or "subjective well-being") of retirees versus older active workers provides little evidence that the retired are systematically less happy than active workers. Retirees on average have more health problems than active workers, but among people who have the same marital status and similar health problems, the retired are about as happy as active workers. Some of the evidence on subjective well-being among the retired is summarized in Loewenstein, Prelec, and Weber (1999).

In sum, there is overwhelming evidence that many households have very little savings as they approach retirement, but this does not help us decide whether workers' saving decisions were based on short-sighted or irrational decision making. Given the uncertainty of preretirement earnings and the availability of means-tested retirement benefits, many forward looking, rational workers will enter retirement with little savings. There is also pervasive evidence that workers experience significant reductions in consumption after they retire, possibly indicating that they were shortsighted in their saving or unpleasantly surprised by the drop in income that followed retirement. Many workers anticipate a fall in consumption after retirement, however, and so another explanation for the fall in consumption is that workers have lower spending needs when they leave work. The drop in consumption spending may not be connected with a decline in welfare.

IMPLICATIONS

Squinting their eyes and looking only at aggregate trends, economists find abundant evidence for rational, farsighted responses to financial incentives for retirement and saving. American retirement patterns at different ages have gradually evolved to reflect the retirement incentives embodied in the nation's most important pension program. Evidence from other industrialized countries and cross-national comparisons of retirement behavior reinforce the findings based on U.S. evidence. Gruber and Wise (1999) and economists from a number of countries recently examined pension systems and retirement behavior in 11 rich countries. Some countries allow workers to begin drawing public pensions at age 60 or earlier, while others do not make old age benefits available until much later. There is also wide variation in the treatment of wage earnings once workers reach the pension-eligible age. Some countries like the United States no longer penalize workers for delaying their retirement beyond the early or normal pension ages. Other countries like France and Belgium offer very generous pensions and impose heavy financial penalties on workers who remain employed after the pension-eligible age. Gruber and Wise et al. find a strong correlation between national retirement patterns and the labor supply incentives that are embodied in national pension systems. Countries with modest pensions and generous treatment of earned income after the pension-eligible age have high employment rates among people between 55–70. In contrast, nations that offer generous pensions and impose heavy penalties on earnings after the pension-eligible age have much lower employment rates. The economists who worked with Gruber and

Wise often found striking age patterns in workers' withdrawal from paid employment. These age patterns frequently corresponded with incentives embedded in the national retirement system. Moreover, as in the United States, the age pattern of actual retirements often moved in parallel with changes in the age pattern of retirement incentives.

The evidence on aggregate retirement patterns seems to dovetail with other recent evidence showing that only a very small proportion of workers enter retirement with wealth that is too low to be consistent with a rational, farsighted plan for lifetime consumption and retirement. Even the evidence that workers reduce their consumption after retirement, which violates a basic implication of the life-cycle model, can be explained by the lower consumption commitments of retirees and by rational saving and consumption responses to unexpected events that can trigger retirement.

Economists' rationalizations of observed behavior are a little harder to square with workers' responses when they are asked about their retirement plans and saving habits. A large percentage of Americans say they have given no thought to retirement, have saved too little for their anticipated old age consumption, and do not know whether they will be able to afford to retire. Moreover, when asked to describe future benefits under their company or Social Security pensions, a majority often show astonishing ignorance of the most basic provisions determining future retirement incomes. If workers do not take the trouble to learn how their pensions are calculated, it is a little hard to believe they use information sensibly to choose an optimal retirement and saving strategy.

There are two ways to reconcile the apparent contradiction between workers' responses to questions about their retirement planning and saving and the aggregate evidence showing that, on the whole, retirement trends and retirement saving are consistent with the predictions of the farsighted life-cycle theory. One explanation is that it does not require a large number of farsighted workers for the aggregate evidence to appear consistent with the main predictions of the model. So long as a modest proportion of workers bases retirement and saving behavior on a rational and farsighted decision-making rule, it may be hard using aggregate evidence to statistically reject the hypothesis that the distribution and trend of retirement ages are determined by one or another version of the life-cycle model. Even if only a small fraction of workers base retirement decisions on the farsighted model, we might still observe the work and retirement patterns shown in Figures 4.2 and 4.3. A second explanation is that many workers follow simple and possibly shortsighted decision-making rules that produce retirement and saving choices that are highly correlated with choices that emerge from a farsighted and rational rule. As noted earlier, if workers decide to retire when their pension income replaces 65% of their preretirement net earnings, the trend and distribution of retirement ages could look like those shown in Figure 4.2. The empirical evidence on worker savings and retiree consumption neither proves nor disproves the hypothesis that retirement and saving decisions are made in a fully rational and farsighted way. The evidence only shows it is hard to rule out rationality and farsightedness using available information on households' consumption and savings.

One explanation for workers' ignorance about retirement incentives and for their lack of retirement planning is that many people anticipate using simple rules of thumb to choose their retirement age. This kind of decision rule may not be farsighted, but it could be rational if workers do not expect to derive much benefit from a big investment in information gathering and retirement planning. The range of uncertainty about workers' future health, wages, and employment prospects is so wide that many people may believe well-informed, deliberative planning is a waste of effort. The process will need to be repeated every time a worker receives fresh news about health or potential earnings. This prospect is clearly unattractive for people who do not enjoy planning or are unskilled at performing it. A simpler and more attractive option for deciding when to retire is to imitate the behavior or follow the advice of older friends who are presumably better informed about the actual consequences of selecting one retirement age over another. As we have seen, both imitation and simple rules of thumb can explain the retirement trends shown in Figures 4.3 and 4.4.

What difference does it make if workers select their saving behavior or choose a retirement age using imitation, simple rules of thumb, or other decision rules that are less than rational? How much is a worker's welfare harmed by use of a poor decision rule? In individual cases, the consequences of a poor choice of retirement age or preretirement saving rate can lead to very poor outcomes in old age. On the whole, however, only a small fraction of Americans faces severe material hardship after they retire. Serious deprivation is currently no more common among the elderly than it is among younger adults (Figure 4.4). Workers who use shortsighted decision rules probably enjoy less comfortable material circumstances in old age than they would enjoy if they based their decisions on rational and farsighted rules. But the shortfall in their retirement income or consumption may be relatively small. Extensive survey evidence on subjective well-being suggests that most people make accommodations to modest changes over time in their income and consumption. People who experience income gains often report temporary increases in subjective well-being, and people who experience economic losses report declines in well-being, but in neither case does the change in well-being appear to persist for very long (Easterlin, 2003). Thus, compared with the happiness that retired workers could obtain under a rational and farsighted retirement and saving plan, the happiness they actually achieve using a less farsighted decision process may not be very different.

Economists' models of retirement and saving behavior should probably be considered helpful guides to sensible decision making rather than realistic descriptions of worker thinking or behavior. In other words, the economic model could help workers think systematically about when to retire and how much to save for retirement, even if most workers apply a different and simpler decision-making rule. Some workers follow an approximation of the life-cycle model in choosing a saving strategy and retirement age. It seems doubtful, however, whether the model describes the actual reasoning of a large percentage of real-world workers, though enough workers follow the model so that it provides a useful explanation of some aggregate patterns in retirement behavior. While it yields helpful predictions of average, long-term responses to changes in retirement incentives, we may not want to rely on the model to describe actual decision making among most workers we encounter in real life—unless we rub shoulders with a lot of workers trained in college economics.

Commentary: Modeling the Retirement Decision

Joseph F. Quinn

Economists love to generate models to explain complex human behavior. The types of behavior discussed by Gary Burtless (this volume) include the allocation of time and income throughout the life cycle, with special attention to the later years. In particular, he asks how people decide how much to work late in life and when and how to retire; that is, when and how to leave the labor force. These decisions in turn help determine their lifetime incomes.

An individual then has to decide when to consume this lifetime income. With lending and borrowing, one can separate earning from consumption. One can consume after earning by saving and later spending the accumulated assets, and one can also consume income before it is earned by borrowing and repaying later. Additionally, one can decide not to consume the income at all and bequeath it to others.

These options are all included in the life-cycle consumption model favored by economists, which is described in detail in the Burtless chapter. The model predicts that people will typically choose consumption patterns over time that are smoother than their income patterns by borrowing when young (for example, to purchase a house or a car), by repaying the debts and then accumulating wealth during peak income years, and finally by consuming these assets when retired, and, ideally, by leaving exactly the desired bequest.

Work, savings, and retirement decisions are obviously interrelated. The more one earns and the more one saves of the earnings, and the better one invests these savings, the earlier one can afford to retire and maintain one's prior standard of living. The more one is willing to let the standard of living drop after retirement, the earlier one can afford to retire.

The study of labor supply and related decisions late in life has been a growth industry in economics, prompted both by the importance of understanding this behavior in a rapidly aging society and by the availability of several fabulous micro data sets, including the Retirement History Study (RHS) in the 1970s and the current Health and Retirement Study (HRS) (Irelan, 1976; Juster & Suzman, 1995). Both of these longitudinal efforts followed large cohorts of older Americans over time, more than 10,000 in each case, reinterviewing them every two years and then linking these survey data to internal Social Security records, and in the case of the current HRS, to employer pension information.

ECONOMIC MODELS

When building models of behavior, economists make many simplifying assumptions. We generally assume that people are well-informed, which they often are not, and that people behave rationally, consistent with their preferences and the information at hand. As Burtless points out, there may be less reason to believe these assumptions when studying retirement than some other types of behavior since most people go through this process only once, unlike buying a car or switching jobs, which one may do many times and thereby learn from the experience. As a result, barring reincarnation, people cannot learn from prior retirement mistakes and get it right the next time. On the other hand, people may be able to learn from other people's experiences, such as older co-workers and friends or relatives who have or have not retired. They may develop rules of thumb based on the experiences of others, for example, not to retire until they can replace a certain percentage of their earnings with retirement income sources.

Rather than critique what I think is an excellent chapter, I will highlight a few points and extend the conversation in a couple of directions. First, let me say that, despite their inadequacies, simple economic models have been very useful in understanding, explaining, and predicting retirement decisions. A simple example, which Burtless describes and which requires only the concept of the present discounted value, leads to a very powerful insight. Retirement income, like Social Security or employer pension benefits, comes as a stream over time, usually in the form of monthly checks. Different retirement choices lead to different income streams. Someone who is eligible for Social Security or employer pension benefits but who delays receipt generally receives less retirement income now (and in some cases, none), but will receive more later. Which stream is worth more, a larger number of smaller checks starting now, or a smaller number of larger checks starting in a year or two? The concept of the present discounted value allows one to translate any future stream of income into today's dollars. The present discounted value is the size of the asset today that could provide that income stream in the future, if invested at market interest rates. The larger that asset today, the more valuable the future income stream, and different assets today are very easy to compare.

Why is this important? It turns out that defined-benefit employer pension plans and, until recently, Social Security, penalized workers who delayed benefit receipt until after some age. This used to happen at age 65 for Social Security and often at the earliest age of eligibility for employer pension plans. Although future monthly benefits were higher if an individual delayed receipt and kept working, the increment in benefits was not sufficient to compensate for what the worker had given up in benefits during the additional year(s) of employment. For example, if a worker declines annual (Social Security or employer pension) benefits of $10,000, and the future increments in retirement benefits because of that additional employment have a present discounted value of $4,000, the employee loses $6,000 in expected lifetime retirement benefits. If he or she earns $30,000 during that additional year of work, the true net compensation is only $24,000—the $30,000 in wages *minus* the $6,000 decline in retirement benefits. This, as Burtless describes, can be viewed as a pay cut. In the prior year, before eligibility for retirement benefits, the worker earned $30,000. This year, by continuing to work while eligible, the worker nets only $24,000.

Defined-benefit employer pensions often work in exactly the same way, and the combined impact of that pay cut and that of Social Security could be large, on the order of 30–40%. Age-based pay cuts like this would violate age discrimination laws if done through a person's paycheck, but they are perfectly legal when imposed through the pension system. This was an important insight by economists, that even if future benefits *increased* as one continued to work, the system could act as a work *dis*incentive—or equivalently, what turns out to be a strong and very effective retirement incentive.

By utilizing the RHS from the 1970s and the current HRS to estimate the size of the actual Social Security or employer pension retirement incentives facing individuals in these samples, economists have established that these incentives work—the larger the penalty for continued work (i.e., the larger the pay cut), the more likely people are to leave their jobs and also to leave the labor force. People *behave* as though they understand these incentives. In many cases, the researcher knows more about the details of the Social Security records and pension plan than the individual in the sample does. He in fact has the programs necessary to calculate the incentives—the exact pension wealth losses that the employee would suffer by working another year, which the individual does not even know! Yet these individuals behave as though they understand the pension calculation rules and their implicit incentives. Why have so many people retired at age 60, 62 or 65? It is because the financial incentives in their Social Security and pension plans encouraged them to do so.

Despite success at the aggregate level, these economic models often do a very imperfect job of predicting *individual* behavior. Many people behave in ways that seem inconsistent with rational planning. For example, some people seem to save too little and some save too much. I think that there are two primary explanations for this—uncertainty and changing preferences over time.

The inability to predict the future (for example, how long we will live and how healthy we will be during our remaining years) means that analysts will observe what looks like, in retrospect, non-optimal behavior. When people die well before their life expectancy would have predicted, they will have saved "too much," planning for the longer life they did not enjoy. Risk-averse people, fearful of outliving their assets, may consume too little and bequeath too much when they die, even if they live to their life expectancy, since they had insured against an even longer life. Similarly, a person goes to the airport, on average, too early, and ends up sitting in the lounge for too long, because of the risk of running into long lines at the security check on this particular day. We often prepare for the worst, which then does not always happen.

Dealing with uncertainty, incidentally, is where insurance is useful. One of the best forms of insurance is Social Security, which is a mandatory social insurance program. One cannot outlive Social Security benefits, even if one outlives one's life expectancy. Not only does Social Security continue as long as a person lives, but it is also fully indexed to changes in cost of living. In addition, since it is mandatory, there is no moral hazard problem, such as those with long life expectancies opting in and those with short expectancies opting out. Unlike a voluntary system in which those with short life expectancies would save on their own and avoid the system, everyone participates in Social Security.

Another problem with traditional economic models is that people's preferences can change with age. With these changing preferences, any pattern of behavior could be logical and optimal. This issue has not been studied in depth, and it would be difficult to do so. Living wills is one area in which there might be some evidence about changing preferences. A person might be willing and even eager to sign a document today that instructs others not to request life-sustaining treatment for him or her under certain circumstances, or never to put him or her in a nursing home. When death is imminent, however, the same person may come to a different decision, one inconsistent with his or her prior behavior. My prior actions were consistent with my preferences when I signed the agreement, but inconsistent with my altered preferences later in life.

Another problem with standard economic models concerns the treatment of work. As Burtless points out, economists usually assume that work is a bad and leisure is a good. Others do not view work in this way. If you ask a sociologist, a psychologist, or a philosopher about work, you are likely to hear a litany of all the *good* things that work provides in addition to a paycheck, such as fulfilling the need to contribute to society, the social interactions at work, or even just a reason to get up in the morning. That said, I think that the economic model is right—at the margin. I would certainly like to work less than I do now. But that does not mean that I would like not to work at all. If I won the lottery, I suspect I would continue working, but fewer hours than I do now.

People's view on leaving the labor force may well change as they age and actually contemplate the decision, or even after they have retired. Once a retiree has cleaned the shed, visited the grandchildren, and gone fishing for a week, he might wonder what he is going to do for the next 17 years. Work provides many social benefits that are not captured in the simple economic model, and their significance may become more important as one contemplates or experiences life without them.

THE RETIREMENT ENVIRONMENT AND RETIREMENT BEHAVIOR

The retirement environment facing older Americans has changed in important ways in recent decades, as we will see below. The relative attractiveness

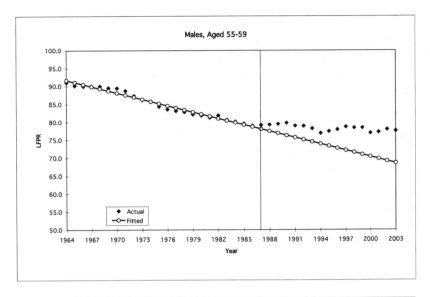

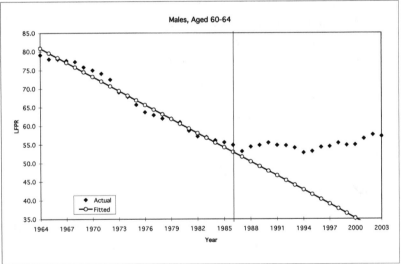

FIGURE 4.5   Labor force participation rates for older men 1964–2003, actual and fitted.

of work and leisure late in life has shifted toward work. Evidence suggests that older Americans are responding to the changing retirement environment and are working longer than prior trends would have predicted (Quinn, 2002). For men aged 60–64 and 65–69, Figure 4.5 shows labor force participation rates from 1964 through the mid-1980s, with those

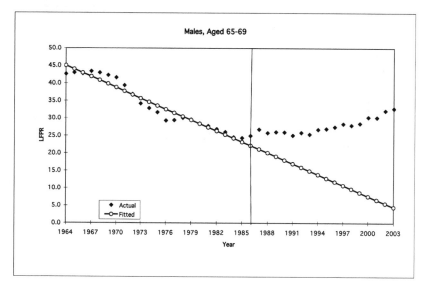

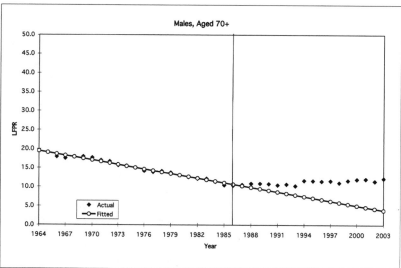

FIGURE 4.5   (Continued)

trends extrapolated to the present (through 2003) and compared to what
actually happened since the mid-1980s. For men, declining participation
rates (on the order of a percentage point per year over these two decades)
have come to a halt. Since then, the participation rates have flattened out
and have increased in recent years, though modestly. The same is true for
men slightly younger (55–59) and older (70 and above).

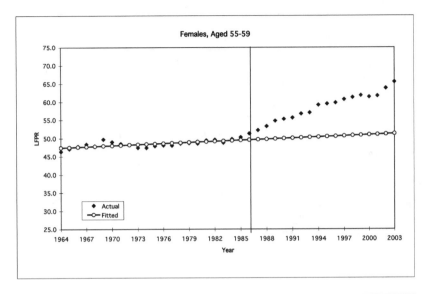

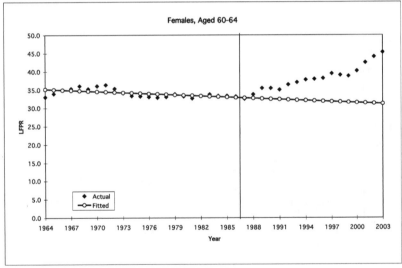

FIGURE 4.6   Labor force participation rates for older men 1964–2003, actual and fitted.

Source: U.S. Bureau of Labor Statistics, and calculations by the author.

For women, the story is both very different and the same. What is different are the trends from the mid-1960s through the mid-1980s. As seen in Figure 4.6 (for women aged 55–59 and 60–64), instead of dramatic decline, older women's labor force participation rates were steady, changing on the order of a percentage point per decade, rather than a percentage point per year as

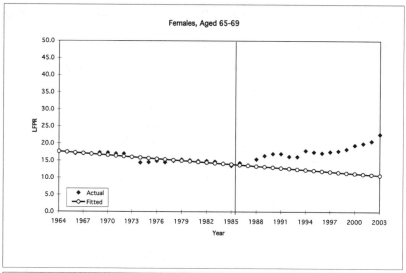

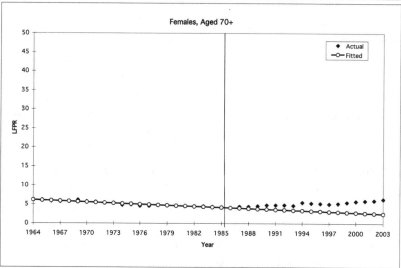

FIGURE 4.6   (Continued)

the men's rates did. This trend was true for women aged 65–69 and 70 and older as well (Quinn, 2002). This probably reflects the combined effects of two factors—earlier and earlier retirement *and* the increasing labor force participation of American women, especially married women. Until the mid-1980s, these trends seem to have just about offset each other. But since then, just like for the men, there is a significant break in the trend—in the women's case, from flat to dramatically upward, showing large increases in the labor force participation of older American women.

Why have these dramatic changes in trends occurred during the past two decades? There are two types of hypotheses about these changes. One focuses on the business cycle and labor demand, and is therefore temporary in nature. The other, which I have emphasized, focuses on permanent changes in the retirement environment—changes that are not expected to disappear the way a low unemployment rate inevitably does.

In 1982 and 1983, the overall unemployment rate in the United States was near 10%. By the end of that decade, it was near 5%, and a decade later, near 4% (Council of Economic Advisors, 2005, Table B-42). This trend describes an era of increasing demand for labor, including the labor of older workers. In this environment, older Americans were able to negotiate terms and conditions of employment that they preferred, and were therefore willing and able to work longer than they might otherwise have done. The implication of this hypothesis is that this change in trend is temporary and that we expect to return to the inevitable decline in participation rates when the strong economy disappears. In fact, this was not the case in the recession years of 2001 and 2002. Why not?

At the same time, some important societal changes occurred that are much more permanent in nature. The earliest age at which mandatory retirement provisions could go into effect was delayed from 65 to 70 in the late 1970s, and then mandatory retirement was outlawed completely for the vast majority of older Americans in the mid-1980s. This was good news for those hoping to stay longer in their career jobs.

As noted above, Social Security regulations used to penalize those who continued to work beyond age 65, because future benefit increments resulting from the additional work were insufficient to compensate for the benefits forgone. How has this changed? The delayed retirement credit, which determines the size of these future benefit increments, is being increased from 3% per year of delay to 8%, and the latter is close to actuarially fair. Social Security is now close to age-neutral for the average worker, meaning that expected lifetime benefits are about the same regardless of when they are first claimed. More recently, the earnings test has been eliminated completely for those working beyond Social Security's normal retirement age (now rising from age 65 to age 66). This is good news for those working beyond this age.

On the employer pension front, traditional defined-benefit plans typically penalize workers who work beyond a certain age (often the earliest age of pension eligibility) in the same way that Social Security (also a defined-benefit plan) did. In contrast, defined-contribution plans, which are basically tax-deferred savings accounts, contain no age-specific retirement incentives, and are age-neutral by their very nature. If a worker decides to work until age 66, an employer cannot reach into that workers' retirement account and extract $6,000, which in essence is what Social Security used to do and defined-benefit plans still can do. As defined-benefit plans decline in importance and defined-contribution plans increase, these strong retirement incentives become less of a factor.

In addition, older workers are living longer and healthier lives, and the nature of occupations in America has changed, with fewer physically demanding jobs (like assembly line positions) and more opportunities in the service sectors. Although some service jobs can be arduous, the occupational mix is becoming more amenable to longer work lives. Technology (such as computers and hearing aids) is also helping, increasing the options about where and how older workers continue to be active in the labor force.

All these factors (cyclical and permanent) are important in explaining the dramatic breaks from trend of older men and women, as seen in Figures 4.5 and 4.6. Business and labor demand cycles will continue to come and go, but these other environmental changes are here to stay. I do not anticipate the return of mandatory retirement provisions, strong age-specific Social Security work disincentives, or a resurgence of defined-benefit employer pension plans. Nor do I expect a decline in life expectancy or in the health status of older Americans. Given these important changes, I think that we have entered a new era of retirement in which many older Americans, anticipating two or three decades of healthy life when they reach traditional retirement age, will decide not to leave the labor force quite yet. Some will remain full-time at their career jobs and others will decide that some combination of reduced work and increased leisure is preferable to either continuing their career jobs full-time or complete labor force withdrawal. As with labor market entry many years before, labor market exit at the other end of the work cycle is a *process* for many Americans—a series of steps involving gradual withdrawal from the world of employment—rather than a single event.

For many older Americans, this decision to work longer is a sensible one. Many fear a less inviting retirement environment in the future. Serious discussion by policy-makers, analysts, and the public is underway on how best to deal with long-run Social Security deficits. Most reform scenarios involve Social Security benefit cuts, or, equivalently, further delays in benefit eligibility ages beyond those legislated in 1983 and currently being implemented. Social Security privatization proposals (individual retirement accounts accompanied by lower traditional Social Security benefits) would create more market risk for future retirees, and the discussion of Medicare reform creates additional uncertainty. Many workers may now foresee a lower level of economic well-being at the planned retirement age than they anticipated when making those plans. How will they respond?

They can leave the labor force as planned and simply consume less in retirement than originally expected. They can try to save more before the planned retirement age, but this requires a change in behavior well in advance of retirement to be very useful. Altering saving behavior at age 30 can make a large difference in wealth at retirement; saving more at age 60 does not. Or, they can decide to delay retirement and work longer. Unlike the increased saving strategy, they can decide this at the last minute.

Given the debate about Social Security and Medicare reform and the recent volatility in the equities markets, this scenario may become increasingly common. I have seen this in my role as Dean of the College of Arts and Sciences at Boston College in which I negotiate retirement agreements with senior faculty. In recent years, interest in these agreements has declined significantly, partly because of the dramatic decline in the stock market several years ago. Faculty members are working longer than they had once planned. Not only did their wealth decline, but their faith in their ability to predict the future has also diminished. Even as the market recovers, I predict that people will remain wary about the future, knowing (and now knowing from personal experience) that it can happen again. Concerns about society's commitment to Social Security and Medicare have the same effect.

In addition to uncertainty and changing expectations, another reason for delayed departure may be asymmetry. If a faculty member could leave a tenured position (or any employee leave a career job) and then return if he or she desired, more people would do so. But this is not the case. If one does leave and then regrets it, one cannot just reverse the decision. A retiree who wishes to return to the labor force will likely return to a very different job, and perhaps to an inferior one. As long as the worker remains employed, he or she has both options (to continue or to leave); once the worker does leave, the option set changes permanently.

SUMMARY

To summarize my thoughts on Gary Burtless's excellent chapter, economic theories are simplifications, indeed over-simplifications, of very complex decision-making processes. They provide insights into human behavior that are very useful in the aggregate, predicting on average how people respond, but less so at the individual level, where the idiosyncrasies lie. For many applications, like the impact of new retirement incentives on elderly labor force participation rates, we are like life insurance firms that do not care who dies in a given year, just how many. For many policy purposes, we care less about exactly who retires than we do about how many do.

Despite their usefulness, economic theories and the behavioral determinants they emphasize, like financial incentives, are only part of the story, but they are usually a very important part. We ignore them at our peril. Burtless has done an excellent job in summarizing the evidence in two very important current research areas: the retirement decision (when and how to leave the labor market late in life), and related decisions about work, consumption, and savings in the preretirement years. His conclusion is exactly right. Economic models are worthwhile guides to sensible decision making. They provide a useful explanation of aggregate patterns in retirement behavior and provide helpful predictions about average long-term responses to changes in retirement incentives.

Paul Samuelson, the first American winner of the Nobel Prize in economics, once defended economic modeling by declaring, "What is the problem? We've predicted nine out of the past four recessions!" I think Gary Burtless has mounted an even more persuasive defense.

Commentary: Numbers Are Just Numbers

Ellen Peters

Making good choices about retirement involves the processing of numbers. In particular, consumers must have easily available, accurate, and timely numbers, and they must also use them. Contrary to the consumer-driven approach, however, the evidence demonstrates that having an abundance of information does not always translate into it being used to inform choices. The challenge is not merely to communicate accurate information to consumers, but to understand how to present that information so that it is actually used in decision making. How do decision makers process information and what formatting strategies increase the likelihood that information will be used in judgments and decisions?

Where economists usually assume decision makers are well-informed, farsighted, and rational, psychologists who study judgment and decision making assume that individuals are "boundedly rational," and may or may not have the cognitive resources or motivation available to process information at the moment of a decision. In other words, while we are capable of great feats of intellect, our intellectual capacity is nonetheless limited. Decision makers are able to process and use only a limited number of variables in any one choice. As the number of options and information increases, the ability to use all of it in choice declines. Although our market economy assumes that more information is better, evidence from decision-making research demonstrates that more information does not always improve decision making, and can in fact undermine it (Garbarino & Edell, 1997; Iyengar & Lepper, 2000; Slovic, 1982; Tversky & Shafir, 1992).

We know, for example, that people have limited resources to deal with complex decisions and the great quantity of information with which they are sometimes faced. As a result, they rely on mental shortcuts to deal with such complexity. The use of mental shortcuts is frequently adaptive (because they are efficient and the resulting judgments or decisions are generally good enough), but it can also be maladaptive (resulting in poorer decisions). Individuals with more limited resources may use mental short-cuts more often (e.g., older adults, Mutter & Poliske, 1994).

A major theme that emerges from judgment and decision research is that we frequently do not know our own "true" values (e.g., the value of working to an older age versus saving more money now). Instead, we construct our values and preferences "on the spot" when asked to form a particular judgment or to make a specific decision (Lichtenstein & Slovic, in press).

With human judgment as a constructive process, individual preferences can be unstable across different contexts, and situational influences can carry great impact. Different presentations of the same information will impact the construction of choices, including retirement choices, making it important for policy makers and others to choose information presentation formats that support better decisions. Burtless (this issue) lists three types of retirement choices (age to retire, percent of wages to set aside, and allocation of savings) that are not well-described by economic models. How can we describe decision making in order to predict decisions and to help people make the best decisions (or at least avoid the worst ones)?

DUAL PROCESS MODES IN DECISION MAKING

Information in decision making appears to be processed using two different modes of thinking: deliberative and affective/experiential (Epstein, 1994; Sloman, 1996). The deliberative mode is conscious, analytical, reason-based, verbal, and relatively slow. It is the deliberative, "high reason" view of decision making that we tend to consider in our attempts to inform choices (e.g., provide more information for better choices). The problem with this view, however, is that we have limited capacity to process information (Simon, 1955) and that capacity declines with age (Salthouse, 1996). A result of focusing on high reasons is that we may also ignore the important influences of the experiential mode. The experiential mode is intuitive, automatic, associative, and fast. It is based on affective (or emotional) feelings, and one of its primary functions is to highlight information important enough to warrant further consideration.

As shown in a number of studies, these affective feelings provide meaning, motivation, and information to choice processes (Damasio, 1994; Osgood, Suci, & Tannenbaum, 1957; Peters, in press). Marketers, who well understand the power of affect, aim their advertisements to evoke an experiential mode of information processing. Ads typically try to associate a product with positive affective images. Try to imagine a car ad without images of freedom, prestige, sex, or power.

Both modes of thinking are important, and good choices are most likely to emerge when both affective and deliberative modes work in concert and decision makers think as well as feel their way through judgments and decisions (Damasio, 1994). Consumers need to consider information carefully, but they also need to be able to understand and be motivated by the meaning that underlies that information.

These multiple needs suggest that the simple provision of information may not be enough to ensure good decisions. The state of Nebraska found this out the hard way. For 30 years they allowed workers to choose either a traditional pension plan or a 401(k) plan that was managed by the individual worker. Workers who chose the 401(k) plan earned average annual returns that were far less than the traditional pension plan, even though Nebraska provided not only information but plenty of education (see Figure 4.7). In 2003, Nebraska eliminated employee choice from its 401(k) plan.

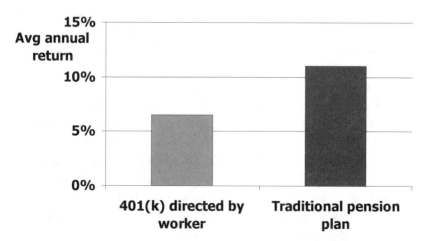

FIGURE 4.7   Average annual returns in Nebraska retirement plans.

Source: Merriman (2002).

POTENTIAL BARRIERS TO USING INFORMATION EFFECTIVELY IN RETIREMENT CHOICES

At least three reasons exist for why simple provision of information may not be effective in retirement choices. First, information can be insufficient, uncertain, and changeable. Burtless (this issue) points out that workers face uncertainty about the path of future earnings, age at death, and the interest rate that can be earned. Second, workers may not comprehend the information when it is sufficient. Some economists, for example, argue that only a small percentage of workers have the capacity or willingness to understand retirement program rules and to interpret their meaning in order to make optimal choices (Burtless, this issue). Results from health plan choice studies support this lack of comprehension and suggest that a proportion of workers, and particularly older workers and retirees, do not always comprehend even fairly simple information. Hibbard, Peters, Slovic, Finucane, and Tusler (2001) presented employed-aged adults (18–64 years old; $n = 239$) and older adults (65–94 years old; $n = 253$) with 34 decision tasks that involved interpretation of numbers from tables and graphs. For example, participants were asked to identify the Health Maintenance Organization (HMO) with the lowest copayment from a table that included four HMOs with information about monthly premiums and copayments. A comprehension index reflected the total number of errors made across the 34 tasks. The youngest participants (aged 18–35) averaged 8% errors; the oldest participants (aged 85–94) averaged 40% errors; the correlation between age and the number of errors was .31 ($p < .001$). Education was protective of comprehension such that those with higher education demonstrated smaller age differences.

A third barrier to using information effectively is that workers may comprehend numerical information without understanding what it means. Bateman, Dent, Peters, Slovic, and Starmer (2005; also reported in Slovic, Finucane, Peters, & MacGregor, 2002) examined how people evaluate the attractiveness of a simple gamble. One group rated a bet that gives a small chance to win $9 (7/36, win $9; otherwise, win $0) on a 0–20 scale; a second group rated a similar gamble with a small loss (7/36, win $9; 29/36, lose 5¢) on the same scale. This second group had an objectively worse bet so that, normatively, they should rate the bet as worse. However, the data were anomalous from the perspective of economic theory. The mean response to the first gamble was 9.4. When a loss of 5¢ was added, the mean attractiveness jumped to 14.9 and there was almost no overlap between the distribution of responses around this mean and the responses for the group judging the gamble that had no loss.

We hypothesize that these curious findings can be explained by affect and affective precision. According to this view, a probability maps relatively precisely onto the attractiveness scale, because it has an upper and lower bound and people know where a given value falls within that range. In contrast, the mapping of a dollar outcome (e.g., $9) onto the scale is diffuse, reflecting a failure to know whether $9 is good or bad, attractive or unattractive. Thus, the impression formed by the gamble offering $9 to win with no losing payoff is dominated by the rather unattractive impression produced by the 7/36 probability of winning. However, adding a very small loss to the payoff dimension puts the $9 payoff in perspective (i.e., makes it more affectively precise) and thus gives it meaning. The combination of a possible $9 gain and a 5¢ loss is a very attractive win/lose ratio, leading to a relatively precise mapping onto the upper part of the scale. Whereas the imprecise mapping of the $9 carries little weight in the averaging process, the more precise and now favorable impression of ($9; −5¢) carries more weight, thus leading to an increase in the overall favorability of the gamble. Participants asked directly about their affect and precision of affect to the $9 had more clear and more positive feelings about the $9 in the $9–5¢ loss condition (Bateman et al., 2005). A follow-up study demonstrated that the effect of the small loss is driven by people high in number ability rather than those low in ability, presumably because highly numerate individuals are more likely or more able to draw meaning from a comparison of numbers (Peters et al., 2006). It is not that these decision makers did not comprehend the $9; everybody knows what $9 is. However, the meaning of the $9 was more clear and more positive in the presence of the five cent loss.

SUPPORTING RETIREMENT DECISIONS

Retirement decisions are much more complicated than a simple bet. And yet even with a simple bet, there are barriers to how decision makers understand the meaning of numerical information. Given this, how can we support retirement decisions and the well-being of the aged? Past research suggests that through an understanding, first, of how people process information and, second, what they will be faced with in a decision situation, decision aids can be designed (if necessary) in order to help support decision making.

Decisions can be supported through various means. First, intermediaries, who have an understanding of the decision that people face and the attributes that may be of importance to them, can help decision makers comprehend the decision situation and its necessary tradeoffs. Second, decisions can be supported through how information and choices are presented. Thaler and Sunstein (2003), for example, discussed the use of default options in retirement plans. Companies offering 401(k) plans to their workers have a choice of what to make the default option, (a default option is defined as what will happen if the employee does nothing at all). As it turns out, this default option makes a big difference. If the workers are automatically out of the plan (and must choose to be in it; this is the norm), about half the workers initially enroll (49%). However, if the default is that the workers are in the plan (but of course they can freely choose not to be), substantially more workers initially enroll (86%; Madrian & Shea, 2001). Automatic enrollment has particularly powerful effects in increasing retirement savings among low-income and younger workers (Munnell & Sundén, 2004).

If you know what people prefer or what is better for their well-being (let's assume for the moment that saving more is better than saving less in this case) and some default option must be chosen, why not design the default to promote better decisions while still allowing free range of choice?

Financial and other information has generally been designed to evoke deliberative processing. However, comprehension, motivation, and the actual use of information can be increased through subtle changes in how information is presented that influence both deliberative and experiential processing. The way information is presented can make a difference in how difficult it is to understand and use. Hibbard and Peters (2003) review a variety of methods to make numbers more meaningful, such as by highlighting affective meaning. An example of highlighting affective meaning is the bets example when adding the five cent loss caused the affective meaning of the $9 to become more clear and more positive. Another way to make numbers more meaningful is by moving the decision maker closer to an experience. The use of narratives can help someone understand what it might be like to live on 60% of their income after retirement. Finally, we can lower the cognitive effort required to understand numbers, for example, by organizing the data for decision makers and ordering it from highest to lowest value (Hibbard, Slovic, Peters, & Finucane, 2002). The use of these three processes (lowering cognitive effort, helping people to understand the experience of choice, and highlighting the affective meaning of information) as design principles in the creation of consumer information products likely will enhance the successful use of information to inform choice.

When designing ways to increase the usability of information, the information provider should also keep in mind the characteristics of the audience receiving the information. An understanding of audience characteristics can help shape the strategy or strategies used. Hibbard et al. (2001), for example, found that many older adults (i.e., Medicare beneficiaries) have more difficulty than younger adults in using information accurately to inform health plan choice. Decision makers who do not have the analytical skills necessary for the task may need additional assistance in lowering the cognitive burden of health decisions. These decision makers may include some older adults, decision makers low in literacy or numeracy, or individuals suffering cognitive decline. In recent research, Hibbard et al. (2001) documented a simple screening device consisting of age, education, and self-reported health that related strongly to older and younger adults' abilities to comprehend and use comparative information. The use of such a screening device may assist information producers in choosing appropriate strategies, particularly when strategies that lower cognitive burden may be needed. Since it is frequently not possible to give numeracy or literacy measures to consumers (e.g., a Medicare beneficiary phones in to get help in choosing a health plan), additional research on simple screening devices would be helpful.

Consumers are going to differ in their ability to handle different types and quantities of financial information. Knowing this and understanding the elements that underlie the usefulness of particular strategies should help information providers design the key ingredients necessary for useable information.

Each of the processes and strategies discussed above has the potential to influence health and financial behaviors and choices. These attempts, by definition, bring up important ethical considerations. Because the way health information is presented is very likely to influence how it is used, information producers have a responsibility to be conscious of that influence and direct it in productive and defensible ways. The alternative is to manipulate people in ways that are unknown, are not thought out, or are not defensible, but are no less manipulative.

Thus, three factors should be considered in selecting information presentation strategies: (a) the complexity and amount of the information; (b) the experience, skill, and motivation of the users; and, (c) the nature of the choice (e.g., the degree to which there is a right or "best" option). These factors can be used to determine which combination of strategies will best facilitate decision making. The testing of consumer information products then should focus on three levels: the degree to which the information is understood; the degree to which the process goals are achieved (reduce cognitive effort, highlight information, help understand the experience of the choice); and the degree to which information is actually used in choice. This too represents a departure from current testing methods. Most consumer information material, if tested at all, assesses consumer preferences for how information is presented. However, consumer preferences for presentation format may not actually support the use of that information in choice.

The conscious use of information presentation strategies to support choice represents a critical departure from how most information producers see their role (i.e., most view their role as providing complete, objective, and accurate information.) To acknowledge that the way information is presented can influence choice is to accept a new level of responsibility. For example, choosing how to display information puts a greater burden on the information provider to summarize or to add "meaning" to the information. However, if the information is going to be weighted and used in choice, information producers must aim beyond providing more and accurate information to providing information in a way that supports decisions. As the preceding discussion demonstrates supporting decisions will require more strategic and sophisticated efforts. While the quantity of information can be voluminous and complex, strategies exist to increase the likelihood that information will actually be used in judgment and choice.

CONCLUSION

Ultimately, we need to develop conceptual models to help us understand and predict what consumers might comprehend, how they decide, and, how then to support and aid those decisions. We may be able to "diagnose" decision situations and aids as well as individuals in order to illuminate the best path to support good decision making in a particular situation.

Numbers appear to be just that—numbers. Research suggests that they may not be information until we compare and contrast the available data and calculate their evaluative meaning for choice or until the data acquire affective meaning through other means. These findings are consistent with the constructed preferences approach in decision making and imply that policy makers cannot present "just the facts." Any method of information presentation manipulates choice; no method presents facts only. It appears that whatever method of presentation we choose will influence how consumers and others find meaning in numbers and construct choices in unfamiliar domains. Policy makers need to make thoughtful choices about how to present information in order to pick a method of data presentation (and therefore preference manipulation) that they can defend, and research scientists need to help them understand how to make that choice. The presentation of simple numbers (a common phenomena in our world of instantaneous data and informed choice) appears to be much more complex than might be thought at first glance. By paying careful attention to how information is presented, information providers can provide additional rationality into retirement choices.

ACKNOWLEDGMENTS

Preparation of this commentary was supported by funds from the National Science Foundation (0339204). It is based in part on Hibbard and Peters (2003). Supporting informed consumer health care decisions: Data presentation approaches that facilitate the use of information in choice. *Annual Review of Public Health, 24,* 413–433.

REFERENCES

Abraham, K. G., & Hausman, S. N. (2004). Work and retirement plans among older Americans. *Pension Research Council Working Paper.* Philadelphia, PA: Pension Research Council, Wharton School.

Ameriks, J., Caplin, A., & Leahy, J. (2002). Retirement consumption: Insights from a survey. *NBER Working Paper 8735.* Cambridge, MA: National Bureau of Economic Research.

Ando, A., & Modigliani, F. (1963). The life cycle hypothesis of saving: Aggregate implications and tests. *American Economic Review, 53,* 55–84.

Axtell, R. L., & Epstein, J. M. (1999). Coordination in transient social networks: An agent- based computational model of the timing of retirement. In H. J. Aaron (Ed.), *Behavioral dimensions of retirement economics* (pp 161–183). Washington, D.C.: The Brookings Institution.

Banks, J., Blundell, R., & Tanner, S. (1998). Is there a retirement savings puzzle? *American Economic Review, 88,* 769–788.

Bateman, I., Dent, S., Peters, E., Slovic, P., & Starmer, C. (2005). *The affect heuristic and the attractiveness of simple gambles.* Manuscript in preparation.

Bernheim, B. D. (1992). *Is the Baby Boom generation preparing adequately for retirement?* New York: Merrill Lynch and Company.

Bernheim, B. D. (1995). *The Merrill Lynch baby boom retirement index: Update '95, Technical Report.* New York: Merrill Lynch and Company.

Burtless, G. (1986). Social Security, unanticipated benefit increases, and the timing of retirement. *Review of Economic Studies, 53,* 781–805.

Burtless, G. (1999). An economic view of retirement. In H. Aaron (Ed.), *Behavioral dimensions of retirement economics* (pp.7–42). Washington, D.C.: The Brookings Institution.

Burtless, G. (2004, February). Pension reform and labor force exit: Cross-national evidence. Brookings working paper prepared for the "International Forum of the Collaboration Projects" meetings in Tokyo, Japan.

Burtless, G., & Moffitt, R. A. (1985). The joint choice of retirement age and postretirement hours of work. *Journal of Labor Economics, 3,* 209–236.

Chan, S., & Stevens, A. H. (2003). What you don't know can't help you: Pension knowledge and retirement decision making. *NBER Working Paper 10185.* Cambridge, MA: National Bureau of Economic Research.

Council of Economic Advisors. (2005). *Economic report of the President, 2005.* Washington, DC: Government Printing Office.

Damasio, A. R. (1994). *Descartes' error: Emotion, reason, and the human brain.* New York: G. P. Putnam's Sons.

Diamond, P. A., & Hausman, J. A. (1984). Individual retirement and savings behavior. *Journal of Public Economics, 23,* 81–114.

Easterlin, R. A. (2003). Building a better theory of well being. *IZA Discussion Paper No. 742.* Bonn, Germany: Institute for the Study of Labor (IZA).

Employee Benefit Research Institute. (2002). *Income of the elderly, 2000.* Washington: Employee Benefit Research Institute.

Engen, E. M., Gale, W. G., & Uccello, C. E. (1999). The adequacy of household saving. *Brookings Papers on Economic Activity, 2,* 65–165.

Epstein, S. (1994). Trait theory as personality theory: Can a part be as great as the whole? *Psychological Inquiry, 5,* 120–122.

Garbarino, E. C., & Edell, J. A. (1997). Cognitive effort, affect, and choice. *Journal of Consumer Research, 24,* 147–158.

Grad, S. (2002). *Income of the population 55 and over, 2000.* Washington, DC: U.S. Social Security Administration.

Gruber, J., & Wise, D. A. (1999). *Social Security and retirement around the world.* Chicago, IL: University of Chicago Press.

Gustman, A. L., & Steinmeier, T. L. (1986). A structural retirement model. *Econometrica, 54,* 555–584.

Gustman, A. L., & Steinmeier, T. L. (2004). What people don't know about their pensions and Social Security: An analysis using linked data from the Health and Retirement Study. In W. G. Gale, J. B. Shoven, & M. J. Warshawsky (Eds.), *Private pensions and public policies* (pp. 57–119). Washington, DC: Brookings Institution.

Gustman, A. L., Mitchell, O. S., & Steinmeier, T. L. (1995). Retirement research using the Health and Retirement Study. *Journal of Human Resources, 30,* S57–S83.

Hamermesh, D. S. (1985). Consumption during retirement: The missing link in the life cycle. *Review of Economics and Statistics, 66,* 1–7.

Hausman, J. A., & Paquette, L. (1987). Involuntary early retirement and consumption. In G. Burtless (Ed.), *Work, health and income among the elderly* (pp. 151–182). Washington, DC: The Brookings Institution.

Hibbard, J. H., & Peters, E. (2003). Supporting informed consumer health care decisions: Data presentation approaches that facilitate the use of information in choice. *Annual Review of Public Health, 24,* 413–433.

Hibbard, J. H., Peters, E., Slovic, P., Finucane, M. L., & Tusler, M. (2001). Making health care quality reports easier to use. *Journal of Quality Improvement, 27,* 591–604.

Hibbard, J. H., Slovic, P., Peters, E., & Finucane, M. L. (2002). Strategies for reporting health plan performance information to consumers: Evidence from controlled studies. *Health Services Research, 37,* 291–313.

Hurd, M. D. (1990). Research on the elderly: Economic status, retirement, and consumption and saving. *Journal of Economic Literature, 28,* 565–637.

Hurd, M. D., & Rohwedder, S. (2004). The retirement-consumption puzzle: Anticipated and actual declines in spending at retirement.

Michigan Retirement Research Center Working Paper 2004–069. Ann Arbor, MI: Michigan Retirement Research Center.

Irelan, L. M. (1976). Almost 65: Baseline data from the Retirement History Study. *Research Report No. 49, Office of Research and Statistics.* Washington, DC: US Social Security Administration.

Iyengar, S. S., & Lepper, M. R. (2000). When choice is demotivating: Can one desire too much of a good thing? *Journal of Personality and Social Psychology, 79*, 995–1006.

Juster, T. F., & Suzman, R. (1995). An overview of the Health and Retirement Study. *Journal of Human Resources, 30*, S7–S56.

Krueger, A. B., & Pischke, J. S. (1992). The effect of Social Security on labor supply: A cohort analysis of the notch generation. *Journal of Labor Economics, 10,* 412–437.

Lichtenstein, S., & Slovic, P. (in press). *The construction of preference.* New York: Cambridge University Press.

Loewenstein, G., Prelec, D., & Weber, R. (1999). What, me worry? A psychological perspective on economic aspects of retirement. In H. J. Aaron (Ed.), *Behavioral dimensions of retirement economics* (pp. 215–246). Washington, DC: The Brookings Institution.

Lumsdaine, R., & Mitchell, O. S. (1999). New developments in the economics of retirement. In O. Ashenfelter & D. Card (Eds.), *Handbook of labor economics,* (Vol. 3, pp. 3261–3308). Amsterdam, The Netherlands: North Holland.

Lumsdaine, R., Stock, J., & Wise, D. A. (1992). Three models of retirement: Computational complexity versus predictive validity. In D. A. Wise (Ed.), *Topics in the economics of aging* (pp. 19–57). Chicago, IL: University of Chicago Press.

Lusardi, A. (2001). Explaining why so many people do not save. *Center for Retirement Research Working Paper 2001–05.* Chestnut Hill, MA: Center for Retirement Research at Boston College.

Lusardi, A., & Browning, M. (1996). Household saving: Micro theories and micro facts. *Journal of Economic Literature, 34*, 1797–1855.

Madrian, B., & Shea, D. F. (2001). The power of suggestion: Inertia in 401(k) participation and savings behavior. *Quarterly Journal of Economics, 116,* 1149–1525.

Merriman, P. (2002). *Lessons learned at Harvard: Easy solutions to baffling problems.* Retrieved March 18, 2006, from http://www.fundadvice.com/FEhtml/PsychHurdles/0206b.html

Modigliani, F., & Brumberg, R. (1954). Utility analysis and the consumption function: An interpretation of cross-section data. In K. K. Kurihara (Ed.), *Post Keynesian economics* (pp. 388–436). New Brunswick, N.J.: Rutgers University Press.

Moore, J., & Mitchell, O. S. (2000). Projected retirement wealth and saving adequacy. In O. S. Mitchell, B. Hammond, & A. Rappaport (Eds.), *Forecasting retirement needs and retirement wealth* (pp. 68–94). Philadelphia, PA: University of Pennsylvania Press.

Munnell, A. H., & Sundén, A. (2004). *The challenge of 401(k) plans.* Washington, DC: Brookings Institution Press.

Mutter, S. A., & Poliske, R. M. (1994). Aging and illusory correlation in judgments of co-occurrence. *Psychology and Aging, 9,* 53–63.

Osgood, C. E., Suci, G. J., & Tannenbaum, P. H. (1957). *The measurement of meaning.* Urbana: University of Illinois.

Peters, E. (in press). The functions of affect in the construction of preferences. In S. Lichtenstein & P. Slovic (Eds.), *The construction of preference.* New York: Cambridge University Press.

Peters, E., Västfjäll, D., Slovic, P., Mertz, C. K., Mazzocco, K., & Dickert, S. (2006). Numeracy and decision making. *Psychological Science, 17,* 407–413.

Quinn, J. F. (2002). Changing retirement trends and their impact on elderly entitlement programs. In H. S. Altman & D. I. Shactman (Eds.), *Policies for an aging society* (pp. 293–315). Baltimore, MD: John Hopkins University Press.

Quinn, J. F., & Burkhauser, R. V. (1994). Retirement and labor force behavior. In L. G. Martin & S. H. Preston (Eds.), *Demography of aging* (pp. 50–101). Washington, DC: National Academy Press.

Quinn, J. F., Burkhauser, R. V., & Myers, D. A. (1990). *Passing the torch: The influence of economic incentives on work and retirement.* Kalamazoo, MI: W. E. Upjohn Institute for Employment Research.

Salthouse, T. A. (1996). The processing-speed theory of adult age differences in cognition. *Psychological Review, 103,* 403–428.

Scholz, J. K., Seshadri, A., & Khitatrakun, S. (2004). Are Americans saving 'optimally' for retirement? *NBER Working Paper 10260.* Cambridge, MA: National Bureau of Economic Research.

Simon, H. (1955). A behavioral model of rational choice. *The Quarterly Journal of Economics, 69,* 99–118.

Sloman, S. A. (1996). The empirical case for two systems of reasoning. *Psychological Bulletin, 119,* 3–22.

Slovic, P. (1982). Toward understanding and improving decisions. In W. C. Howell & E. A. Fleishman (Eds.), *Human performance and productivity* (Vol. 2, pp. 157–183). Hillsdale, NJ: Erlbaum.

Slovic, P., Finucane, M., Peters, E., & MacGregor, D. G. (2002). The affect heuristic. In T. Gilovich, D. Griffin, & D. Kahneman (Eds.), *Heuristics and biases: The psychology of intuitive judgment* (pp. 397–420). New York: Cambridge University Press.

Thaler, R. H., & Sunstein, C. R. (2003). Libertarian paternalism. *The American Economic Review, 93,* 174–179.

Tversky, A., & Shafir, E. (1992). Choice under conflict: The dynamics of deferred decision. *Psychological Science, 3,* 358–361.

U.S. Department of Commerce, Bureau of the Census. (1975). *Historical statistics of the United States: Colonial times to 1970.* Washington, DC: U.S. Government Printing Office.

Vroman, W. (1985). Some economic effects of the Social Security retirement test. In R. Ehrenberg (Ed.), *Research in labor economics* (pp. 31–89). Greenwich, CT: JAI Press.

Warshawsky, M., & Ameriks, J. (2001). What does financial planning software say about Americans' preparedness for retirement? *Journal of Retirement Planning, (May-June),* 27–37.

5

Race and Self-Regulatory Health Behaviors: The Role of the Stress Response and the HPA Axis in Physical and Mental Health Disparities

James S. Jackson and Katherine M. Knight

INTRODUCTION

Race, ethnicity, and sociocultural factors form the context and the sources of important influences on normal development and on the nature, expression, and course of poor physical and psychological health and mental disorders (Jackson, 1991). Research on ethnic and racial disparities in both physical and mental health has largely ignored important contextual variation, such as socioeconomic resources, living conditions, and discrimination (Geronimous & Thompson, 2004; Schnittker & McLeod, 2005). We believe that they are important sources of observed racial and ethnic physical and mental health disparities (Jackson, 2002; Schnittker & McLeod, 2005). Prior research suggests that disparities between African and non-African Americans in resources and environmental stressors contribute to critical differences in physical and mental health statuses (e.g., Aneshensel, Rutter, & Lachenbruch, 1991; Jackson, 2002; Neighbors, Jackson, Campbell, & Williams, 1989). Thus, greater attention has to be placed on studying these factors in the course of normative human development, physical morbidity, and psychopathology (Clark, Anderson, Clark, & Williams, 1999).

Recent work addresses discrete mental disorders and pathways into treatment, diagnostic divergence, and treatment efficacy outcomes (Jackson et al.,

Supplemental graphs and charts are available upon request; contact jamessj@umich.edu. The authors thank Jane Rafferty for contributions to data analyses.

2004). There is clearly a need for research that assesses risk factors, individual and family strengths, individual psychopathology, and service use all within a context that stresses a focus on multiple (individual, family, community, organizational) levels of research and analysis (Thompson & Neville, 1999). One consistent theme is a concern with the influence of racial, cultural, and social psychological factors on these processes and their explication and empirical examination (Schnittker & McLeod, 2005).

The purpose of this chapter is to address one possible causal pathway by which the stress of daily living may have differential effects among different race and ethnic groups on physical and mental health outcomes (Geronimus & Thompson, 2004; Massey, 2004). It is widely documented that living under negative environmental conditions and with the attendant stressful outcomes results in higher rates of physical health disparities (Geronimus & Thompson, 2004; Schnittker & McLeod, 2005). An interesting conundrum in the health literature, however, is that while large racial disparities exist in the nature and distribution of physical health disparities, favoring non-Hispanic whites over African Americans (Massey, 2004), epidemiological and clinical data have long revealed that African Americans, in comparison to non-Hispanic whites, suffer the same or lower rates of mental disorders, even while suffering higher rates of psychological distress and depressive symptoms (Jackson, 2002). These divergent disparities in physical and mental health statuses raise questions about the assumed relationship between negative life conditions, stressors and stressful experience, and negative physical and mental health outcomes (Geronimous & Thompson, 2004; Massey, 2004).

Succinctly, we propose and explore in this chapter the theory that, under stressful living conditions, individuals often engage in a large number of negative health behaviors, for example, smoking, alcohol use and abuse, drug use, and overeating, in attempts (conscious or unconscious) to cope with the stressors of daily life (Jackson, 2002; Winkleby & Cubbin, 2004). We suggest that the symptoms of stressful life conditions and physiological stress are more available to conscious thought than the concomitant mechanisms that eventuate in physical health ailments and chronic health conditions, such as heart disease, diabetes, and cancer. Thus, when individuals are faced with stressful conditions of life (e.g., poverty, disorganized living conditions, poor housing, financial difficulties, etc.), they will engage in behaviors that alleviate the immediate stressful reactions to these environmental exposures; the same environmental exposures that are affecting (silently) pathways to eventual negative physical health morbidity and mortality. Consequently, though somewhat perverse, while engaging in negative health behaviors whose immediate effects are to alleviate or distort the symptoms of stress associated with poor living conditions, those same poor living conditions and negative health behaviors are contributing to the development of poor health and chronic health disorders (Warner & Hayward, 2002). We propose that these behaviors may interfere with or mask the physiological cascade of stressful responses through the hypothalamic-pituitary-adrenalcortical (HPA) axis that eventuate in serious mental disorders (Barden, 2004). While these negative behaviors may have salubrious effects on the diagnosis of mental disorders among some race and ethnic groups, such as African Americans (small negative, no disparities, or positive disparities), the direct effects of stressful living (Dohrenwend, 2000), combined with the direct effects of the negative behaviors themselves, create higher rates of serious physical health morbidity and mortality (large and unfavorable negative disparities) (Hayward, Crimmins, Miles, & Yang, 2000).

The relative social and economic deprivation of Blacks and many other minority groups (e.g., Puerto Rican, Vietnamese, etc.) compared to Whites and other ethnic minorities (e.g., Chinese, Japanese, etc.) are thought to influence the distribution of psychopathology among ethnic and racial minorities (Williams, 2001). Despite recent improvements in education and income, for example, the socioeconomic status of African Americans is still relatively low in comparison to Whites and several other minority groups (e.g., Chinese, Japanese, etc.; Farley, 1995; Massey, 2004). Black Americans are less likely to graduate from high school, and have lower family incomes, lower levels of occupational prestige, and higher levels of unemployment (Harrison & Bennett, 1995; Jackson, 2000). These trends are exacerbated by high levels of residential segregation, with poor Blacks much more likely than poor Whites (and even poor Latinos) to reside in census tracts with high concentrations of poverty (Bureau of the Census, 1995). Consequentially, poor Blacks, to a much greater degree than other poor groups, live in neighborhoods that suffer from problems such as high rates of crime, low quality schools, high unemployment, chronic teenage pregnancy, inadequate housing, and inferior health care (Browning & Cagney, 2003). Recent data reveal that the decline in the economic status of Blacks relative to Whites during the 1980s resulted in a widening of the gap in health status, driven in part by an absolute decline in some health status indicators for the African American population (Williams & Collins, 1995).

Based on these social indicators, social and other health scientists have long argued that the stress associated with disadvantaged status and exposure to discrimination increases the vulnerability of African Americans and other ethnic/racial minorities to mental and physical disorders (e.g., Geronimous & Thompson, 2004; Massey, 2004). Although studies of psychological distress have routinely revealed significantly higher prevalence and severity of symptoms among Blacks compared to Whites, these differences appear to be accounted for by differences in socioeconomic status (SES) (e.g., Hayward et al., 2000; Vega & Rumbaut, 1991). Some researchers have used these race-by-SES findings to argue that race, per se, is unimportant in the psychiatric epidemiologic arena (e.g., Warheit, Holzer, & Arey, 1975). Other findings indicate, however, that the epidemiologic picture is more complex. Kessler and Neighbors (1986) and Ulbrich, Warheit, and Zimmerman (1989) found that at lower levels of SES, African Americans did evidence higher rates of psychological distress than Whites. Despite the attention given to the importance of estimating the relative effects of ethnicity and SES on morbidity, we still do not fully understand how race and SES interact to produce observed patterns of distress (Dohrenwend, 2000).

Reliance upon global constructs like psychological distress provides only limited information on group differences in psychiatric morbidity. The Epiedemiological Catchment Area (ECA) study of prevalence rates of specific psychiatric disorders used methods that addressed some of the ambiguity inherent in the symptom checklist approach, and thus was less encumbered by the selection bias compared to clinical studies (Neighbors, 1984). With the exceptions of schizophrenia and phobias, the ECA found roughly comparable rates of mental disorders for Blacks and Whites (Robins & Regier, 1991). For example, age-adjusted analyses by sex and ECA site did not show any consistent Black excess in lifetime or 6-month prevalence of depression (Somervell, Leaf, Weissman, Blazer, & Bruce, 1989). Even more striking, results from the National Comorbidity Study (NCS) found that rates of disorders for African Americans were consistently *below* those of Whites; these differences were particularly pronounced for depression and substance abuse disorders (Blazer, Kessler, McGonagle, & Swartz, 1994; Kessler et al., 1994). The only exception to this trend was in the rates of phobia, where Blacks had slightly but significantly higher rates of agoraphobia than Whites (Magee, Eaton, Wittchen, McGonagle, & Kessler, 1996). Historically, Blacks have consistently exhibited higher rates of phobias than Whites. As far back as the mid-1970s, Warheit et al. (1975) reported significantly higher rates of phobic symptomatology for African Americans than Whites. Similarly, Brown, Eaton, and Sussman's (1990) ECA analysis showed that African Americans were more likely than Whites to report recent phobia. In general, however, psychiatric epidemiologic studies have shown that the mental health of African Americans is better than would be expected based on the assumed effects of discrimination and disadvantaged status (Jackson, 2002; Neighbors, 1984; Williams, 1995).

STRESS AND ADAPTATION OVER THE LIFE COURSE

Historically, we have employed a stress, coping, and social resource model to guide data collection, analyses, and interpretation in mental health studies (Jackson, Neighbors, & Gurin, 1986). This approach has focused on how both diffuse and specific symptom reactions are defined by the general public (lay diagnostic inference), and how these definitions of personal problems influence the nature of coping and responses, particularly help-seeking behaviors. Stress and adaptation are viewed as arising from discrepancies between the demands impinging upon a person and the capacity of that person to effectively cope with those demands (e.g., Cohen, Kessler, & Gordon, 1995; Myers, 1982). High levels of discrepancies are commonly associated with the onset of psychological distress. This orientation places equal emphasis on environmental/situational and individual factors as explanations for possible causes of psychological distress (Neighbors, Jackson, Bowman, & Gurin, 1983). The stress and adaptation model also examines one of the more positive aspects of minority mental health—successful problem solving.

Specifically, this work has focused on the relative importance of race, ethnicity, SES, and gender, as well as factors like acculturation, as antecedents for understanding the nature of stress and its influences on, for example, mental health and services use. Just as an example of the needed subtlety of defining and assessing potential mediating and moderation factors, we recognize that the effects of SES must be assessed not only at the level of the individual and household, but also at the level of the neighborhood (e.g., Krieger, Williams, & Moss, 1997). Regardless of individual or household characteristics, Black, White, Latino, Caribbean, and Asian neighborhoods differ dramatically in the availability of jobs, crime, family structures, opportunities for marriage, and exposure to conventional role models (e.g., Wilson, 1996). These geographical, area-based characteristics capture important aspects of the physical and social contexts that may adversely affect mental health over and above the aggregation of individual characteristics. These demographic and aggregate characteristics are also expected to directly influence the specific types of mental health problems, help-seeking behaviors, and service use patterns, one may observe. Although we expect a direct relationship between psychological and social resource factors and mental health outcomes, we are particularly interested in how these and other resources moderate the relationship between acute and chronic stress and mental health. We also acknowledge important research in this field (e.g., Thoits, 1995; Wheaten, 1985) that suggests that mediation and moderation can occur individually, as well as in tandem, to buffer the impact of stress on mental health. For example, previous analyses of the original 1979–1980 National Survey of Black Americans (NSBA) cross-section study and subsequent NSBA panel data (Williams, Lavizzo-Mourey, & Warren, 1994) suggest that psychological and social resources are important mediators and moderators of the relationship between stress and mental health for African Americans. Finally, the impact of having a serious mental disorder and high levels of distress and impairment are expected to directly influence patterns of help-seeking and service use, patterns that may differ markedly across different minority groups.

There is little information from national studies concerning the impact of life events on the distribution of psychopathology among ethnic and racial minorities. Chronic stressors (i.e., lack of income, chronic problems in work, marriage, and parenting) may be as important determinants of mental health as acute life events (Pearlin, 1989). Recent developments in the measurement of stress highlight the need to broaden the assessment of stress beyond life events and chronic stressors (Dohrenwend, 2000). Childhood and adult traumatic events, daily hassles, and the absence of desired events have effects on mental health beyond those of life events and chronic stressors (Wheaton, 1994). This comprehensive approach to the measurement of stress accounts for substantially more variability in mental health status than previous work suggested (Turner, Wheaton & Lloyd, 1995). Unfortunately, prior studies have not assessed the relationship among comprehensive measures of stress and especially comparative studies across a wide range of America's ethnic and racial population (e.g., Williams, 2001).

One critical issue is the extent to which minority status itself increases risk for health and mental health problems (e.g., Vega & Rumbaut, 1991; Williams & Fenton, 1994). For example, previous research has long argued that discrimination adversely affects the mental health of African Americans (e.g., McCarthy & Yancey, 1971). However, stressors that may be unique to, or more prevalent among, African Americans have not always been incorporated into the assessment of stress (Essed, 1991; Feagin, 1991; Jackson et al., 1996; McLean & Link, 1994; Pearlin, 1989). Several studies indicate that discrimination, as measured by subjective reports, adversely affects the emotional well-being (and physical health outcomes such as blood pressure) of African Americans and other minorities (e.g., Amaro, Russo, & Jackson, 1987; Jackson et al., 1996; James, LaCroix, Kleinbaum, & Strogatz, 1984; Krieger, 1990; Krieger & Signey, 1996; Saldana, 1995; Salgado de Snyder, 1987). Other evidence suggests that the experience of unfair treatment, irrespective of race or ethnicity, may have negative consequences for health (Harburg et al., 1973a; Harburg et al., 1973b).

STRESSFUL LIFE EXPERIENCES AND COPING

In addition to the daily stressors of living, Blacks and other racial minorities are often confronted with the additional stress of racial discrimination (Clark et al., 1999). Our ongoing research attempts to identify the types and amounts of discrimination that affect mental health in an attempt to explain how racial/ethnic bias combines with other types of stressors to affect mental health among ethnic/racial minority populations. Exposure to stress, either race related or not, does not always adversely affect mental health (Cohen et al., 1995). Social and psychological resources that can mitigate the impact of stress on health include social relationships, self-esteem, perceptions of mastery or control, anger or hostility, feelings of helplessness or hopelessness, and repression or denial of emotions (Kessler et al., 1994; Mirowsky & Ross, 1980; Mirowsky & Ross, 1989; Rogler, Malgady, & Rodriguez 1989; Williams, 1990; Williams & Fenton, 1994). Analyses of data from a 1995 Detroit

Area Study highlight the importance of understanding coping processes (Williams, Yu, Jackson, & Anderson, 1997). In this study, the mental health outcomes of Blacks exceeded that of Whites when adjusted for the effects of race-related stress. This pattern is consistent with the suggestion that stressful experiences may more adversely affect the mental health of Whites than Blacks. Kessler (1979) documented a similar pattern for the relationship between stressful life events and psychological distress for non-Whites (mainly Blacks). While Blacks were more likely to be exposed, comparable stressful events more adversely affected the mental health of Whites. Kessler (1979) suggested that compared to Whites, African Americans may have earlier and more frequent exposure to adversity, which lessens the impact of stress, greater emotional flexibility that facilitates recovery, and access to culturally-based psychological coping resources.

In a prospective study, Breslau, Kilbey, and Andreski (1993) found that Blacks are nearly twice as likely as Whites to experience a traumatic event, while the black/white odds ratio for retrospective reporting of lifetime traumatic events was only 1.22, suggesting that Blacks may have lower rates of recall or reporting of negative events. Thus Blacks may be suffering exposure to and the deleterious effects of stressful events at rates greater than those observed through self-report methodologies.

A broad range of other coping resources, including family support and religious involvement, play an important role in buffering minority populations from the negative effects of stress. Prior research suggests that religion can have a positive impact on psychological well-being by providing systems of meaning that help individuals make sense of stressful experiences. Further, involvement in religious communities can be an important source of social integration and social support (e.g., Chatters & Taylor, 1989; Williams, 1994).

In addition to religion, a number of other social and psychological resources may play a special role in adaptation to stress for racial and ethnic minority groups. These include John Henryism (James, 1994), interracial contact (Rosenberg, 1979), racial self-esteem, internalized racism (Taylor, Chatters, Hardison, & Riley, 2001), and system blame (Neighbors, Jackson, Broman, & Gurin, 1996). Racial self-concept and identity is a neglected resource that can buffer the relationship between stress and health. We recently documented that keeping group identity salient protected African Americans from some of the adverse effects of discrimination on their health. The John Henryism scale measures an active predisposition to master environmental challenges (James, 1994). Research documents that John Henryism is unrelated to the blood pressure levels of Whites and higher SES Blacks. There is, however, a strong positive relationship between John Henryism and blood pressure among lower SES Blacks. Prior research has given insufficient attention to the potential mental health consequences of John Henryism.

The mental health consequences of buying into the dominant society's stigma of inferiority of one's own racial group are also important to assess. For example, research across a broad range of societies (in the United Kingdom, Japan, India, South Africa, Israel) indicates that groups that are socially unequal perform more poorly on standardized tests (Fischer, 1969). Similarly, the performance of African Americans on difficult intellectual examinations is adversely affected when the stereotype of black intellectual inferiority is made salient (Blascovich, Spencer, Quinn, & Steele, 2001). Research on stereotype threat has been largely confined to intellectual test performance. It is conceivable that the salience (and persistence) of negative racial stereotypes may have effects beyond this domain. For example, research by Blascovich et al. (2001) suggests that stereotype threat effects may extend to negative influences on blood pressure. In addition, Taylor et al. have found that Blacks who score highly on internalized racism—that is, they believe Blacks are inferior—have higher levels of psychological distress and alcohol use. A similar pattern of results was found in the NSBA (Williams & Chung, in press).

Social scientists have long speculated about the protective implications of system-blame for Blacks as an explanation for their relative disadvantaged status. The presumed benefit to African Americans of casting themselves as victims of oppression, thereby lessening the degree of personal responsibility for low status, has led social psychiatric epidemiologists to employ the system-blame concept to explain the lack of racial differences in mental health status (Neff, 1985). Unfortunately, there has been no direct test of this hypothesis to date. In fact, the opposite may be true; system-blame may actually diminish individual feelings of self-efficacy, leading to a fatalistic attitude that reduces coping effort in the face of adversity (Jones & Matsumoto, 1982).

In sum, while race and ethnic groups employ a wide range of coping strategies to address both race and non-race related stressors of daily life, it is not clear that they are always effective in alleviating the debilitating effects of stressors and stress (Jackson, Williams, &

Torres, 2003). In fact, we suggest in this chapter that there is no clear, known physiological pathway for the range of social coping strategies discussed above to have their effects in alleviating stress. On the other hand, there is a range of negative behaviors (overeating, alcohol, drug use, etc.), often examined within the context of "self-medication" (Winkleby & Cubbins, 2004) that do have a clear physiologic pathway and may serve, as we discuss later, to buffer the effects of stress on poor psychological health while simultaneously affecting health morbidity and eventually mortality.

STRESS RESPONSE

The term *stress response* refers to the cascade of behavioral and physiological changes that aim to reestablish homeostasis (Sapolsky, 2002). It is assumed this response evolved to deal with acute stressors, particularly those that threatened life and were short in duration, by mobilizing energy for immediate use and suppressing nonessential systems (Sapolsky, 1998; Sapolsky, 2002). Humans respond not only to physical stressors such as hunger, but also to psychological stressors such as fear. Both physical and psychological stressors activate the same stress response, but the nature of psychological stressors is such that they tend to be longer in duration than physical stressors. While the response is well-adapted to deal with short-term stressors, chronic activation of this system can result in negative physiological and health outcomes (McEwen, 1998a). Thus, psychological stressors provide a unique path for chronic activation of the stress response.

The term stress refers to a disruption in the homeostasis of an organism. A stressor is the specific thing that is responsible for the disruption (e.g., hunger, anxiety). While the research discussed in this chapter focuses largely on surveys and lay interviewer measures of mental disorder, we believe that it is important to consider the effect that factors such as discrimination have on a person's physiology (Clark et al., 1999). We propose that to fully explain racial discrepancies in both physical and mental health, research must also focus on physiological mechanisms related to certain behaviors. In particular, we believe that certain negative health behaviors (e.g., smoking, overeating, etc.) may actually put into action a chain of physiological events that result in an individual becoming more resilient to mental illness by their actions on the stress system.

Many systems are activated by stress. We focus on the response of the HPA axis to stress, and the implications this system may have for the buffering effects of negative health behaviors on mental disorder. Following a stressor, inputs from sensory areas and limbic structures in the brain stimulate the release of corticotropin releasing factor (CRF) and arginine vasopressin (AVP) from the paraventricular nucleus (PVN) of the hypothalamus. Corticotropin-releasing hormone (CRH) is believed to be the primary coordinator of the stress response, and it modulates the release of adrenocorticotropin (ACTH) from the anterior pituitary. ACTH then stimulates the release of the glucocorticoid cortisol from the adrenal cortex. Through a system of negative feedback, cortisol regulates the further release of CRF by binding to glucocorticoid receptors in the brain, most importantly, to receptors located in the PVN.

This explanation is simplified and it is important to recognize that interactions between endocrine and neurological actors are complex and not completely understood. The HPA axis has been widely researched in the fields of physiology/neurology (e.g., McEwen, 1998a; Sapolsky, 1998) and psychology (e.g., Dickerson & Kemeny, 2004); therefore, we believe that it is an appropriate starting point for a theory combining the two fields. We believe that it is through this system that negative health behaviors, such as eating comfort food, smoking, consuming alcohol, and taking illicit drugs, may buffer against negative affective/mental states.

HPA Axis and Comfort Food

Eating certain types of foods, known as comfort foods, cheers people up and may improve functioning while making them feel better (Cannetti, Bachar, & Berry, 2002). But why this relationship exists and its relation to stress reduction is just beginning to be understood. Recent research (Dallman et al., 2003a; Dallman et al., 2003b) suggests that consuming comfort foods (foods that are high in fat and/or carbohydrates) reduces anxiety via feedback to the HPA axis. During times of chronic stress, the negative feedback loop through which cortisol regulates further release of CRF breaks down as glucocorticoid receptors are downregulated and the release of CRF continues. This continued release of CRF is associated with feelings of anxiety as CRF mRNA expression in the amygdala (an important area of the emotional brain) is increased (Dallman et al., 2003a).

Consuming foods that are high in fat appear to aid in the shutdown of the stress response by regulating the release of CRF. Dallman et al. (2003a, 2003b) propose that chronically high levels of cortisol increase stimulus salience (desire to consume foods that taste good) and increase abdominal obesity, which results in an inhibitory metabolic feedback to CRF in the PVN, reducing HPA axis activity. Simply put, under times of stress we feel anxiety (because of activation of CRF in the amygdala) and have increased circulating levels of cortisol because negative feedback is not working (increasing compulsion and abdominal fat deposits). These effects of cortisol result in the consumption and storage of comfort foods that act to reduce CRF levels (through the inhibitory metabolic feedback signal), resulting in a reduction of anxiety (as CRF in the amygdala is lowered). Eating comfort food reduces anxiety by inhibiting the release of CRF (Dallman et al., 2003a, 2003b).

High rates of obesity are observed in black populations, particularly among women (Kahng, Dunkle, & Jackson, 2004) and it is believed that consuming large amounts of comfort foods may be responsible for this trend. Being larger and even obese may be more socially accepted among Blacks than among Whites, and so consuming foods may be a socially accepted (and gender appropriate) way of dealing with stress. Because of neighborhood effects, comfort food may be more convenient because of the proliferation of fast food outlets, but chronic stress would most likely cause the seeking of such food even if it were not readily available. The chronic stress present in the lives of many African American women, especially among those who live in urban areas, leads to frequent anxiety (Geronimus & Thompson, 2004). Consuming foods high in fat and carbohydrates may reduce this anxiety by inhibiting CRF release, but relying on this stress-reduction technique does not come without cost. For example, when the HPA axis is chronically activated, stress hormones promote insulin resistance in fat cells (Raikkonen, Keltikangas-Jarvinen, Adlercreutz, & Hautanen, 1996; Sapolsky, 1998). If other risk factors exist, or if the stress persists long enough, this resistance may develop into Type II, or insulin resistant, diabetes. Furthermore, eating foods high in fat and carbohydrates is also related to stroke, cardiovascular disease, and other negative health outcomes.

While eating comfort foods may have the short-term benefit of reducing feelings of anxiety in times of chronic stress, this short-term benefit comes at a significant cost. Managing anxiety in this manner may well result in negative long-term health outcomes that affect not only vitality but also mortality.

HPA Axis and Alcohol Use

We propose that the use of alcohol buffers, in the short term, the stress of everyday life that accompanies minority status and urban life. Many researchers and laypeople have assumed that alcohol intake reduces anxiety and relieves tension (for discussion, see Lender, 1987; Peyser, 1993). Rats that have had access to alcohol, but that have been abstinent, will begin alcohol-seeking behavior following a stressor (Le et al., 1998). In humans, studies have indicated that stress levels and negative psychological states influence alcohol consumption (Peele & Brodsky, 2000; Pohorecky, 1991). Examination of the research testing the tension-reduction hypothesis of alcohol use indicates that the relationship between alcohol use and stress is more complicated (Peyser, 1993). Alcohol consumption can both reduce and produce anxiety (Pohorecky, 1981) and has both depressive and excitatory effects on the HPA axis. We believe that while alcohol consumption may result in an increased activation of the HPA axis, its simultaneous elevation of dopamine and beta-endorphin levels in the brain results in a feeling of relaxation and subjective release from stress.

Ethanol ingestion stimulates the release of CRH, affecting the stress response. However, this increase in CRH stimulates not only the release of ACTH from the anterior pituitary, but also the release of beta-endorphin. Beta-endorphin is an endogenous opioid that shares a precursor (proopiome-lanocortin; (POMC)) with ACTH and is released from the pituitary. Endogenous opioids are associated with pain relief, euphoria, and the rewarding and reinforcing effects of drugs and alcohol (Akil & Cicero, 1986). This release of beta-endorphin via radiating axons into other areas of the brain (e.g., nucleus accumbens, nucleus accumbens (NAc); ventral tegmental area, (VTA)) likely results in a feeling of calmness.

Glucocorticoids released following alcohol consumption may also act on the mesolimbic dopaminergic system, resulting in an increase of dopamine in regions such as the NAc (Piazza & LeMoal, 1998). The rewarding effects of many drugs, including alcohol, may be the result of dopamine release in this region (Koob et al., 1998). Thus, while alcohol consumption results in activation of the HPA axis, it also results in an increased release of dopamine and beta-endorphins, which likely reduce feelings of stress. The long-term outcomes of excessive alcohol use are negative, but in the short-term the use of alcohol likely alleviates stress.

HPA Axis and Nicotine

Tobacco use is the leading cause of preventable death in the United States (U.S. Department of Health and Human Services, 2001), and is responsible for roughly one out of every five American deaths (CDC, 2002; CDC, 2003). Individuals who smoke are at higher risk of developing lung cancer, emphysema, bronchitis, heart disease, chronic airway obstruction, and other forms of cancer, and research indicates that adult smokers have a life expectancy that is 13–14 years less than nonsmokers (CDC, 2002). However, despite wide public knowledge of the negative health outcomes associated with tobacco use, many Americans continue to regularly use tobacco.

Individuals who use tobacco cite a variety of reasons for engaging in the activity. For example, smoking results in a mild euphoria (Pomerleau & Pomerleau, 1992), increased energy, and a suppressed appetite (Benowitz, 1996; Stolerman & Jarvis, 1995). Nicotine, a potent ingredient in tobacco, also induces a sense of well-being (Jones, 1987). At typical levels, nicotine improves physical and intellectual performance (Pritchard, Robinson, & Guy, 1992) while also increasing moodiness (Breslau, Kilbey, & Andreski, 1993) and reducing stress-related anxiety (Wesnes & Warburton, 1983). Because many smokers report that smoking relaxes them when they are under stress (Benowitz, 1988), researchers have focused on how the HPA axis is affected by tobacco use.

Research in both humans and animals has found evidence that nicotine (the primary addictive component of tobacco products) increases levels of stress hormones (e.g., Andersson, Siegel, Fuxe, & Eneroth, 1983; Kirschbaum, Wust, & Strasburger, 1992; Porcu et al., 2003). This increase in stress hormones would indicate that nicotine has an anxiogenic effect; however, nicotine also has neurological effects that may explain the anxiolytic effects reported by individuals who use tobacco.

Animal studies have found that the mesolimbic dopamine (DA) system plays an important role in addiction to psychostimulants and other drugs of abuse (e.g., Piazza & LeMoal, 1996). Nicotine has been found to stimulate dopamine release from the ventral tegmental area and the shell of the NAc, and that both of these areas are related to the DA system (Nisell, Nomikos, & Svensson, 1994). This increase in dopamine, and subsequent activation of the DA system, likely gives rise to the pleasant experiences reported by smokers and reinforce the behavior.

Hormones associated with the HPA appear to mediate the response of the DA system to nicotine. In animals that have been self-administering drugs, adrenalectomy ends drug-seeking behavior. When glucocorticoids are injected into these adrenalectomized rats, their drug-seeking behavior is reinstated. These findings indicate that glucocorticoids are an essential ingredient for drug-seeking behavior (Piazza & LeMoal, 1996). Supporting this hypothesis, studies have shown that rats that had their previous self-administration of stimulant drugs extinguished began seeking drugs following a stressor (e.g., Piazza & LeMoal, 1998; Stewart, 2000). Therefore, it appears, although somewhat paradoxical, that the release of stress hormones in response to nicotine actually mediates the response of the DA system, giving rise to feelings of relaxation, reduced anxiety, and calm.

HPA Axis and Drugs

The effects of drugs on the HPA axis are closely related to the effects of licit drugs. Similar to alcohol and nicotine, we believe that using psychostimulant drugs may protect the individual against negative psychological states in the short-term at the expense of long-term physical health. Stress is related to an increase in psychostimulant self-administration in rats (see Piazza & LeMoal, 1998, for review), and this finding indicates that such drugs may give relief from stress or are made more salient by stress.

A recent paper (DeJong & De Kloet, 2004) concluded that the synaptic changes produced by glucocorticoids in the mesolimbic dopaminergic system mimic those caused by psychostimulant drugs, and that glucocorticoids may "act synergistically with drugs of abuse or prime the brain reward system for the subsequent actions of these compounds" (p.195); however, more research is needed to elucidate specific pathways and interactions. Drugs also increase levels of dopamine in the shell of the NAc (Barrot et al., 2000). This dopamine increase may reduce anxiety directly or it may enhance the effects of drugs (for discussion, see Marinelli & Piazza, 2002).

We propose that by acting on the mesolimbic dopaminergic system, both directly and via the HPA axis, psychostimulant drug use reduces the psychological effects of stress by "releasing the individual"; that is, while under the influence of illicit or licit drugs, an individual may well be released from anxieties, self-criticism, self-doubt, and ruminations. The troubles that drove the person to the activity are slowly reduced or removed while intoxicated. Additionally, such drug use results in the release of both dopamine and beta-endorphins in the brain and activates the system associated with reward. These neurological underpinnings help to reinforce the behavior as one that is associated with feelings of stress-release. In addition, these drugs also further the activation of the HPA axis, which may increase the allostatic load of the individual. While individuals are *psychologically* released from the stress, they are not *physically* released from the effects of stress (Dallman, 2003).

CONCLUSION

Our review of the literature and research leads us to the model proposed in Figure 5.1. In this model we postulate that the environment serves as a source of stressors (Browning & Cagney, 2003; Roux, 2003; Williams & Jackson, 2005) as well a source of available structures that facilitate or afford the availability of negative health behaviors (Morland, Wing, & Roux, 2002; Morland, Wing, Roux, & Poole, 2002). In addition, we believe that the environment can have direct effects on the development of physical disorders (Cagney & Browning, 2004; Roux, 2003) and perhaps psychological health disorders as well (Dohrenwend, 2000). As noted above, stressors and negative health behaviors have been shown to activate the HPA axis. As we have also reviewed, the chronic activation of this axis has deleterious effects on physical disorders and if not buffered psychological health disorders.

As we have also discussed, many African Americans live under conditions that are chronically stressful (Geronimous & Thompson, 2004; Massey, 2004). The environment serves to produce stressful conditions and provide opportunities (or affordances) for the alleviation of this concomitant stress through behaviors and actions thought to be negative (smoking, drinking, drug use, etc.). As we have reviewed, these behaviors may serve to alleviate stress, or at least its symptoms, through the same mechanism that is hypothesized to contribute to at least some mental disorders—the HPA axis (Barden, 2004). What is certain is that those negative health behaviors, such as smoking, drinking, and drug use, also have direct and negative effects on physical health status. Thus, while the engagement in these activities has the salubrious effects of alleviating at least the ostensible symptoms of stress, they are contributing to the mortality and morbidity differential observed among African American and non-Hispanic white populations. In fact, in some recent empirical research we find that negative health behaviors directly buffer the effects of stressful events on *DSM* depression (Jackson, 2002). Succinctly, among African Americans who live in stressful situations, engaging in negative behaviors (smoking drinking, etc.) actually significantly reduces the probability of being a major *DSM* depression case, while African Americans who have more stressful events and do not engage in these negative behaviors have higher odds of having major depression. In general, we do not believe that this effect is inherently linked to race. On the contrary, we believe that the effect observed among African Americans is due to the disproportionately greater distribution of negative environmental and stressful events and the availability of structures that facilitate negative health behaviors than is found in white populations. We believe that Whites who live under similar situations and facilitating structures will show the same effects as we have found for African Americans.

As we have intimated throughout this chapter, the life course of black Americans is fraught with challenges to healthy physical and psychological

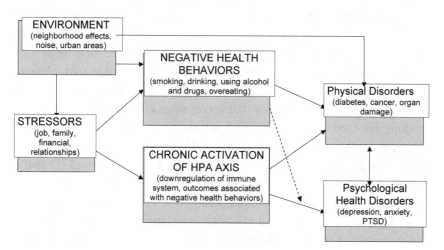

FIGURE 5.1 Possible interrelationships among environment, stressors, negative health behaviors, and physical and mental health disorders.

life (Geronimous & Thompson, 2004; Hayward et al., 2000; Massey, 2004). It is no accident that consistent and large physical health disparities separate Blacks and non-Hispanic whites and that they emerge largely in middle age and beyond (Geronimous & Thompson, 2004). At younger ages, Blacks are able to employ a variety of strategies that, when combined with more robust physical health, prove to be effective in masking the cascade to disparities that appear after middle age. During younger years, social support and other strategies discussed earlier in this chapter work, even imperfectly, to alleviate stressful conditions. However, we also suggest that early on, black Americans begin to employ more effective strategies that are stress reductive through the HPA-axis. These behaviors are differentiated by social class, culture, and gender (Jackson, 2002). For example, black American women show clear signs early in life of heightened rates of obesity (Kahng et al., 2004). As we have noted in this chapter, overeating, especially comfort foods, is an effective method for coping with chronic stress. Because the behaviors are effective for black women, they become a well-learned response to environmental stressors and only strengthen over the life course. Analyses of national data from the National Household Surveys on Drug Abuse reveal a string linear trend for increased obesity with age among black women. On the other hand, these same data reveal no such trends for black men; they do not have large prevalence rates for obesity at any age. Culturally, black men tend to have active, athletic lives until middle age. At middle age, the effectiveness of this dopamine-producing coping strategy is reduced by physical decline. It is at middle age that the age difference analyses show that black men begin to increase rates of smoking, alcohol consumption, and illicit drug use.

For both black men and women, the life course is filled with chronic stressors. Overeating, which is learned early in life among black women, is a culturally acceptable behavior that serves as an effective chronic stressor antidote. For men, reaching middle age diminishes an effective dopamine-releasing coping strategy, and in the face of continuing race and non-race related life stressors, other effective methods must be found. Thus the age-related rise in drinking, smoking, and drug use (Jackson, 2002).

In order to develop successful interventions to reduce the use of negative health behaviors in ethnic and minority populations over the life course, it is important to recognize that such behaviors may have salutatory, neurological effects that alleviate negative psychological (and physiological) states. For many individuals, especially among disadvantaged race and ethnic groups, the short-term benefits of reducing states such as anxiety, depression, and frustration that have been implicated in the etiologic pathways to mental disorders, may outweigh the risk of poor long-term physical health from behaviors such as overeating, consuming alcohol, using tobacco, and over the counter or illicit drug use (Heisler, Rust, Pattillo, & Dubois, 2004).

The most effective methods of addressing what we have argued to be an important source of physical health disparities in this country would be the reduction of environmentally mediated and produced race and non-race related stressors, improving living conditions, creating real job opportunities, eliminating poverty, and improving the poor quality of inner-city urban life. Changes in the context of life for millions of poor and black Americans have been difficult, if not intractable, because of the cost, lack of concern, and missing political will (Jackson, 1993). Paradoxically, the lack of attention to these large macro and environmental conditions has forced populations living under stressful life circumstances to employ a range of behaviors, both legal and illegal, that while ensuring better mental health, contribute over the life course to gradually worsening physical health morbidities and eventual early mortality (Hayward et al., 2000; Heisler et al., 2004)

ACKNOWLEDGMENTS

The research on which this chapter is based was funded by a grant from NIMH (5-U01 MH057716), OBSSR and NIA (3-R01 AG 020282). The data presented and views expressed are solely the responsibility of the authors.

Commentary: Mechanisms of Health Disparities: Variations in Health Care Provider Attitudes and Their Impact on Older Minority Adults

Stephanie L. Garrett and Toni P. Miles

INTRODUCTION

Traditionally, health disparities affecting American minority populations have most consistently been attributed to a complex set of external forces—either psychosocial-economic consequences or racism. Recently proposed empirical models, which utilize national survey samples, provide evidence for a significant impact of negative structural and environmental conditions on poor self-reported health as well as poor chronic health. See Jackson (this volume) for a more complete discussion.

Using three examples, we explore the often problematic and sometimes antagonistic interaction between physicians and patients. This interaction has its own potential to create disadvantageous outcomes for minority patient populations. First, we discuss the disadvantage created by the educational inequality between physician and patient. This can also be seen as differences in cognitive approach to information and the impact of this training on minority patients. This is particularly significant for those who have no medical expertise and are likely to have a different style of processing health information. Second, we compare strategies that physicians use when sharing health information—the authoritarian versus the consultant. Another way to express this tension is in the process of medical decision making and the concepts of autonomy and shared consent. Finally, we consider the potential for disadvantage created by the emerging emphasis in health care on the patient as a consumer and the ability of minority patients to afford emerging medical technologies. Health promotion and disease prevention has led many physicians to change their view of patients from passive health care recipients to active health consumers. Older adults, minority adults in particular, oftentimes operate from the perspective of health care recipient or one who *receives* care. The consumerist approach carries with it a personal responsibility for health related decision making that disempowered minority adults may not be familiar with or comfortable exercising. These examples illustrate how the physician-patient interaction has the potential to create disadvantage for older minority patients.

EDUCATIONAL INEQUALITY/COGNITIVE TRAINING

Research has demonstrated that order and format of clinical evidence presented to patients can bias patient understanding. To illustrate, older and less educated patients prefer proportions to percentages. Saying "one in 10 women/men will get X" is felt to be more people-oriented than explaining the probability of getting X (Epstein, Alper, & Quill, 2004). Patients also tend to prefer bar graphs (Elit et al., 1996), highlighting a preference by older persons for images rather than numbers. It is therefore critical that health care providers are aware of older patients' preferences as they relate to the processing of information. Patients can experience disadvantage when providers who are trained to express patient risk of disease in quantitative terms communicate their evidence to older adult patients who prefer graphs. Consider the situation where a patient who was doing well on antidepressant therapy for 12 months inquires about the possibility of discontinuing the medication. In this discussion, the provider decides to give the patient a choice by presenting the evidence for return of depressive symptoms. This presentation can take on at least two distinct forms. One presentation is structured so that the patient is told that the average risk for relapse is 18% with continued active treatment compared to 41% with placebo. An alternative strategy for comparing risk of relapse could proceed as follows: 41 out of 100 people who stop medication will experience a new episode of depression. If medication is continued without stopping, then only 18 out of 100 have a new onset. This second formulation is people-oriented and graphically based. It is very likely that the patient receiving the first explanation would discontinue the medication and the same patient receiving the second report might choose to continue the medication.

EDUCATIONAL INEQUALITY

There is always inequality of information content between physician and patient. Failing to fully describe a medical procedure or the reason for performing a particular therapy does not give a patient enough information to make a decision to accept or reject a specific procedure. To illustrate, physicians can exacerbate the gap in medical knowledge between themselves and their patients by not adequately explaining pertinent details and purposes of procedures. Consider the example of an elderly person requesting "everything done" when asked about choice concerning receipt of a feeding tube at a future point in the course of their illness. The physician knows that the placement of this tube is through a hole in the abdominal wall, that this invasive procedure carries a risk of infection, and that it may be medically inappropriate within the context of a terminal illness at a later point in the disease process. The patient is unaware of the potential for pain, suffering, and additional complications from this procedure. The patient is also unaware that a feeding tube may be inappropriate or ineffective at a later stage in care.

Educational inequality can also lead to the opposite situation. A patient may refuse what they perceive as heroic measures when there is every indication that it is medically necessary and a potentially effective treatment. It is quite common for patients to a priori refuse support with mechanical ventilation. Sometimes this treatment is used to correct a significant acid-base imbalance rather than to assist with breathing difficulty. Under these conditions, the support is temporary and will be removed as soon as the balance is restored. However, physicians may not be sufficiently skilled or comfortable explaining this use of the ventilator to patients perceived as being poorly educated (Mueller, Hook, & Fleming, 2004).

AUTONOMY AND SHARED CONSENT

When patients exhibit autonomy, they typically investigate medical therapies via library or internet searches, seek medical opinions from a second physician, and make their own health care decisions. There are instances when patients feel that they possess inadequate decision-making ability to make health care decisions on their own. Under these circumstances, they engage their physician in shared decision making and shared consent. There has been little research documenting the extent to which older minority adults exhibit autonomy in directing their medical care. However, the financial and technological resources required to support autonomy diminish the likelihood that elders on limited income will seek additional information. In this section, we will discuss the potential for disadvantage during the process of shared decision making and shared consent.

Advance Directives in Persons with Dementia

Without a living will, it is impossible to truly know what a person with cognitive impairment would want in a present or particular situation. Unfortunately, too many vulnerable elders find themselves in such a position. Without this kind of advance directive, these individuals are unable to participate in the process of shared decision making, causing disparity with respect to autonomy.

Medical and legal advocates, in their attempt to implement beneficence as well as justice, complicate circumstances by transferring patient autonomy to next of kin. Even if next of kin do accurately predict what the patient would want, they take from the patient his or her own choice concerning self determination.

To illustrate, an approach to provide a just surrogate for patient autonomy is proposed in a philosophical approach called an *ethic of care* (Messer, 2004). This approach outlines five characteristics: (a) Moral attention to "the situation in all its complexity" (p. 98); (b) sympathetic understanding, willing to identify with the persons in the situation, becoming aware of their wishes and best interests; (c) relationship awareness; (d) accommodation of the needs of all involved; and (e) response to needs of others (Manning, 1998). Although the intent of this ethic of care is certainly not to draw the attention and focus away from the patient, its effect contributes to the patient's lack of participatory capacity and highlights how physician biases in other areas become really important—sexism, racism, and ageism.

Physicians may further diminish patient autonomy by intentionally omitting critically important information necessary for a patient to make an informed choice. In doing so, the physician takes away choice from the patient, even if he or she strongly feels that he or she is in some way protecting the patient. Medical areas of uncertainty are particularly problematic, as proven testing, procedures, and/or therapy are unknown. Consider the controversy and physician behaviors surrounding prostate cancer screening as one important example (Miles, 2005).

The certainty that prostate cancer is now the leading cause of cancer mortality among men aged 65 years and older (CDC, 2002) is in opposition to the conventional uncertainty of prostate cancer truly being *the* life limiting disease in the context of other frequent comorbidities (heart disease, Chronic Obstructive Pulmonary Disease (COPD), etc.). Inaccurate judgments surrounding the seriousness of prostate cancer diagnosis can lead to disparities, as different physicians screen for prostate cancer with different frequency. Also, a physician who feels that it is unreasonable to start prostate cancer screening based on the lack of consensus that routine screening decreases mortality does not choose to share with his African American patient that African American men have a higher risk of dying from prostate cancer, partly due to the fact that they are at increased risk of getting more aggressive cancers. As a result this patient is not given the appropriate choice or advice, and is at risk from dying prematurely from a cancer that is manageable if not curable.

HEALTH RECIPIENT VERSUS HEALTH CONSUMER

The nature of our health care workforce is such that providers include an array of professions—doctors, nurses, nurse practitioners, and medical assistants—any individual who either prescribes, assists, or helps to deliver medical care. Medical care includes medical treatment, therapy, or any service that is provided to impact a person's physical or emotional condition. Conversely, consumers are more broadly defined to not only include patients but others who purchase medical supplies, medications, or treatment services. It is important to clarify who directs the movement of health services and who is subsequently affected, in order to appreciate additional external forces that create new and exacerbate current health disparities.

Patients are now able to directly purchase screening computed tomography (CT) or ultrasound scans without a physician diagnosis and subsequent referral (Fenton & Deyo, 2003). This single example of direct purchase of medical services highlights issues of access to medical technology, control of that access, patient empowerment and, ultimately, class differences—lower classes are less likely to exercise this option.

While the above example exposes potential health disparities, it also demonstrates how having the power to purchase technology can have some negative outcomes. None of the marketed screening tests (whole-body CT, CT-based heart scans, heel ultrasound for osteoporosis, and carotid duplex sonography for carotid stenosis) are accurate for screening in low-risk populations, and none has been proven to lead to early, beneficial intervention.

In the worst case, someone who has the money to pay for such a scan may receive a normal result, enjoy a false sense of security, and not follow-up for routine screening with a physician, resulting in a missed early diagnosis for some form of cancer. On the other hand, when someone is at high risk for cardiovascular disease and does not have the money, there is a possibility that person could not be offered a heart scan. This test, when abnormal, is usually followed by referral to a cardiologist. This process often leads to the diagnosis of significant disease prior to a heart attack. Other examples of technology access and disparities include access to specialists who offer the latest treatments as well as access to health care institutions with Electronic Medical Record (EMR) technology.

EMR systems are information technology considered necessary to maintain the ever increasing mass of patient information. Using new electronic record systems to document patient histories affords fast access to massive amounts of information, quicker access to patient histories during emergencies, and easy compilation of patient data (Walsh, 2004). Patients receiving care from health systems not able to afford EMR technology may experience longer times to accurate diagnoses. This can lead to delays in treatment, increased risks of polypharmacy, and premature mortality. EMR is a very recent addition to health care technology and its full impact on the creation of health disparities is not known. By 2008, all health care institutions that receive Medicare funds will be required to have EMR.

SUMMARY

In this commentary, we propose that educational inequalities, autonomy and shared consent, and consumerism in health care have the potential to create health disparities. The impact that these factors have on the interaction between physicians and patients may approach or exceed any effect that ethnicity, culture, or the social construct of race contributes to the development of health disparities.

Commentary: Adding Paths to Resilience and Daily Accounts to an Already Rich Field of Inquiry: A Brief Commentary on James Jackson's "Social Structure and Health Disparities"

Alex J. Zautra, Kate E. Murray, and Brendt P. Parish

In absolute terms, there have been improvements in social resources for all racial and ethnic groups in the United States. The rise in education levels among Blacks and Hispanics, for instance, suggests a lessening of the gap between classes, beginning in the later part of the 1960s (Kao & Thompson, 2003). Yet the divide in income, and to a lesser extent, education, between peoples who differ in gender, skin color, and ethnic origin continues, and in many ways is greater now than ever (Danziger & Gottschalk, 1997; Gottschalk, 1997). The psychological distance between those high and those low in social-economic status continues unabated and threatens to undermine the capacity of communities to foster the positive architecture of hope, optimism, and equal opportunity that holds us together as a nation.

In his chapter, James Jackson presents a comprehensive case for the importance of social structure as an underlying factor in health and mental health disparities within our nation. Indeed, health disparities follow the patterns of income distribution and discrimination, although they do not show linear concordance in every case. There are complexities in the data of course, and Jackson suggests that these are the clues to follow in uncovering the mechanisms of influence. He notes the apparent paradox in health disparities between rates of mental disorder (relatively low among

---

A previous version of this commentary was presented at the Penn State Gerontology Center Conference on Social Structures, Aging, and Self-Regulation in the Elderly, October 4–5, Pennsylvania State University, State College, PA. The authors wish to thank members of the Resilience Solution Group (www.asu.edu/resilience) for their intellectual guidance on the meaning and measurement of resilience.

some minority populations such as Blacks) juxtaposed against the backdrop of higher rates of all cause mortality among Blacks and other racial and ethnic minority groups. How might we best understand anomalies like these?

Even the more straightforward questions regarding the effects of race on health are not easily answered. Are racial disparities in chronic illness due to constitutional differences wired into genetic codes for different racial groups? Even highly heterogeneous racial groups such as United States black populations have propensities for illnesses that differ from European American groups. Among the social-environmental influences on health outcomes are a number of potential sources of health care disparities, including differential access to health care, higher rates of exposure to pathogens, and higher rates of social stress for low income and minority populations. What is needed is a careful examination of the potential mediators of the relationships obtained between race and ethnicity, on the one hand, and health outcomes, on the other.

Jackson advocates a biopsychosocial approach to the identification of underlying factors responsible for the observed differences among ethnic and racial groups based on a well-established stress and coping paradigm. The examination of stressful events and unhealthy patterns of coping behavior as potential mediators of the effects of social class and discrimination is likely to yield many findings that help us understand these disparities in health and develop social policies that are useful to further a more equitable distribution of sickness and health across ethnic and racial lines. He brings us back to the thoughtful discourse about the interplay between social causation and social selection (Dohrenwend & Dohrenwend, 1974) that underlies findings that show high income racial minorities at times better off than wealthy non-minorities, but that may find middle and lower class minority groups substantially worse.

Jackson points out that large scale survey research holds much promise for understanding differences among groups in physical and mental health. Indeed, there are likely to be many as yet undiscovered differences between subgroups within ethnic and racial groups in their adaptations to health and illness. By drawing upon large representative samples of communities with diverse ethnic and racial groups like those Jackson et al., have managed to recruit, it is possible to have a sufficient sample size with which to discriminate subgroups within an ethnic or racial cohort and test for differences in health and mental health. Data from these studies will go far down the path of understanding differences between and among racial and ethnic groups in our country.

Informative national studies of health and income disparities have been conducted in Great Britain that challenge us to adopt a comprehensive approach to the health of populations (Marmot & Wilkinson, 1999). Through the Whitehall studies, Marmot and Wilkinson have demonstrated that the differences in health extend across all levels of social class. Even those with many financial resources are not immune to early death in comparison to those higher in social position. Wilkinson and Pickett (2005) in their analysis of nations have shown that relative deprivation has remarkable influence on mortality. This further substantiates the case that Jackson builds for racial and ethnic disparities in health.

Yet the Whitehall studies also raise questions that are not fully addressed by the conceptual framework that Jackson offers, and the national survey methods, as extensive as they are, do not provide the kind of detailed inquiry into everyday life processes necessary to identify the biopsychosocial mediators responsible for differential rates of health and mental health problems as a function of racial and ethnic groups. If the social gradient influences health even among those who bear no chronic strain from economic hardship and who have adequate access to health care, then we must look to influences other than the frequency of social stressors and elevations in psychological distress to explain health disparities. Our research laboratory has embarked on a set of studies on resilience that we think will provide the kind of approach needed to identify additional mechanisms underlying social structural influences on health.

The Resilience Research Paradigm differs from the standard paradigmatic approach offered by a stress and coping model of adaptation in two ways. First, it pays greater attention to how people are able to sustain their ongoing plans and hopes for the future in the face of stressful events. Individual resilience may be defined in part by the amount of distress that a person can endure without a fundamental change in his or her capacity to pursue goals and purposes that give their life meaning. Here we may ask how much provocation a person can tolerate before responding with behaviors that change the nature of the relationships that person has fostered. The more reserve capacity to stay on a satisfying life course, the greater the resilience.

Second, resilience research suggests that we do not necessarily learn what we need to know about resilience from studies of adaptation failures.

For most outcomes of interest, people will show successes alongside failures on adaptation. Personal, social, and community resourcefulness define a separate dimension of adaptation that is often independent of the personal, social, and community vulnerabilities. To fully understand how people are resilient, we need to adopt measures of resourcefulness like hope (Snyder, 2002) and social engagement (Etzioni, 1993) that are distinct from measures of psychosocial vulnerability such as helplessness and anomie. This bi-dimensionality has implications for assessment at the level of the independent variable side and also the dependent variable side of the equation. Thus, what sometimes appears as a paradox in adaptation such as greater self-worth and sense of purpose but also higher risk for cardiovascular disease may reflect separate parallel processes influencing different outcomes rather than compensatory processes that are inexorably linked.

To illustrate what we mean, we report on data we have been collecting from two studies of women with chronic pain due to arthritis-related illnesses. These studies were multiyear projects that assessed a range of mental and physical health variables. Participants were 205 women between the ages of 21–86 ($M = 56.01$, $SD = 11.79$) with rheumatoid arthritis, osteoarthritis, and fibromyalgia , who completed a battery of self-report measures at the onset of participation and completion of nightly diary assessments for 30 days. In the diary reports, participants completed ratings of the extent to which they had experienced various positive and negative emotions, and the number of positive and negative interpersonal events that happened over the course of the day.

In these analyses, we wanted to understand the independent influences of sets of resilience resources and risk factors in conjunction with basic demographics (gender, age, and SES) in predicting physical and mental health outcomes. The Resilience Resources (RR) included individual ratings of Purpose in Life (Ryff & Keyes, 1995), average ratings of Positive Affect on the Positive and Negative Affect Schedule (PANAS; Watson, Clark, & Tellegen, 1988), and the average number of total Positive Interpersonal Events from the Inventory of Small Life Events (ISLE; Zautra, Guarnaccia, & Dohrenwend, 1986) from the diary measures. The Risk Index included ratings of negative social ties based on prior factor analytic work (Finch & Zautra, 1992), average ratings of Negative Affect (PANAS) and the average number of total Negative Interpersonal Events from the ISLE taken from the diary measures. Stepwise regression was used to predict physical functioning and mental health, subscales on the SF-36, a widely used measure of health status (Ware & Sherbourne, 1992). In these analyses, the demographic variables were entered in step I, the Risk Index in step II, and the RR Index in step III.

The data suggest a bi-dimensional model improves the ability to understand physical and mental health functioning in this sample. That is, health status is better understood when the independent indices of risk and resilience were simultaneously considered. In predicting physical health, the demographic variables accounted for 11%, the Risk Index accounted for 14.6%, and the RR Index accounted for 14% of the variance. In predicting mental health, the demographic variables accounted for 7.2%, the Risk Index accounted for 23%, and the RR Index accounted for 21% of the variance. When the order was reversed and the RR Index was entered in step II of the equation, resilience factors accounted for 23.8% of the variance in physical health and 36% of the variance in mental health. The resilience factors provide additional information that is not captured by an environmental and risk-based model. Their effects are mediated through psychosocial risk and relative resources.

Taken individually, the various risk and resilience factors were differentially important in predicting mental and physical health outcomes. That is, different factors were more or less important depending on the outcome being predicted. For example, in the complete model including demographics, risk, and resilience factors, individuals with higher ratings of purpose in life had significantly better scores of mental health ($t = 5.33, p < .001$), but not significantly higher levels of physical health ($t = 1.85, p = .07$). On the other hand, perceived criticism was a significant predictor of lower physical functioning ($t = -2.20, p = .03$) but not mental functioning ($t = -1.52, p = .13$). The differential impact of risk and resilience factors suggests previous anomalies may be better understood by more fully specified models. Phenomena such as the Hispanic Paradox may have been the result of using a risk-based model that ignores the other half of the equation, drawing attention to the processes of resistance and recovery. Future research should continue to build theoretical models that incorporate important positive and negative factors that influence health and illness, respectively. For example, Figure 5.2 includes positive as well as negative factors found in Jackson's original risk-based model. By including both resources and risk factors, we may better understand how some are able to both withstand and to bounce back from stressors in their lives.

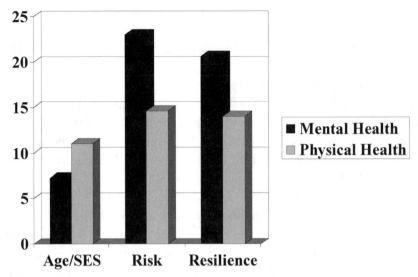

FIGURE 5.2   Proportion of variance accounted for by each set of variables using stepwise regression.

Overall, the findings suggest resilience resources play an important and independent role in predicting physical and mental health outcomes, implying distinct mediators of health versus illness outcomes. In fact, in the complete model (demographics + risk + resilience resources) a person's educational background, level of income, and the number of negative stressful events they reported on a daily basis (including events related to work, family, friends, and partners) were not significant in predicting mental health outcomes. Of these, only income was a significant predictor of lower physical health status ($t = 2.58$, $p = .01$). This suggests that lower income appears to negatively impact physical health more than it depreciates mental health, which corresponds with Jackson's research. The impact on physical health makes sense given the number of factors related to lower income, such as a lack of access to health care, reduced access to healthy foods, and attempts to self-regulate the HPA axis, as Jackson hypothesizes. Although this is a rough calculation of socioeconomic status and environmental stress, the overall lack of predictive power among these variables makes it clear that environmental deprivation is not enough to understand the disparities in health among this sample.

Jackson's research program offers the opportunity to further explore the impact of risk and resilience factors at both the individual and community level. As Jackson alludes, the risk factors among African Americans are often greater, as they are more often living in poverty and more likely to experience violent crime. There are also deficits in resources that accompany low income neighborhoods, such as inferior school systems, reduced access to healthy foods, and unsafe neighborhood streets. At a community level, there may be community variables that have been mistakenly attributed to racial and ethnic differences. Upcoming research in our lab will purposefully sample individuals across diverse communities, examining the heterogeneity within and between communities on health outcomes. It is important to be able to examine the independent contribution of community level variables on individual and community outcomes, such as social capital and collective efficacy. For example, Kawachi, Kennedy, and Glass (1999) found that even after accounting for individual differences (e.g., education, income, poor health behaviors), there was a significant effect of social capital on self-rated health. This means that within communities where there were higher levels of social trust and social cohesion, individuals reported better health than individuals living in communities with lower levels of trust and cohesion. Advances in multi-level modeling, which permits the simultaneous examination of person and community level effects, are critical for large-scale community research to more thoroughly examine and understand the role of neighborhood effects on individual health outcomes.

At an individual level, research and interventions must target other modifiable psychosocial resources that promote healthy outcomes across diverse populations. Jackson suggests the critical psychosocial resource factors for African Americans might well be different than those of highly White samples, such as the sample we have reported here. Other important resource factors might include variables such as religiosity and sources of support from neighborhood, community, and extended family. This suggests that although the bi-dimensional structure of the resilience model will be the same, the critical components may vary across racial and ethnic groups. This follows developmental resilience research that suggest there are developmental differences in what children and adolescents need at various stages to be resilient to developmental challenges (Hawkins, Catalano, & Miller, 1992; Masten & Powell, 2003; Rutter, 1985, 1993). Research that allows for heterogeneity across and within racial and ethnic groups is essential if we are to tease apart the relative importance of positive and negative aspects of individuals, families, and communities, and perhaps shed light on previous anomalies in the data.

THE IMPORTANCE OF EVERYDAY PROCESSES

In addition to advocating a paradigmatic shift toward the study of resilience as well as illness, we think much may be learned if great attention is paid to the study of everyday life processes. Our team advocates the use of daily, even within day, assessments in the study of racial and ethnic disparities in health and health care. This advance is primarily methodological—the introduction of multiple repeated measures on the same person permits us to examine the role of key mediators of health and illness disparities among racial and ethnic groups of the kind that Jackson proposes in his model, and also permits probing of resilience capacity as manifested by speed and depth of recovery and sustainability of ongoing personal goal-directed behavior. We are not alone in advocating their use (Almeida, 2005), and there is now sufficient evidence to show not only that participants from all walks of life are willing and able to complete daily measures, but also that the reports of events, behavior, affect, and cognitions are less biased than retrospective accounts.

Daily recording is not only an improvement in the methods of assessment of behavior. This method also focuses the research question on adaptation problems that arise in everyday life rather than the study of major life stressors and their consequences. There is now ample evidence that small but chronically recurrent stressors are among the most troubling challenges, and represent the kind of stressors that provoke health behaviors that are particularly harmful (McEwen, 1998b). Further, there is growing evidence that socioeconomic status differentials may reveal their impact on patterns of adaptation by providing relative richness versus deprivation in everyday response options for self-regulation and support of family members in need (Gallo, Bogart, Vranceanu, & Matthews, 2005). Further still, in order to properly trace the physiological mechanisms that may link behavioral responses to stress with health outcomes, we need to provide methods of assessment of those links close in time to the occurrence of the stressors and adapt to adjust to those stressors.

Our lab has advanced this work through the development of methods of assessment of everyday life events and their consequences. This work was informed early on by the need to consider not only the relative occurrence and coping responses to stressful events, but also to develop means to assess the occurrence and relative staying power of everyday events that are positive in their impact on psychological well-being. Early evidence from our community studies revealed that the regular diet of positive life experiences, particularly those that were the result of the person's own efforts, constituted a resilience resource not accounted for by the number of negative events and how well the resident coped with those stressors. Such resilience resources have been linked not only to psychological well-being, but also to physiological processes thought to be important to the lightening of allostatic load by restoring homeostasis (Steptoe, Wardle, & Marmot, 2005).

To illustrate how such inquiries may be conducted and the unique findings that they may reveal, we return to the data we have collected among women in chronic pain. In this second set of analyses, we wanted to look at the role of minority status and daily reports of pain as they relate to physical and mental outcomes. Because our data set did not include a large number of any single minority group, we combined those participants who identified as being part of a minority group and compared them to those who solely identified as white European Americans (EA). With exception of demographic information gathered in the initial questionnaire, both outcome and predictor variables examined were taken from the 30-day diary mentioned earlier. Outcome measures consisted of ratings of Positive Affect (PA) and Negative Affect (NA) (Watson, Clark, & Tellegen, 1988) and physical functioning was assessed using items adapted from the Role Physical subscale of the SF-36 (Ware & Sherbourne, 1992). Daily pain as a predictor variable was measured on a 100-point scale where 0 meant "no pain" and 100 meant "pain as bad as it could be".

For these analyses, we used three separate multilevel modeling analyses using SAS PROC MIXED (Littell, Milliken, Stroup, & Wolfinger, 1996) to predict daily outcomes of PA, NA, and physical functioning. For all three equations, we control for any effect of socioeconomic status using income level and age to control for differences in disease progression. Further, we examined both within person and between person levels of pain to determine whether there were differences between participants' average pain as well as if there were differences within a participants' daily report of pain.

In the first equation, predicting daily PA, after controlling for income, age, and NA, we found that within person ($t = -7.91$, $p < .01$) and between person ($t = -4.67$, $p < .01$) ratings of pain were significant predictors though age and income were not. More interestingly, we found that though EA alone did not predict PA, there was a significant pain by

EA interaction ($t = 2.80, p < .01$). This interaction indicates differences between groups as their pain varied such that greater pain brought significantly lower positive affect from non-EA participants.

Second, in predicting daily NA, after controlling for age, income, and PA, within person ($t = 5.74, p < .01$) and between person ($t = 3.40, p < .01$) ratings of pain significantly predicted NA. Again, while EA did not individually predict NA, there was a significant pain by EA interaction ($t = -2.53, p < .01$): greater NA in response to pain for non-EA participants. Income was not a significant predictor of NA, however age was significant ($t = -2.73, p < .01$).

In predicting daily physical functioning, after controlling for age and income, both within ($t = 14.41, p < .01$) and between person ($t = 7.55, p < .01$)reports of pain were significant. Age was not a significant predictor of physical functioning, however income was ($t = 2.82, p < .01$). Yet again, EA was not a significant predictor of physical functioning but, there was a significant pain by ethnicity interaction ($t = -2.59, p < .01$). This suggests that the presence of pain has a stronger influence for non-EA participants on their physical functioning.

In these findings, while we consistently found no simple *between* racial/ ethnic group differences in affect or physical functioning, there were significant differences between groups *when* they were in pain. Figure 5.3 illustrates the nature of these findings by (14.2) graphing the interaction of pain with EA's in predicting physical functioning. Here, we see that as pain increases, non-EA's will report worse physical functioning. The data show that racial/ethnic groups differ when they are experiencing high pain; non-EA's experience lower levels of physical functioning than EA's. Finally, the finding of a loss in physical functioning during pain periods greater for non-EA than EA participants points to a relative absence of resilience resources among non-EA pain patients even after accounting for income differences.

The findings we present illustrate the richness of the inquiry possible with more intensive study of the everyday lives. Our methods provide a means of documenting specific differences in the profiles due to race (Green et al., 2003). We do not have answers yet to the reasons behind these differences, but we believe we are closer to asking the right question with regard to racial/ethnic disparities in health and emotional well-being. We urge further study of these processes as potential links to understanding the problems of adaptation that beset those in

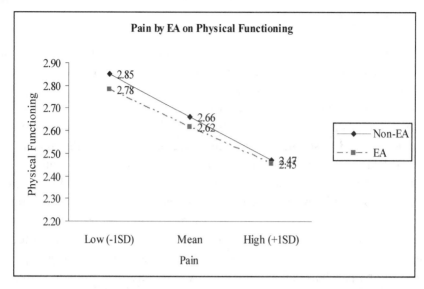

FIGURE 5.3   The effects of pain on daily physical functioning for European American (EA) and non-EA women with musculoskeletal conditions.

disadvantaged groups. One of us has discussed previously the problems inherent with alcohol, drug use, and overeating as affect regulation strategies (Zautra, 2003). These health behaviors, when used as a means of recovery of mood during stressful or other occasions, invite dependency. With repeated use, the person conflates two fundamentally different motivational processes: the need to cope/avoid/escape following negative affective experiences and the need to approach sources of positive emotion. Thus they misinterpret the affective principles underlying their own behavior, and this leads to further errors in judgment about the utility of drinking, smoking, eating, and so forth. Doing so makes it all the more difficult to self-regulate, thus placing them at greater risk for illness as a consequence of overdoing behaviors harmful when engaged in excess. The lack of social capital in the communities appears to invite this kind of "one-stop shopping" for affect modulation. Through closer on time assessments of behaviors, their antecedents and their consequences, we gain not only the means of testing hypotheses like those stated above, we also introduce the beginnings of intervention frameworks based on real life contingencies associated with the problems of self-regulation in resource-poor environments.

CONCLUSION

Jackson's work provides us with both reason and motivation to put racial disparities in health and mental health under the microscope. A focus on the social, ethnic, and racial divide leads us down many paths. One such path is the examination of the culture of health and illness, and the means by which social structure encourages behaviors that increase and/or decrease vulnerability. Jackson furthers our discourse down that road through gathering data across the nation on health and illness from peoples of all colors and ethnic heritage. Paradigms provide directions to follow, and the stress and coping paradigm that Jackson follows leads us to uncover key risk factors that distinguish populations. We suggest examination of the paths to resilience as a paradigmatic approach that adds to the directions afforded us by the stress and coping models of health and illness in its urging us to examine psychosocial and community resources that promote sustainability and recovery. Further, we suggest that the broad knowledge gained from national surveys is enhanced through the study of everyday lives with methods that allow us to capture the standing waves of social life as it is lived for the peoples of our nation.

ACKNOWLEDGMENTS

The authors wish to acknowledge the support of two grants from the National Institute of Arthritis, Musculoskeletal, and Skin Diseases, Alex Zautra, Principal Investigator, "Adaptation to pain and interpersonal stress in Fibromyalgia" (5R01AR046034), and "Stress Adaptation in Rheumatoid Arthritis" (2R01AR/AG41687).

REFERENCES

Almeida, D. M. (2005). Resilience and vulnerability to daily stressors. *Current Directions in Psychological Science, 14–2,* 64–68.

Amaro, H., Russo, N. F., & Johnson, J. (1987). Family and work predictors of psychological well-being among Hispanic women professionals. *Psychology of Women Quarterly, 11,* 505–521.

Andersson, K., Siegel, R., Fuxe, K., & Eneroth, P. (1983). Intravenous injections of nicotine induce very rapid and discrete reductions of hypothalamic catecholamine levels associated with increases of ACTH, vasopression, and prolactin secretion. *Acta Physiologica Scandinavica, 118*, 35–40.

Aneshensel, C. S., Rutter, C. M., & Lachenbruch, P. A. (1991). Social structure, stress, and mental health: Competing conceptual and analytic models. *American Sociological Review, 56*, 166–178.

Barden, N. (2004). Implication of the hypothalamic-pituitary-adrenal axis in the physiopathology of depression. *Journal of Psychiatry and Neuroscience, 29*, 185–193.

Barrot, M., Marinelli, M., Abrous, D. N., Rouge-Pont, F., Le Moal, M., & Piazza, P. V. (2000). The dopaminergic hyper-responsiveness of the shell of the nucleus accumbens is hormone-dependent. *European Journal of Neuroscience, 12*, 973–979.

Benowitz, N. L. (1988). Pharmacologic aspects of cigarette smoking and nicotine addiction. *New England Journal of Medicine, 319*, 1318–1330.

Benowitz, N. L. (1996). Pharmacology of nicotine: Addiction and therapeutics. *Annual Review of Pharmacology and Toxicology, 36*, 597–613.

Blascovich, J., Spencer, S. J., Quinn, D., & Steele, C. (2001). African Americans and high blood pressure: The role of stereotype threat. *Psychological Science, 12*, 225–229.

Blazer, D. G., Kessler, R. C., McGonagle, K. A., & Swartz, M. S. (1994). The prevalence and distribution of major depression in a national community sample: The National Comorbidity Survey. *American Journal of Psychiatry, 151*, 979–986.

Breslau, N., Kilbey, M. M., & Andreski, P. (1993). Nicotine dependence and major depression: New evidence from a prospective investigation. *Archives of General Psychiatry, 50*, 31–35.

Brown, D. R., Eaton, W., & Sussman, L. (1990). Racial differences in the prevaence of phobic disorders. *Journal of Nervous and Mental Diseas, 178(7)*, 434–441.

Browning, C. R., & Cagney, K. A. (2003). Moving beyond poverty: Neighborhood structure, social processes, and health. *Journal of Health and Social Behavior, 44*, 552–571.

Bureau of the Census. (1995). *Statistical brief: Poverty areas.* Washington, D.C.: U.S. Department of Commerce, Economics and Statistics Administration.

Cagney, K. A., & Browning, C. R. (2004). Exploring neighborhood-level variation in asthma and other respiratory diseases. *Journal of General Internal Medicine, 19*, 229–236.

Cannetti, L., Bachar, E., & Berry, E. M. (2002). Food and emotion. *Behavioral Processes, 60*, 157–164.

Centers for Disease Control (CDC). (2002). Annual smoking-attributable mortality, years of potential life lost, and economic costs—United States, 1995–1999. *Morbidity and Mortality Weekly Report, 51*(14), 300–303.

Centers for Disease Control (CDC). (2003). *Health United States, 2003, with chartbook on trends in the health of Americans*. Hyattsville, MD: CDC, National Center for Health Statistics.

Chatters, L. M., & Taylor, R. J. (1989). Age differences in religious participation among black adults. *Journals of Gerontology. Series B, Psychological Sciences and Social Sciences, 44*, S183–S189.

Clark, R., Anderson, N. B., Clark, V. R., & Williams, D. R. (1999). Racism as a stressor for African Americans: A biopsychosocial model. *American Psychologist, 54*, 805–816.

Cohen, S., Kessler, R. C., & Gordon, L. G. (1995). *Measuring stress.* New York: Oxford University Press.

Dallman, M. F. (2003). Stress by any other name . . . ? *Hormones and Behavior, 43*, 18–20.

Dallman, M. F., Pecoraro, N., Akana, S. F., la Fleur, S. E., Gomez, F., Houshyar, H., et al. (2003a). Chronic stress and obesity: A new view of "comfort food". *Proceedings of the National Academy of Sciences, 100*, 11696–11701.

Dallman, M. F., Akana, S. F., Laugero, K. D., Gomez, F., Manalo, S., Bell, M. E., et al. (2003b). A spoonful of sugar: Feedback signals of energy stores and corticosterone regulate responses to chronic stress. *Physiology and Behavior, 79*, 3–12.

Danziger, S., & Gottschalk, P. (1997). *America unequal.* Cambridge, MA: Harvard University Press.

De Jong, I.E.M., & De Kloet, R. (2004). Glucocorticoids and vulnerability to psychostimulant drugs: Toward substrate and mechanism. *Annals of New York Academy of Sciences, 1018*, 192–198.

Dickerson, S. S., & Kemeny, M. E. (2004). Acute stressors and cortisol responses: A theoretical integration and synthesis of laboratory research. *Psychological Bulletin, 130*, 355–391.

Dohrenwend, B. P. (2000). The role of adversity and stress in psychopathology: Some evidence and its implications for theory and research. *Journal of Health and Social Behavior, 41*, 1–19.

Dohrenwend, B. P., & Dohrenwend, B. S. (1974). Social and cultural influences on psychophathology. *Annual Review of Psychology, 25,* 417–452.

Elit, L. M., Levine, M. N., Gafni, A., Whelan, T. J., Doig, G., Streiner, D. L., et al. (1996). Patients' preferences for therapy in advanced epithelial ovarian cancer: Development, testing, and application of a bedside decision instrument. *Gynecolic Oncology, 62,* 329–335.

Epstein, R. M., Alper, B. S., & Quill, T. E. (2004). Communicating evidence for participatory decision making. [The patient physician relationship.] *Journal of the American Medical Association, 291,* 2359–2366.

Essed, P. (1991). *Understanding everyday racism.* Newbury Park, California: Sage Publications.

Etzioni, A. (1993). *The spirit of community: Rights, responsibilities and the communitarian agenda.* New York: Crown Publishers.

Farley, R. (Ed.). (1995). *State of the union: American in the 1990s, economic trends* (Vol. 1). New York: Russell Sage.

Feagin, J. R. (1991). The continuing significance of race: Anti-black discrimination in public places. *American Sociological Review, 56,* 101–116.

Fenton, J. J., & Deyo, R. A. (2003). Patient self-referral for radiologic screening tests: Clinical and ethical concerns. *Journal of the American Board of Family Practice, 16,* 494–501.

Finch, J. F., & Zautra, A. J. (1992). Testing latent longitudinal models of social ties and depression among the elderly: A comparison of distribution-free and maximum likelihood estimates with nonnormal data. *Psychology and Aging, 7,* 107–118.

Fischer, J. (1969). Negroes and whites and rates of mental illness: Reconsideration of a myth. *Psychiatry, 32,* 428–446.

Gallo, L. C., Bogart, L. M., Vranceanu, A., & Matthews, K. A. (2005). Socioeconomic status, resources, psychological experiences, and emotional responses: A test of the reserve capacity model. *Journal of Personality and Social Psychology, 88,* 386–399.

Geronimus, A. T., & Thompson, P. J. (2004). To denigrate, ignore or disrupt: Racial inequality in health and the impact of a policy-induced breakdown of African American communities. *Du Bois Review, 1,* 247–279.

Gottschalk, P. (1997). Inequality, income growth, and mobility: The basic facts. *The Journal of Economic Perspectives, 11,* 21–40.

Green, C. R., Anderson, K. O., Baker, T. A., Campbell, L. C., Decker, S., Fillingim, R. B., et al. (2003). The unequal burden of pain: Confronting racial and ethnic disparities in pain. *Pain Medicine, 4,* 277–294.

Harburg, E., Erfurt, J., Chape, C., Havenstein, L., Schull, W., & Schork, M. A. (1973a). Socioecological stressor areas and black-white blood pressure: Detroit. *Journal of Chronic Disease, 26,* 595–611.

Harburg, E., Erfurt, J. C., Huenstein, L. S., Chape, C., Schull, W. J., & Schork, M. A. (1973b). Socio-ecological stress, suppressed hostility, skin color, and black-white male blood pressure: Detroit. *Psychosomatic Medicine, 35,* 276–296.

Harrison, R., & Bennett, C. (1995). Racial and ethnic diversity. In R. Farley (Ed.), *State of the union: America in the 1990's, social trends* (Vol. 2). New York: Russell Sage.

Hawkins, J. D., Catalano, R. F., & Miller, J. Y. (1992). Risk and protective factors for alcohol and other drug problems in adolescence and early adulthood: Implications for substance abuse prevention. *Psychological Bulletin, 112,* 64–105.

Hayward, M. D., Crimmins, E. M., Miles, T. P., & Yang, Y. (2000). The significance of socioeconomic status in explaining the racial gap in chronic health conditions. *American Sociological Review, 65,* 910–930.

Heisler, M., Rust, G., Patillo, R., & Dubois, A. M. (2004). Improving health, eliminating disparities: Finding solutions for better health care for all. *Ethnicity & Disease, 15,* S2-1–S2-4.

Jackson, J. S. (1991). *Life in Black America.* Newbury Park: Sage Publications.

Jackson, J. S. (1993). African American experiences through the adult years. In R. J. Kastenbaum (Ed.), *The encyclopedia of adult development* (pp. 18–26). Phoenix, Arizona: Oryx Press.

Jackson, J. S. (Ed.). (2000). *New directions: African Americans in a diversifying nation.* Washington, D.C.: National Policy Association & Program for Research on Black Americans.

Jackson, J. S. (2002). Health and mental health disparities among black Americans. In M. Hager (Ed.), *Modern psychiatry: Challenges in educating health professionals to meet new needs* (pp. 246–254). New York: Josiah Macy Jr. Foundation.

Jackson, J. S., Brown, T. B., Williams, D. R., Torres, M., Sellers. S. L., & Brown, K. B. (1996). Racism and the physical and mental health status of African Americans: A thirteen year national panel study. *Ethnicity & Disease, 6,* 132–147.

Jackson, J. S., Neighbors, H. W., & Gurin, G. (1986). Findings from a national survey of black mental health: Implications for practice and training. In M. R. Miranda, H. L. Kitano (Eds.), *Mental health research and practice in minority communities: Development of culturally sensitive training programs* (pp. 91–115). Rockville, MD: NIMH DHHS Pub. No. (ADM) 86–1466.

Jackson, J. S., Torres, M., Caldwell, C. H., Neighbors, H. W., Nesse, R. M., Taylor, R. J., et al. (2004). The National Survey of American Life: A study of racial, ethnic and cultural influences on mental disorders and mental health. *International Journal of Methods in Psychiatric Research, 13,* 196–207.

Jackson, J. S., Williams, D. R., & Torres, M. (2003). Discrimination, health and mental health: The social stress process. In A. Maney (Ed.), *Socioeconomic conditions, stress and mental disorders: Toward a new synthesis of research and public policy.* Bethesda, MD: NIH Office of Behavioral and Social Research.

James, S. A. (1994). John Henryism and the health of African Americans. *Culture of Medicine and Psychiatry, 18,* 163–182.

James, S. A., LaCroix, A. Z., Kleinbaum, D. G., & Strogatz, D. S. (1984). John Henryism and blood pressure differences among black men: The role of occupational stressors. *Journal of Behavioral Medicine, 7,* 259–275.

Jones, E., & Matsumoto, D. (1982). Psychotherapy with the underserved: Recent developments. In L. Snowden (Ed.), *Reaching the underserved: Mental health needs of neglected populations* (pp. 207–228). Beverly Hills: Sage Publications.

Jones, R. T. (1987). Tobacco dependence. In H. Y. Meltzer (Ed.), *Psychopharmacology: A generation of progress, twenty-fifth anniversary volume, ACNP* (pp. 1589–1595). New York: Raven Press.

Kahng, S. K., Dunkle, R., & Jackson, J. S. (2004). The relationship between the trajectory of body mass index and health trajectory among older adults: Multilevel modeling analyses. *Research on Aging, 26,* 31–61.

Kao, G., & Thompson, J. S. (2003). Racial and ethnic stratification in educational achievement and attainment. *Annual Review of Sociology, 29,* 417–442.

Kawachi, I., Kennedy, B. P., & Glass, R. (1999). Social capital and self-rated health: A contextual analysis. *American Journal of Public Health, 89,* 1187–1193.

Kessler, R. C. (1979). Stress, social status, and psychological distress. *Journal of Health and Social Behavior, 20,* 259–273.

Kessler, R. C., McGonagle, K., Zhao, S., Nelson, C., Hughes, M., Eshleman, S., et al. (1994). Lifetime and 12-month prevalence of DSM-III-R psychiatric disorders in the United States: Results from the National Comorbidity Survey. *Archives of General Psychiatry, 51,* 8–19.

Kessler, R. C., & Neighbors H. W. (1986). A new perspective on the relationships among race, social class and psychological distress. *Journal of Health and Social Behavior, 27,* 107–115.

Kirschbaum, C., Wust, S., & Strasburger, C. J. (1992). 'Normal' cigarette smoking increases free cortisol in habitual smokers. *Life Sciences, 50,* 435–442.

Koob, G. F., Roberts, A. J., Schultheis, G., Parsons, L. H., Charles, J. H., Hyytia, P., et al. (1998). Neurocircuitry targets in ethanol reward and dependence. *Alcoholism: Clinical and Experimental Research, 22,* 3–9.

Krieger, N., (1990). Racial and gender discrimination: Risk factors for high blood pressure? *Social Science and Medicine, 30,* 1273–1281.

Krieger, N., & Signey, S. (1996). Racial discrimination and blood pressure: The CARDIA study of young black and white adults. *American Journal of Public Health, 86,* 1370–1378.

Krieger, N., Williams, D. R., & Moss, N. (1997). Measuring social class in U.S. public health research: Concepts, methodologies, and guidelines. *Annual Review of Public Health, 18,* 341–378.

Le, A. D., Quan, B., Juzytch, W., Fletcher, P. J., Joharchi, N., & Shaham, Y. (1998). Reinstatement of alcohol-seeking by priming injections of alcohol and exposure to stress in rats. *Psychopharmacology, 135,* 169–174.

Lender, M. B. (1987). Alcohol, stress and society: The 19th century origins of the tension reduction hypothesis. In E. Gottheil, K. A. Druley, S. D. Pashko, & S. P. Weinstein (Eds.), *Stress and addiction* (pp. 13–23). New York: Brunner/Mazel.

Littell, R. C., Milliken, G. A., Stroup, W. W., & Wolfinger, R. D. (1996). *SAS system for MIXED models.* Cary, N.C.: SAS Institute, Inc.

Magee, W. J., Eaton, W. W., Wittchen, H., McGonagle, K. A., & Kessler, R. C. (1996). Agoraphobia, simple phobia, and social phobia in the National Comorbidity Survey. *Archives of General Psychiatry, 53,* 159–168.

Manning, R. (1998) A care approach. In H. Kuhse, & P. Singer (Eds.), *A companion to bioethics* (pp. 512). Oxford: Blackwell: 98–105.

Marinelli, M., & Piazza, P. V. (2002). Interaction between glucocorticoid hormones, stress and psychostimulant drugs. *European Journal of Neuroscience, 16,* 387–394.

Marmot, M., & Wilkinson, R. G. (1999). *Social determinants of health.* New York: Oxford University Press.

Massey, D. S. (2004). Segregation and stratification: A biosocial perspective. *Du Bois Review , 1*(1), 7–25.

Masten, A. S., & Powell, J. L. (2003). A resilience framework for research, policy and practice. In S. S. Luthar (Ed.), *Resilience and vulnerability: Adaptation in the context of childhood adversities* (pp. 1–25). Cambridge, MA: Cambridge University Press.

McCarthy, J., & Yancey, W. (1971). Uncle Tom and Mr. Charlie: Metaphysical pathos in the study of racism and personal disorganization. *American Journal of Sociology, 76,* 648–672.

McEwen, B. S. (1998a). Protective and damaging effects of stress mediators. *New England Journal of Medicine, 338,* 171–179.

McEwen, B. S. (1998b). Stress, adaptation and disease: Allostasis and allostatic load. *Annals of the New York Academy of Sciences, 840,* 33–44.

McLean, D. E., & Link, B. G. (1994). Unraveling complexity: Strategies to refine concepts, measures, and research designs in the study of life events and mental health. In W. R. Avison & I. H. Gotlib (Eds.), *Stress and mental health: Contemporary issues and prospects for the future* (pp. 15–42). New York: Plenum Press.

Messer, N. G. (2004). Professional-patient relationships and informed consent. *Postgraduate Medical Journal, 80,* 277–283.

Miles, T. P. (2005). Correctable sources of disparities in cancer among minority elders. *Medical Clinics of North America, 89,* 869–894.

Mirowsky, J., & Ross, C. (1980). Minority status, ethnic culture, and distress: A comparison of Blacks, Whites, Mexicans and Mexican-Americans. *American Journal of Sociology, 86,* 479–495.

Mirowsky, J., & Ross, C. E. (1989). *Social causes of psychological distress.* New York: Aldine de Gruyter.

Morland, K., Wing, S., & Roux, A. D. (2002). The contextual effect of the local food environment on residents' diets: The atherosclerosis risk in communities study. *American Journal of Public Health, 92,* 1761–1767.

Morland, K., Wing, S., Roux, A. D., & Poole, C. (2002). Neighborhood characteristics associated with the location of food stores and food service places. *American Journal of Preventive Medicine, 22,* 23–29.

Mueller, P. S., Hook, C. C., & Fleming, K. C. (2004). Ethical issues in geriatrics: A guide for clinicians. *Mayo Clinic Proceedings, 79,* 554–562.

Myers, H. F. (1982). Stress, ethnicity, and social class: A model for research with black populations. In E. E. Jones & S. J. Korchin (Eds.), *Minority mental health* (pp. 118–148). New York: Praeger.

Neff, J. (1985). Race and vulnerability to stress: An examination of differential vulnerability. *Journal of Personality and Social Psychology, 49,* 481–491.

Neighbors, H. W. (1984). The distribution of psychiatric morbidity in black Americans: A review and suggestions for research. *Community Mental Health Journal, 20,* 5–18.

Neighbors, H. W., Jackson, J. S., Bowman, P. J., & Gurin, G. (1983). Stress, coping and black mental health: Preliminary findings from a national study. *Prevention in Human Services, 2,* 5–29.

Neighbors, H. W., Jackson, J. S., Broman, C. L., & Thompson, E. (1996). Racism and the mental health of African Americans: The role of self and system blame. *Ethnicity & Disease, 6,* 167–175.

Neighbors, H. W., Jackson, J. S., Campbell, L., & Williams, D. (1989). The influence of racial factors on psychiatric diagnosis: A review and suggestions for research. *Community Mental Health Journal, 25(4),* 201–311.

Nisell, M., Nomikos, G. G., & Svensson, T. H. (1994). Systemic nicotine-induced dopamine release in the rat nucleus accumbens is regulated by nicotinic receptors in the ventral segmental area. *Synapse, 16,* 36–44.

Pearlin, L. I. (1989). The sociological study of stress. *Journal of Health and Social Behavior, 30,* 241–256.

Peele, S., & Brodsky, A. (2000). Exploring psychological benefits associated with moderate alcohol use: A necessary corrective to assessments of drinking outcomes. *Drug and Alcohol Dependence, 60,* 221–247.

Peyser, H. S. (1993). Stress, ethyl alcohol, and alcoholism. In L. Goldberger & S. Breznitz (Eds.), *Handbook of stress: Theoretical and clinical aspects* (2nd ed., pp. 532–549). New York: The Free Press.

Piazza, P. V., & Le Moal, M. L. (1996). Pathophysiological basis of vulnerability to drug abuse: Role of an interaction between stress, glucocorticoids, and dopaminergic neurons. *Annual Review of Pharmacology and Toxicology, 36,* 359–378.

Piazza, P. V., & Le Moal, M. L. (1998). The role of stress in drug self-administration. *Trends in Pharmacological Science, 19,* 67–74.

Pohorecky, L. A. (1981). The interaction of alcohol and stress. *Neuroscience and Behavioral Reviews, 5,* 209–229.

Pohorecky, L. A. (1991). Stress and alcohol interactions: An update of human research. *Alcoholism: Clinical and Experimental Research, 15,* 438–458.

Pomerleau, C. S., & Pomerleau, O. F. (1992). Euphoriant effects of nicotine in smokers. *Psychopharmacology, 108,* 460–465.

Porcu, P., Sogliano, C., Cinus, M., Purdy, R. H., Biggio, G., & Concas, A. (2003). Nicotine-induced changes in cerebrocortical neuroactive steroids and plasma corticosterone concentrations in the rat. *Pharmacology, Biochemistry, and Behavior, 74,* 683–690.

Pritchard, W. S., Robinson, J. H., & Guy, T. D. (1992). Enhancement of continuous performance task reaction time by smoking in non-deprived smokers. *Psychopharmacology, 108,* 437–442.

Raikkonen, K., Keltikangas-Jarvinen, L., Adlercreutz, H., & Hautanen, A. (1996). Psychosocial stress and the insulin resistance syndrome. *Metabolism: Clinical and Experimental, 45,* 1533–1538.

Robins, L., & Regier, D. (1991). *Psychiatric disorders in American: The Epidemiologic Catchment Area Study.* New York: The Free Press.

Rogler, L. H., Malgady, R. G., & Rodriguez, O. (1989). *Hispanics and mental health: A framework for research.* Malabar, Florida: Robert E. Krieger Publishing.

Rosenberg, M. (1979). *Conceiving the self.* New York: Basic Books.

Roux, A. D. (2003). Residential environments and cardiovascular risk. *Journal of Urban Health: Bulletin of the New York Academy of Medicine, 80,* 569–589.

Rutter, M. (1985). Resilience in the face of adversity. Protective factors and resistance to psychiatric disorder. *British Journal of Psychiatry, 147,* 598–611.

Rutter, M. (1993). Resilience: Some conceptual considerations. *Journal of Adolescent Health, 14,* 626–631, 690–626.

Ryff, C. D., & Keyes, C. L. (1995). The structure of psychological well-being revisited. *Journal of Personality and Social Psychology, 69,* 719–727.

Saldana, D. H. (1995). Acculturative stress. In D. H. Saldana (Ed.), *Hispanic psychology: Critical issues in theory* (pp. 43–56). New York: Sage Publications.

Salgado de Snyder, V. N. (1987). Factors associated with acculturative stress and depressive symptomatology among married Mexican immigrant women. *Psychology of Women Quarterly, 11*, 475–488.

Sapolsky, R. M. (1998). *Why zebras don't get ulcers: An updated guide to stress, stress-related diseases and coping* (2nd ed.). New York: W. H. Freeman & Company.

Sapolsky, R. M. (2002). Endocrinology of the stress-response. In J. B. Becker, S. M. Breedlove, D. Crews, & M. M. McCarthy (Eds.), *Behavioral Endocrinology* (pp. 409–450). Cambridge, MA: Massachusetts Institute of Technology Press.

Schnittker, J., & McLeod, J. D. (2005). The social psychology of health disparities. *Annual Review of Sociology, 31*, 75–103.

Snyder, C. R. (2002). Hope theory: Rainbows of the mind. *Psychological Inquiry, 13*, 249–275.

Somervell, P. D., Leaf, P. J., Weissman, M. M., Blazer, D. G., & Bruce, M. L. (1989). The prevalence of major depression in black and white adults in five United States communities. *American Journal of Epidemiology, 130*, 725–735.

Stewart, J. (2000). Pathways to relapse: The neurobiology of drug- and stress-induced relapse to drug-taking. *Journal of Psychiatry and Neuroscience, 25*, 125–136.

Steptoe, A., Wardle, J., & Marmot, M. (2005). Positive affect and health-related neuroendocrine, cardiovascular, and inflammatory processes. *Proceedings of the National Academy of Sciences of the United States of America, 102*, 6508–6512.

Stolerman, I. P., & Jarvis, M. J. (1995). The scientific case that nicotine is addictive. *Psychopharmacology, 117*, 2–10.

Taylor, R. J., Chatters, L. M., Hardison, C. B., & Riley, A. (2001). Informal social support networks and subjective well-being among African Americans. *Journal of Black Psychology, 27*, 439–463.

Thoits, P. A. (1995). Stress, coping and social support processes: Where are we? What next? *Journal of Health and Social Behavior, (Extra Issue)*, 53–79.

Thompson, C. E. & Neville, H. A. (1999). Racism, mental health, and mental health practice. *The Counseling Psychologist, 27*, 155–223.

Turner, R. J., Wheaton, B., & Lloyd, D. A. (1995). The Epidemiology of Social Stress. *American Sociological Review, 60*, 104–125.

U.S. Department of Health and Human Services. (2001). *Mental health: Culture, race, and ethnicity – A supplement to mental health: A report of the Surgeon General.* Rockville: U.S. Department of Health and Human Services, Substance Abuse and Mental Health Services Administration, Center for Mental Health Services.

Vega, W. A., & Rumbaut, R. G. (1991). Ethnic minorities and mental health. *Annual Review of Sociology, 17,* 351–383.

Walsh, S. H. (2004). The clinician's perspective on electronic health records and how they can affect patient care. *BMJ (Clinical Research Ed.), 328,* 1184–1187.

Ware, J. E., Jr., & Sherbourne, C. D. (1992). The MOS 36-item short-form health survey (SF-36). I. Conceptual framework and item selection. *Medical Care, 30,* 473–483.

Ulbrich, P., Warheit, G., & Zimmerman, R. (1989). Race, socioeconomic status and psychological distress. *Journal of Health and Scoial Behavior, 30,* 131–146.

Warheit, G., Holzer, C., & Arey, S. (1975). Race and mental illness: An epidemiologic update. *Journal of Health and Social behavior, 16,* 243–256.

Warner, D. F., & Hayward, M. D. (2002, May). *Race disparities in men's mortality: The role of childhood social conditions in a process of cumulative disadvantage.* Presented at the Population Association of American Annual Meeting, Atlanta, Georgia.

Watson, D., Clark, L. A., & Tellegen, A. (1988). Development and validation of brief measures of positive and negative affect: The PANAS scales. *Journal of Personality and Social Psychology, 54,* 1063–1070.

Wesnes, K., & Warburton, D. M. (1983). The effects of cigarettes of varying yield on rapid information processing performance. *Psychopharmacology, 82,* 338–342.

Wheaten, B. (1985). Models for the stress-buffering functions of coping resources. *Journal of Health and Social Behavior, 26,* 352–364.

Wheaton, B. (1994). Sampling the stress universe. In W. R. Avison & I. H. Gotlib (Eds.), *Stress and mental health: Contemporary issues and prospects for the future* (pp. 77–114). New York: Plenum Press.

Wilkinson, R. G., & Pickett, K. E. (2005). Income inequality and population health: A review and explanation of the evidence. *Social Science & Medicine, 62,* 1768–1784.

Williams, D. R. (1990). Socioeconomic differentials in health: A review and redirection. *Social Psychology Quarterly, 53,* 81–99.

Williams, D. R. (1994). The concept of race in Health Services Research: 1966–1990. *Health Services Research, 29*, 261–274.

Williams, D. R. (1995). African American mental health: Persisting questions and paradoxical findings. In R. J. Taylor (Ed.), *African American research perspectives, An Occasional Report of the Program for Research on Black Americans, Ann Arbor: University of Michigan Institute for Social Research. 2(1):8–16.*

Williams, D. R. (1996). Racism and health: A research agenda. *Ethnicity and Disease, 6*, 1–6.

Williams, D. R. (2001). Racial variations in adult health status: Patterns, paradoxes, and prospects. In N. J. Smelser, W. J. Wison, & F. Mitchell (Eds.), *America Becoming: Racial trends and their consequences* (Vol. 2, pp. 371–410). Washington, D.C.: National Academy Press.

Williams, D. R., & Chung, A-M. (in press). Racism and health. In R. C. Gibson & J. S. Jackson (Eds.), *Health in Black America.* Thousand Oaks, CA: Sage Publications.

Williams, D. R., & Collins, C. (1995). Socioeconomic and racial differences in health. *Annual Review of Sociology, 21*, 349–386.

Williams, D. R., & Fenton, B. (1994). The mental health of African Americans: Findings, questions, and directions. In I. L. Livingston (Ed.), *Handbook of Black American health: The mosaic of conditions, issues, policies, and prospects* (pp. 253–268). Westport, CT: Greenwood Publishing.

Williams, D. R. & Jackson, P. B. (2005). Social sources of racial disparities in health: Policies in societal domains, far removed from traditional health policy, can have decisive consequences for health. *Health Affairs, 24*, 325–334.

Williams, D. R., Lavizzo-Mourey, R., & Warren, R. C. (1994). The concept of race and health status in America. *Public Health Reports, 109*, 26–41.

Williams, D. R., Yu, Y., Jackson, J. S., & Anderson, N. B. (1997). Racial differences in physical and mental health: Socio-economic status, stress and discrimination. *Journal of Health Psychology, 2*, 335–351.

Wilson, W. J. (1996). *When work disappears: The world of the new urban poor.* New York: Knopf.

Winkleby, M. A. & Cubbin, C. (2004). Racial/ethnic disparities in health behaviors: A challenge to current assumptions. In N. B. Anderson, R. A. Bulatao, & B. Cohen (Eds.), *Critical Perspectives on racial and ethnic disparities in health in later life* (pp. 171–226). Washington, DC: National Research Council.

Zautra, A. J. (2003). *Stress, emotions and health.* New York: Oxford University Press.

Zautra, A. J., Guarnaccia, C. A., & Dohrenwend, B. P. (1986). Measuring small life events. *American Journal of Community Psychology, 14,* 629–655.

Index

Activity
  cognitive, 5–6, 10–11
  physical, 2–3, 6, 9, 11–12, 88
Adrenocorticotropin (ACTH), 199, 201
Affect Balance Scale, 100
Affect regulation strategies, 225
African-American, 192, 200, 205, 213
Age
  declines in memory and, 96, 99, 109
  differences of, 95, 97–99, 103–109, 111–112,
    144, 178
  stereotypes of, 57–58, 197
Age-associated cognitive decline (AACD), 2
Age-associated memory impairment (AAMI), 2
Aging, cognitive, 9–13, 15, 22, 87
Alcohol, 11, 71, 88, 190, 197–199, 201–203,
  206–207, 225
Alzheimer's disease (AD), 1–8, 11, 16–17
Arginine vasopressin (AVP), 199
Autonomy, 209, 211–212, 214
Average life expectancy, 135, 142

Baby boomers, 21, 150
Benign senescent forgetfulness, 2

Cardiovascular disease, 88, 200, 214, 218
Cohorts
  differences and, 21
  trajectories and, 21
Comfort food, 199–200
Conscientiousness, 71, 77, 79–82, 87–93
Corticotropin releasing factor (CRF), 199–200
Council of Economic Advisors, 170

Decline
  cognitive, 1–5, 7–10, 21, 24, 58, 181
  physical, 206
Deliberative mode, 176
Delphi procedure, 44
Dementia, 2–10, 13, 15–16, 212
Developmental changes, 95
Disparities
  ethnic, 217, 222, 224
  health, 189–190, 206–207, 209, 213–215, 217
  racial, 189–190, 216, 226
Distance, psychological, 215
Distress
  end day, 101, 103, 105–106

  monthly distress recall, 101
  peak day, 100, 103, 105–107, 110
  psychological, 95–112, 190, 192–193,
    196–197, 217
  recalling, 103
  weekly aggregate, 100, 103, 106
  weekly distress recall, 101
Drugs, 199, 201–204
Dysregulation, 73–74

Education
  attainment of, 3–4, 10, 16, 18–19
  inequality of, 209–211
Electronic Medical Record (EMR), 214
Emotional regulation, 96, 98, 112
Emotions
  negative, 96–97, 108, 110–112, 218
  positive, 110–111
Epidemiological Catchment Area (ECA),
  192–193
Ethic of care, 212
401 (K) plan, 177, 180
Function, cognitive, 1, 3–7, 19
Fundamental change, 217

GI bill, 16

Health
  consumer, 209, 213
  disparities of, 189–190, 206–207, 209,
    213–215, 217
Health and Retirement Survey (HRS), 139,
  145–147, 149–151, 153–155, 162–163
Health conditions, chronic, 190
Health disorders, chronic, 191
Hispanics, 190, 205–206, 219
Hyperreactivity, 72, 77
Hypothalamic-pituitary-adrenalcortical (HPA)
  axis, 74, 77, 189, 191, 199–204, 206, 220

Individual investment accounts, 125
Inductive reasoning, 18–21, 23
Intelligence quotient (IQ), 10
Internalized racism, 196–197
Inventory of Small Life Events (ISLE), 218

Kindling effects, 74–77, 79, 86

Life cycle
  consumption model of, 129, 131, 161

framework of, 139, 144
saving of, 148
Lifestyle factors, 2–3, 7, 13, 19
Lifetime earnings, 130, 132, 152
Living will, 212
Longitudinal Retirement History Survey
  (LRHS), 139, 153
Longitudinal studies of cognition, 13

Manifest Anxiety Scale, 100
Mild cognitive impairment (MCI), 2, 13, 15
Mood regulation, 69–72, 77, 81–82
Morbidity, 189, 191–192, 198, 205
Mortality, 15, 69, 71, 77, 79–80, 88, 191, 198,
  201, 205, 207, 212–214, 216–217

National Comorbidity Study (NCS), 192
National Household Surveys on Drug Abuse,
  206
National Study of Daily Experiences (NSDE),
  75, 99–100
National Survey of Black American (NSBA),
  194, 197
National Survey of Midlife in the United States
  (MIDUS), 96–97, 99–101
Negative affect (NA), 69, 72–79, 81–83, 95–97,
  199, 218, 223, 225
Negative health behaviors, 190–191, 198–199,
  204–206
Negative interpersonal events, 218
Neuroticism, 70–81, 86–87, 89–90
Nicotine, 202–203
Non-Hispanics, 190, 205–206
Non-Specific Psychological Distress Scale,
  100, 102
Normal aging, 1–2, 9, 13, 16
Nun Study, 4, 10
Nutrition, 2–3, 6–7, 9, 11–12, 19

Obesity, 11, 88, 200, 206
Occupational attainment, 2–5, 9, 16, 90
Occupational status, 18–20

Pain, chronic, 74–75, 218, 223
Paraventricular nucleus (PVN), 199–200
Peak-end recollection process, 98, 108
Performance, cognitive, 4, 10, 40
Poor health, 88, 127, 191, 221
Poor living conditions, 191
Positive Affect (PA), 96, 177, 218, 223–224
Positive interpersonal events, 218
Private charity, 128
Public aid, 128

Quality of life, 1, 96

Racial self-esteem, 196
Religion, 196
Resilience Research Paradigm, 217
Resilience Resources (RR), 218–220, 223–224
Reasoning ability, 18–19
Retirement
  age of, 124, 126–128, 131, 133, 136–137, 139,
    140–147, 151–152, 157–159, 170–172
  behavior in, 139, 142, 144, 149, 156, 159,
    165, 173
  environment of, 165–166, 170–171
  incentives for, 133, 147, 156–159, 163, 171,
    173
  nest eggs for, 125–126, 131
  planning of, 123, 157–158
  rules of thumb for, 123–125, 144, 158, 162
Retirement History Study (RHS), 139, 153,
  162–163
Risk index, 218–219

Seattle Longitudinal Study (SLS), 13, 22
Self-regulation, 36, 42, 69–73, 76–78, 80–83,
  85–88, 90–93, 95, 98, 112, 123, 215, 222,
  225
Self-regulatory behavior, 69, 80, 82, 89, 91–93
Self-stereotypes, 57
Shared consent, 209, 211–212, 214
Single domain non-amnestic MCI, 2
Social contexts
  exosystem, 39
  macrosystem, 39
  mesosystem, 39
  microsystem, 38–39
Social Security, 126, 133–137, 140–144, 147,
  150–151, 153, 157, 162–165, 170
Societal influences, 80
Society
  engagement with, 218
  norms of, 35, 123
  resources of, 194, 215, 221
  status in, 13
  structure of, 69, 76, 85, 87, 91–91, 93, 215, 226
  economic status in, 215
Socioemotional selectivity theory, 46, 96
Spatial ability, 21
Standard of living, 161
Stress
  and coping, 216–217, 226
  of daily living, 190
  experience of, 95, 112, 190, 196
  life experiences and, 195
  outcomes of, 190
  living conditions and, 190
  reactivity effect and, 72–73, 76

response to, 189, 198–201
Stressors, 72, 75–77, 189–190, 194–195,
    197–198, 204–207, 217, 219, 222–223
  chronic, 77, 194, 206
  physical, 198
  psychological, 198
Successful aging, 1, 15
Survival in old age, 1
System blame, 196–197

Temporal integration process, 97–98, 104, 110
TIAA-CREF, 155
Traditional pension plan, 177
Training, cognitive, 210
Trajectories
  of aging, 9
  cognitive, 13–14, 22, 24

U.S. Census Bureau, 138, 153
Unsuccessful aging, 15

Verbal ability, 18–21, 23
Vietnam War, 43

White European Americans (EA), 223–225
Whitehall studies, 217
Wisdom
  action side of, 37
  acquisition of, 40, 43, 45, 50
  agents of, 39
  and age, 41, 44, 55–57
  Berlin wisdom paradigm, 33, 37, 41, 43, 50–52

carriers of, 39
concept of, 51–52
consensual recognition, 50–51
development of, 41–42, 50, 53
elicitation of, 39
evolution of, 40–41
fundamental source of, 38
general, 33–38, 41–43, 46–49, 51
heuristics for growth, 36
interrelating the self, 36
life-insight, 34, 37, 44
life-management, 34, 37, 71
microgenesis, 38, 40, 45–46
ontogenesis of, 38, 41, 43, 45
performance, 56–59
personal, 34–37, 42–43, 48–53, 56
profession, 44
recognition of, 38–39
and related insight, 40–42, 45, 52
and related performance, 35–37, 39, 42,
    45–47, 52
and self-insight, 34, 36–37
and self-relativism, 36
social function of, 38, 51–52, 55
social nature of, 33, 37, 39–40, 51–52
social sources of, 40
theories of, 38, 52
tolerance of ambiguity, 36
Word fluency, 21
World War II, 16, 43–44